THE WARRIOR'S Bride

PRAISE FOR
THE WARRIOR'S BRIDE

"*The Warrior's Bride* is a MUST READ for every military wife! While Carrie and Kathy have not sugar-coated the many challenges of military life, they have generously shared the HOPE they have found and the "road map" for thriving! This book contains so many important lessons that could save your marriage or that of someone you know. Read it and pass it along!"

—Kathleen Dees, wife of
Major General (Army Retired) Robert F. Dees

"I love how every chapter feels like it relates to me and what I am going through in my life and walk with Christ. This book will touch and impact so many lives!"

—Heather Osgood, wife of an active duty soldier

"I found your life stories and growth in your understanding and commitment to God's purpose in marriage to be inspiring and insightful! Your testimonies will encourage many military spouses!"

—Paula Van Antwerp, Army spouse for 39 years,
married to Lieutenant General (Retired) R.L. Van Antwerp

THE WARRIOR'S Bride

BIBLICAL STRATEGIES
TO HELP THE MILITARY SPOUSE THRIVE

Kathy Barnett | *Carrie Daws*

AMBASSADOR INTERNATIONAL
GREENVILLE, SOUTH CAROLINA & BELFAST, NORTHERN IRELAND

www.ambassador-international.com

The Warrior's Bride

ISBN: 978-1-62020-287-6
eISBN: 978-1-62020-390-3

Cover Photo by Kristen Huntley Photography
Page Layout by Hannah Nichols
eBook Conversion by Anna Raats

AMBASSADOR INTERNATIONAL
Emerald House
427 Wade Hampton Blvd.
Greenville, SC 29609, USA
www.ambassador-international.com

AMBASSADOR BOOKS
The Mount
2 Woodstock Link
Belfast, BT6 8DD, Northern Ireland, UK
www.ambassadormedia.co.uk
The colophon is a trademark of Ambassador

This book is not ours to dedicate. All that is in these pages came from the Lord and goes back to Him for His glory and for Kingdom advancement.

I would like to give thanks, however, to the Lover of my Soul, and to the Warrior He gave me to share life with. I love them both immeasurably.

"My beloved is mine, and I am his."
—Song of Songs 2:16

And to Carrie . . . words escape me for once!
Thank you sister.

-Kathy

A NOTE FROM THE AUTHORS

Political correctness permeates many areas of our society. While we're certain that it helps soothe feathers that would otherwise be easily ruffled, to be honest with you, neither of us is particularly good at it. With God's help, we find moments of grace, mercy, and even tact, but rarely political correctness.

We are military wives, writing to military wives, simply because it's what we know and who we are. We've never served a day in uniform, never deployed outside the places our families need us to be, and never put our physical lives on the line for the benefit of others. Yet we do not fail to recognize that many women do serve their country proudly within the military. We honor all those within the ranks of the Department of Defense, regardless of gender.

In the pages that follow, you will read phrases like *military man* or pronouns designating the male species being the one in uniform. Please understand our hearts: we do not intend to negate or even diminish the burden placed on our military women and their civilian spouses. We recognize that about twenty percent of the United States Military is comprised of women, and many of those women are married with families.

Throughout this book you will read what we have learned, often the hard way. We encourage you to learn from us without having to travel the roads we traversed. And we ask for grace from those military women and their civilian husbands when we use the terms and pronouns that seem to convey that the military is only comprised of men. It is not a political statement, and we mean no disrespect.

We merely speak from our lives.

CONTENTS

MARRIED TO THE SUPERSUIT

FROM KATHY

(A scene from *The Incredibles*, a Disney Pixar movie released in 2004)

LUCIUS (FROZONE): Honey?

HONEY: What?

LUCIUS (FROZONE): Where's my supersuit?

HONEY: What?

LUCIUS (FROZONE): Where is my supersuit?

HONEY: I, uh . . . put it away.

LUCIUS (FROZONE): Where?

HONEY: Why do you need to know?

LUCIUS (FROZONE): I need it!

HONEY: Uh-uh! Don't you think about running off doing no derrin'-do! We've been planning this dinner for two months!

LUCIUS (FROZONE): The public is in danger!

HONEY: My evening's in danger!

LUCIUS (FROZONE): You tell me where my suit is, woman! We are talking about the greater good!

HONEY: *Greater good?* I am your wife! I'm the greatest good you are ever gonna get!

One of the greatest frustrations about being married to a military man is knowing that you cannot plan your own life. Your husband, and thus your marriage, is owned by the United States Government, and you are forced to accept the plans for the greater good over your own.

In the movie scene above, Lucius's wife is freshly reminded of this fact. It had been many years since Frozone's supersuit was put away, and I'm certain that part of Honey had relaxed into a false perception that the days of the supersuit were over. However, as Frozone later shows up in full regalia to save the world, we can only assume that his wife dealt with her feelings and pulled out the supersuit, allowing him the freedom to do his job to the best of his ability. I can so totally relate to her.

I can't count the number of plans that Hubby and I have had to scrap because an urgent call came down the Chain of Command for him to put on his supersuit and save the world from some imminent threat. Or at least go take a class to learn how to save the world from imminent threat. And sometimes I am less than graceful in my acceptance of the inevitable. But I still do it. I still dig out whatever he needs, sometimes grudgingly and other times squelching my thoughts in the breathless whirlwind of trying to get him out the door in whatever time the government has dictated.

I know now, after many years of being a military spouse, that I married a man who isn't *normal*. I've learned over the years that I didn't just marry him; I married his supersuit too. And because his supersuit is so much a part of who he is, I have to love it and all its baggage. That doesn't mean that I run around wearing red, white, and blue, singing the "Star Spangled Banner" twenty-four hours a day.

While I am very proud of my soldier, sometimes I get frustrated or angry. And sometimes I feel a lot of disappointment or despair. Sometimes I just want to go buy my own private island and set up my own tin-pot dictatorship that doesn't involve deployment or TDYs (temporary duty). But I think that even if we had our own country, Hubby would form an alliance with some other country that would require him to put on his supersuit and rush off to save the world. It's just who he is.

And me? I'm the greatest good he is ever going to get.

That simple ending to the movie scene above expresses my world on so many levels. Just as Honey ends up laying down her own feelings and plans, families of military men are asked to sacrifice much. We sacrifice having our husbands around for holidays and birthdays. We sacrifice their presence when we give birth to their children. We sacrifice them missing our babies taking their first steps, cutting their first teeth, and starring in the holiday show. Of course, they also tend to miss the other joys of life when their presence would be convenient, such as stomach flus, cars breaking down, and major house repairs.

As difficult as all those things are, sometimes it's our own hearts and minds that are the biggest battlefield. Like wondering if your husband still loves you when you have gone three weeks without a word from him, knowing your marriage was shaky before he left for this deployment to a war zone. Wondering if he found someone else to warm his bed on the other side of the planet. Wondering if he wants to come home to you at all. How do you fight for the man when you can't see him? When you can't control when you will see him? Or even, heaven forbid, if you will see him again. I hope you are not in this hard place, but I have been. It is so hard to see your man run off to sacrifice for this country when you aren't even sure he wants to sacrifice anything for you.

The truth is that the men we married are willing to lay down their lives for their country, and in so doing, for you, their wives. This is the epitome of Christlikeness. As the Bible says, "Greater love has no one than this: to lay down one's life for one's friends" (John 15:13). When your husband goes running off to follow orders, he is laying his life down for this country and all of the people God has bestowed upon it. Including you.

I know that it frequently doesn't feel that way. I often fight the feeling that the only thing he sacrifices *is* me. I often feel left out of the loop in his "HOO-AHH" world, and I resent the time he spends training and fighting for everyone else.

When I look at the lives of my civilian friends, I want to scream, because their marriages all seem so reliable, while I am forced to live in uncertainty and flexibility. To be able to pick up a cell phone and always have my husband answer is surreal to me. To have him home every night for dinner, spending time with me and our children, is like asking for the moon. I often fail to see value in the supersuit.

But that does not mean the value isn't there. It does not mean you are forgotten. And it does not mean that life would be better without it. If you are ready to consider this, to lay down your feelings and let God work on you and your life with your supersuit spouse, I encourage you to begin praying now. Pray for your heart to be open to the Word and for your ears to hear the truth God has for you.

The burden God has given us in writing this book is to help you find hope and joy in your marriage. We promise that we don't have all the answers, but we have discovered secrets to finding joy in our trials. We have learned to not only love our own men, but to love the calling of those men. And we have learned to love our calling as military wives.

Join us as we share our journey.

CHAPTER 1

IT STARTS WITH YOU

The things you have heard me say in the presence of many witnesses entrust to reliable people who will also be qualified to teach others.
—2 Timothy 2:2 (the Apostle Paul to his student Timothy)

FROM CARRIE

Have you ever considered how much of your life is ruled by your own filters and perceptions? For example, if I told you I recently took a trip through Charleston, what comes to mind? Those who live in the northeast may think of West Virginia, while those in the south probably think of South Carolina. Perhaps someone in the Navy recalls the ship bearing the name USS Charleston. A quick search on the Internet revealed a town named Charleston in twenty-two different states, in addition to four other countries!

The Charleston that came to your mind depends upon your background and experiences.

We can have similar problems within our marriages. Imagine your husband coming home to laundry all over the family room and asking, "What did you do all day?" You may assume he thinks you lazed about when you know you cared for three sick children, trying to do the laundry as quickly as they were dirtying it. Knowing he doesn't usually find the house in such a state, the intent of your husband's question may have been motivated out of love and concern. Acting on a false perception could leave you hurt and angry as you push away the help you desire.

Filters and perceptions color our world. If you believe the national media with their constant bombardment of bad news, how can you possibly hold on to hope that your marriage will last into old age? If you perceive that your husband is more committed to his job than to you, why should you lay your heart open before him? If you are constantly filtering negative emotions onto his every word, why should you trust that he loves you?

This is where we all need truth. We must find absolutes to hang onto so that no matter what we feel, think, or fear, we can continue to love and serve the very person with whom we long to grow old. In our many years of living as military wives, Kathy and I have survived everything life has thrown at us so far. But along the way, each of us anchored ourselves to the realization that Jesus is Truth and God provides Hope.

We aren't going to argue the legitimacy of Christ or the reality of Him as the only path to salvation. We also will not debate the Bible's validity. We are simply going to present it that way. If you are skeptical, many good books provide ample evidence for the historical reality of Jesus, the authenticity of His crucifixion, and the certainty of His resurrection. (see appendix)

Many Americans want to cling to God's loving nature. Even those who never enter a church building boldly proclaim that God is love. Exodus 34 says, "The LORD, the LORD, the compassionate and gracious God, slow to anger, abounding in love and faithfulness, maintaining love to thousands, and forgiving wickedness, rebellion and sin" (verses 6–7). If the story ended there, we'd be good! Heaven's just on the other side of death.

But one thing about this reasoning always bothered me. If God truly forgives that easily, if God is merely love, then what about the men who shamelessly torture and murder millions? Are they going to be in Heaven too? Is there no ultimate accountability for those who steal, kill and destroy on this earth? Fortunately, Exodus has more to say. Verse seven continues by saying, "Yet He does not leave the guilty unpunished." Obviously, the picture of an all-loving God who lets everyone into Heaven is distorted.

Psalm 99:5 says, "Exalt the LORD our God and worship at His footstool; He is holy." The key that most people want to ignore is God's holiness, and that His holy nature both deserves and requires perfection. The word holy means "to be set apart, separated from sin." The book of Romans says that "all have sinned and fall short of the glory of God" (Romans 3:23). If we have sinned, then God must separate His holy self from us. We cannot live with Him in heaven. Are we doomed?

Because love is such an integral part of God's nature, He could not help but provide a way for us to reach Him. He sent Jesus. Jesus lived a sinless life and died an excruciating death on a Roman cross, accepting the penalty for our mistakes. While God offers this gift to everyone, He does not make anyone accept it. You see, if I propose to give you my truck, it is yours only if you obtain the title and keys. The gift is there, waiting for your response. I will not pressure you to take the vehicle any more than God will compel you to welcome Jesus's sacrifice.

1 John 1:9 says, "If we confess our sins, He is faithful and just and will forgive us our sins and purify us from all unrighteousness." When you ask for forgiveness, wanting nothing more than to be forgiven, Psalm 103 assures us that "as far as the east is from the west, so far has He removed our transgressions from us" (verse 12). God truly loves you that much. He wants to save you and give you knowledge of the truth (1 Timothy 2:4). He longs to spend eternity with you.

You may be thinking, "I'm a Christian. I believe that Jesus died on a cross and rose from the dead 2,000 years ago. I heard it in mass or Sunday School or Vacation Bible School when I was a kid."

You may believe in Jesus as Savior, but are you prepared to let Him be Lord of your life? Do you believe His Word is absolute truth? Could you learn to trust in that Word for freedom in your marriage instead of trusting in your own filters, perceptions, and feelings? Much of this book hinges on your response to Jesus and your answers to these questions.

Or you may be thinking, "I don't want anything to do with a Heavenly Father. My experience with my dad wasn't so great." Although Kathy and I had good dads growing up, we know our experience isn't as commonplace as we'd like it to be. And perhaps more than anyone else, you need to understand how your filters and perceptions are coloring your view of other people.

In our marriages, Kathy and I both faced times when we thought divorce was around the corner. We have feared for our husband's safety and we've contemplated what he was doing on the other side of the world without us. Thoughts of infidelity invaded our minds, frustration with being a single parent has overwhelmed some of our days, and the stress of moving again has dominated sleepless nights. But God holds the answer and Jesus is the key. We take Paul's words in 2 Timothy 2:2 seriously (written out for you at the top of this chapter), and in the pages ahead we will share more than just some funny stories, moments we failed miserably, and encouragement to stay the course. We will entrust you with what we have learned, what Christ has taught us.

FROM KATHY

> *The Lord God said, "It is not good for the man to be alone. I*
> *will make a helper suitable for him."*
> —Genesis 2:18

Before reading further in this book, you must understand that there are principles attached to being a wife, a framework to how marriage is supposed to look. Most of us are just trying to survive, particularly since we may be living six months or more of every year away from the man we are supposed to be one with. If you don't understand how Christ wants your marriage to look, then you are going to be miserable trying to make it work outside the realm of how He is calling you to operate. It doesn't help if your husband doesn't love God. It can also cause you grief if you have some ideas of what the Word says, but you know your husband isn't following those guidelines for God's prescription for marriage. However, the circumstances surrounding your situation do not negate the principles for how you are supposed to live and operate within that marriage. Whether or not your husband is living in a godly manner does not determine if you get to choose to live as a godly wife.

Jesus lived a life of sacrifice. And then He died to show us life. We too are asked to sacrifice. Matthew 16:24–27 says,

> Whoever wants to be My disciple must deny themselves and take up their cross and follow Me. For whoever wants to save their life will lose it, but whoever loses their life for Me will find it. What good will it be for someone to gain the whole world, yet forfeit their soul? Or what can anyone give in exchange for their soul? For the Son of Man is going to come in His Father's glory with His angels, and then He will reward each person according to what they have done.

We are called to lay down our lives within our marriage as a sacrifice to God. To lay down our ideas, or perceptions, as Carrie said, of what we may think marriage is supposed to look like. Sacrifice usually involves pain and death.

I am certain some will not want to hear this. You are convinced that, due to your marital circumstances, your life is different. You may have already made presupposed judgments that I couldn't possibly relate to the trials you are facing. Perhaps your husband is anxious to deploy, or he doesn't appreciate the fact that you are working hard within the home. Maybe your husband thinks nothing of cussing or is into porn or has had an affair or two. Or three.

But the reality is that I've been there too. My marriage was once on the rocks. My husband was not walking with God when we got married. He had a foul mouth, refused to go to church, was into porn, and had been involved in extra-marital affairs. As a result of the pressure and trials, I lost complete control and ended up involved in an affair myself.

And I'm here to tell you that if you think your marriage is lost, it isn't. If you think God isn't bigger than your situation, you are wrong. Christ has hope for you and your husband. I submit that you must also have some hope or you wouldn't be reading this book. If you truly felt that all the problems were the fault of your husband, his career choice, or the Chain of Command, you wouldn't get a book to help you be a better wife.

We will challenge you in this book that the biggest changes in your marriage will not take place within your husband. At least, not at first. The changes have to start in you, in the heart of the woman who loves the man who is often unlovable and who likely doesn't understand the amazing call God has on his life. That is why God gave him a helper. That is why God gave him you! You are important. You are valuable to this man. But you must understand your role and purpose according to God's Word, if you are to fulfill your role and find joy doing it.

If you read Genesis 2:15–25, take note that God made man and then gave him a job. In fact, He gave him the job before He gave him the woman. He had already created all the other living things, both male and female, and He knew the man would need a suitable helper. But God waited.

Imagine Adam looking around at the pairs of animals, only to realize that he was the only one of his kind. He was in the image of God and had fellowship with God, but I believe he came to see his own need for a companion. I believe God allowed him to desire for her in that short span of time he was without her. Adam sacrificed part of himself, perhaps unwillingly and unknowingly at first, so that she might be formed. God could have created her the same way He made Adam, but He chose to make her from the man. She was a part of him from the beginning. She knew from the moment she opened her eyes and took her first breath that she was called *from* the man and *to* the man for the purpose of blessing and helping him.

Do you see yourself called to the purpose of being united with your man, helping him to fulfill the purpose God gave him? This is how God designed marriage. Just as Christ came to lay down His life for you, you are to lay your life down for those who God brings into your world. And if you are married, after your relationship with Christ, you are first and foremost to lay your life down for that man.

Ouch! You may be thinking about how you feel you are always the one to lay down for him and he never lays down for you. But remember, you aren't working on changing him. You are allowing God to shine His light of truth on you. I know this is hard. It was hard for me at first. But God didn't call us to an easy life. He called us to be a living sacrifice for Him (Romans 12:1).

I can hear some of you crying out, wondering about your hopes and dreams. I hear you! I have dreams too. In fact, I was well on my way in a career that I loved when I began learning all of this. There were moments when I thought about walking out on my marriage to follow what I wanted for myself. I got tired of waiting for my husband to lead me and love me.

But please listen: if you want true freedom in your heart and in your marriage, then you must understand that Christ desires more for you and more for your husband than you can fathom. God's desire to bless you and see your marriage prosper will always far exceed your own.

How do you attain that blessing? How do you see the desires of your heart fulfilled? It is simple, really. You must obey the Lord. He has set Himself out to capture your heart and love you like no other. He wants to show you what true love is, so that you might better love the gift He has given you in your husband. In order for Him to do this, you must learn from Him how to love.

The greatest way our Jesus showed us that He loved us was to die for us. And now, He is asking you to die. He knows it is hard. He knows it is painful. He didn't want to do it anymore than you do, but He waits to show you. Jesus did what He did on the cross so that you might be able to walk into the abundant life He promised. Just as salvation is yours for the asking, so is the peace and joy that you are longing for—but it has to be achieved God's way.

The trials you face as a military wife are often unique, compared to what other marriages face. But in all of this, Christ knew you could carry your cross and walk in the way He prepared for you (Luke 14:25–27). God wants you to find freedom; He has a plan. He intimately knows the heart of the one in your life wearing the supersuit. He waits to tell you how to reach out and love that man. He knows how to usher that man into loving you as he was called to do.

But it will start with you. You must let go of worrying about how well your husband serves you, and focus on how well you serve him. This book will continually point you back to the cross and how to exchange your yoke for the one Christ has for you (Matthew 11:28–30). It will challenge you to die to yourself, your desires, your opinions, and your disappointments. But it will also encourage you to know that your heart is the most important thing Christ is after. He wants your heart so much that He died for it. He will ask you to receive His love, and then you can learn to give His love sacrificially to your man.

At some point, you fell in love with the man you married. At the moment you spoke your vows, you decided to lay your life down and embrace oneness with him. You chose to submit to his headship and the life God was calling him to live. In so doing, you sealed your own calling: you are his wife. You are to walk alongside him and whatever God calls him to do. If he is a warrior in the Armed Forces, then you are called to be a warrior bride. It is a hard calling. But it is a high calling.

The big question is: What will you do? Will you hold onto your dreams and plans, resentments and canceled dinners? Or can you get past your filters and perceptions, taking the chance that you might not be seeing things clearly? Will you consider that God might have something better in store for you?

CHAPTER 2

WHO'S IN CHARGE HERE?

Do not conform to the pattern of this world but be trans-
formed by the renewing of your mind. Then you will be able to
test and approve what God's will is—His good, pleasing and
perfect will.

—Romans 12:2

FROM CARRIE

According to The Pew Forum on Religion and Public Life, almost eighty percent of people in the United States in 2010 claimed
to be Christian.[1] If that statistic surprises you, Barna Research
helps shed light on it. Their 2003 survey probed the minds of
those who said they accepted Jesus as Savior and believed they
would go to Heaven when they died. Questions were asked to find

1 The Pew Forum on Religion and Public Life, "Global Christianity:
A Report on the Size and Distribution of the World's Christian
Population," A Project of the Pew Research Center, December 19,
2011, accessed May 5, 2014, http://www.pewforum.org/2011/12/19/
global-christianity-exec/.

out how many of this group of Americans held a biblical world-view interpreted as belief in the following:

1. Absolute moral truth exists and is defined by the Bible

2. The Bible is accurate

3. Jesus Christ lived a sinless life

4. God is the Creator of the universe and still rules today

5. Salvation is a free gift from God

6. Satan is real

Out of the 2,033 adults polled, only 9% held fast to the above concepts.[2]

In popular culture today, everything is said to be relative: people tend to see more ethical and moral grey areas than clearly defined black and white absolutes. The Christian who is determined to follow God should ask if this cultural thinking lines up with the Bible. 2 Timothy 3:16–17 says, "All Scripture is God-breathed and is useful for teaching, rebuking, correcting and training in righteousness, so that the servant of God may be thoroughly equipped for every good work." Either this is true or it isn't. The phrase "all Scripture" doesn't leave any wiggle room. If it's an exaggeration, then everything, including the resurrection and hope of Heaven, must also be called into question. But if the Bible is

2 Barna Group, "A Biblical Worldview Has a Radical Effect on a Person's Life," December 1, 2003, accessed May 6, 2014, https://www.barna.org/barna-update/5-barna-update/131-a-biblical-worldview-has-a-radical-effect-on-a-persons-life.

God's Word, if it is sound truth from the Architect of the universe to His people, then it should govern our entire life.

1 Corinthians 6:19–20 states, "Do you not know that your bodies are temples of the Holy Spirit, who is in you, whom you have received from God? You are not your own; you were bought at a price." Although most of us struggle to varying degrees with trusting God to direct our lives, I've learned that giving up control is not a negative. If God is responsible for leading me, then He is responsible for all the details along the path. (Not that this knowledge makes following Him easier all the time.)

Mankind began exalting itself over God in the Garden of Eden. We pride ourselves in thinking that we are wise and powerful, acting as if we know more than the Creator. But we must be careful to follow His Word, else we will bring the negative promises of Scripture down on ourselves. As Isaiah warns, "The arrogance of man will be brought low and human pride humbled . . . Stop trusting in mere humans, who have but a breath in their nostrils. Why hold them in esteem?" (Isaiah 2:17, 22).

Do you believe God knows everything? Do you trust that He wants only what is best for you? These are tough questions that I tend to wrestle with during those times when my life is interrupted with a problem. But all other issues aside, if God really knows everything and He wants only what is best for me, then why do I fight being obedient?

Moses often comes to mind when I think about this issue. In Exodus 3, Moses meets God in a burning bush. God gives him very simple instructions: go to Pharaoh and bring the Israelites out of Egypt. Many are familiar with Moses's 101 excuses as to why he was not the right man for the job (Exodus 3:12–4:17). He showed doubt in his importance, disbelief that anyone would believe him, and uncertainty in his abilities given his physical limitations. Yet God persisted and eventually Moses conceded. When Moses trusted and obeyed, God took care of the details.

So often I claim "Jesus is Lord" but then act like Moses, submitting rationalizations as to why God must be wrong. I've noticed that sometimes it doesn't even matter what the size of the job is that God wants me to do. By nature, I am a quiet introvert who hates to talk on the phone. In my younger days, when God would ask me to stop working around the house long enough to call a friend, I would sit and argue with Him. I'd act as if God knew everything about the universe except the one fragment of information that prevented me from participating in His plan. If God would simply understand my natural limitations and insecurities, I thought, then He would agree with me that I was not the right person for the job.

Sometimes I think more like Jonah. God showed up in Jonah's life, and, just as with Moses, He gave very simple instructions: go to Nineveh and preach (Jonah 1:1–2). After trying to run away and earning three days in the belly of a huge fish for his effort (verse 17), Jonah finally presents himself in Nineveh and delivers God's message (Jonah 3:3–4). Then, instead of rejoicing at the repentance going on throughout town, Jonah is furious when God shows compassion (chapter 4).

Occasionally when God does not meet my expectations, I throw grand tantrums like Jonah. I act like God doesn't always have my best interests in mind. Deep in my heart, I conclude that every once in awhile, God ignores me, forgets about me, or simply lets something slip by that ultimately causes me more harm than good. After all, how can God honestly tell me that it is in my best interests to unpack that house in a new town with a toddler and preschooler underfoot while my husband searches for bombs in a danger zone half a world away?

The truth is that God does know our strengths and weaknesses, and He still wants to use us. One of the things I love about the Bible is that it shows us real people, including their shortcomings, scruples, fears, and doubts. Abraham was a liar, but he had the faith that started a nation. Moses was a murderer, but he led the children of Israel to the Promised Land. Rahab was a prostitute, but she protected the Israelite spies. The list just continues throughout the Bible. God molded one unknown, imperfect person after another and asked them to enlist into active Kingdom service. When they stepped up to do exactly what God asked of them, He intervened and provided miraculous stories that we still read today.

For every name we recognize, I imagine a hundred more who never received a single verse. Noah's wife, unnamed in the Bible, stood faithfully by her man for years while he built a monstrous boat in the desert. Imagine the persecution she endured from the town busybodies! Many women remained at Jesus's side during his ministry years simply to provide for His needs, yet the Bible records few of their names. Just think about the sacrifice these women willingly endured, not just serving a group of men for months on end, but leaving their hometown, their family, perhaps everything they grew up knowing and loving. Sounds a lot like a military wife, doesn't it?

The point is not worldly recognition, but perfect obedience. Sometimes others will see what is asked of you and sometimes they will not. Often God's instructions will be inconvenient, require great discipline, or just seem goofy. But if we truly love God, then we must obey. John records Jesus as saying, "Anyone who loves Me will obey My teaching. My Father will love them, and We will come to them and make Our home with them. Anyone who does not love Me will not obey My teaching. These words you hear are not My own; they belong to the Father who sent Me" (John 14:23–24).

Notice that Jesus puts no limitations or restrictions on His words. God doesn't provide us a free pass on any area of life. This isn't a Sunday-only verse that applies during church services and special fellowships. If we love God, we will obey His Word; and by obeying His Word, we show that we love God. If you want your life to accomplish extraordinary things and your marriage to fulfill all your girlish dreams, then you must allow Jesus to be both Savior and Lord.

FROM KATHY

> *Why do you call Me, "Lord, Lord," and do not do what I say?*
> —Luke 6:46

The Greek word for "Lord" used in Luke 6 is *Kurios*. Its Hebrew counterpart, the word most frequently substituted for the holy title YHWH in the Old Testament, is *Adonai,* and was used by the Jews to describe the sovereign God of the universe who had the right to exercise authority over his creation. Both the New Testament word *Kurios* and the Old Testament term *Adonai* embrace the concepts of honor, power, and glory (Revelation 4:11) being intricately tied to the makeup of the Supreme Authority, who had not only the right, but the responsibility, of mastering His creation.

In our modern English, we have the unfortunate disadvantage of not seeing the differences in semantics through the translation of many words in Scripture. For example, sometimes what we see translated as *Lord* is the Greek word *Rhabboni* (from the Aramaic *Rabboni*), which is a title of honor, denoting a master or a teacher. While *Rhabboni* can be used to describe men, and it conveys ideas of competency, wisdom, and greatness, *Kurios* is used only for the supreme, self-sufficient God who possesses all authority and to whom ultimately every knee will bow in submission (Philippians 2:9–11).

Most of us don't understand this concept of lordship, yet it would have been familiar to those Jesus was addressing. The Jewish people were indoctrinated with the concept of Yahweh being the only God to worship and follow. The word *Lord* as a title of honor would have never been confused with the word used for *Jehovah,* the eternal, self-existing God they had followed out of Egyptian slavery to the Promised Land.

It was from this Lord God that they eagerly awaited the promised Messiah. They understood, as Carrie said, that there was no wiggle room in serving more than the one true God. They were reminded again and again throughout their law to serve only the Lord (see Deuteronomy chapters 6–7, 10–11, and 13), and their experiences had proven the veracity of His promises. When they obeyed, blessings followed. When they didn't, they slipped into their own sin-filled destruction. The Jews had no doubt what their jealous Creator thought of sharing His glory with another.

Because they took God's laws so seriously, the concept of Lordship pervaded every area of their lives. Being a Jew wasn't just a religion. It defined who they were culturally, racially, spiritually, and relationally. Lordship flowed out of their submission to and trust of God, and was evident within marriages, families, and friendships. It permeated their history and culminated in Christ's declaration that the most important commandment is to "love the Lord your God with all your heart, soul, mind, and strength" (Matthew 22:36–40, Luke 10:25–28).

God seeks to show Himself in all our relationships. Parents, siblings, mentors, disciples, and friends all portray examples of God's love for us and remind us of our roles with our Creator. But ultimately, over time, those relationships all change. As the years pass, we displace obedience to our parents with honor for them. We will change from stewarded caretakers of our children to becoming wise counselors for them, even perhaps eventually becoming dependent upon their care for us.

But marriage most clearly depicts the beauty of the positional authority that God wants with us. Just as Paul outlines in Ephesians 5:21–33, where he compares marriage to how Christ and the church are to operate, the biblical model of marriage reflects the gentleness and kindness of one who rules and leads as well as the trust and submission of one who serves and follows. While the husband is called to lay his life down for his wife and to deal gently with her, the wife is called to submit to her husband, trusting and respecting him, following him as her leader throughout their life together. And it is here that we need to spend some time, discovering more clearly our role as wives.

The Apostle Peter uses the example of Sarah and Abraham, the great Patriarch of the Jewish nation. Peter says,

> Your beauty should not come from outward adornment, such as elaborate hairstyles and the wearing of gold jewelry or fine clothes. Rather, it should be that of your inner self, the unfading beauty of a gentle and quiet spirit, which is of great worth in God's sight. For this is the way the holy women of the past who put their hope in God used to adorn themselves. They submitted themselves to their own husbands, like Sarah, who obeyed Abraham and called him her lord.
>
> —1 Peter 3:3–6

I don't know about you, but I really have a hard time with those verses. Given our modern American culture, I have struggled to understand it on many levels. In modern-day America, women's liberation and personal rights are magnified as the essential key to our personal happiness and success. We are encouraged to pursue anything that will bring us pleasure. Along with trying to satisfy the desires of our flesh, we also are expected to maintain a level of appearance that the world will deem attractive. I have a difficult time not letting the world's standards determine my beauty, but added to that I now have the supreme challenge of trying to have a gentle and quiet spirit. Trust me—I am the furthest thing from gentle or quiet.

With my overwhelming personality, I often think of myself as a bull in a china shop. While I can be the life of the party, I can also easily take over all the festivities, not allowing anyone else to participate in the conversation. Additionally, I'm hard-headed, strong-willed, and very independent. These are not the traits of the ideal biblical wife. Imagine my husband's struggle to lead me—and my strife in being led! But this does not negate what God is trying to convey to me through Peter.

Although our culture interchanges *Lord* and *God* quite readily, Sarah would never have equated Abraham with God. She would have understood the positional authority her husband held as head of the house and master over her life. By acquiescing to Abraham, she followed the role God laid out for her, therefore ultimately submitting to Jehovah Himself. And she did this even when Abraham had less than stellar ideas.

The Bible tells us that Abraham was declared righteous because he believed God and was willing to sacrifice his son. (Genesis 15:1–6, Genesis 22:1–18, Romans 4:3, Galatians 3:6, James 2:20–24). He not only knew who the one true God was, he was intimately involved with Him. In person-to-person conversations with the Lord, Abraham spoke of his own limitations. He knew God was his shield who fulfilled promises he couldn't begin to comprehend (Genesis 15).

If Abraham knew his own shortcomings, surely Sarah did too. Yet, she didn't focus on what Abraham couldn't, wouldn't, or didn't do. She focused on what she was supposed to do. Her culture and training induced her to serve her husband without questioning his worthiness of being served. In other words, just because he had weaknesses and may not have always led her perfectly, she knew her role as a wife was to trust him, serve him, and follow him unconditionally.

FROM CARRIE

Perhaps to Americans, one of the more familiar examples of *lordship* is medieval England. After William the Conqueror won control of the country, he had to figure out a way to govern it, particularly since he wasn't popular with the citizens. His solution, feudalism, was to divide the land and give each section to one of his most loyal men. These were the dukes, earls, and barons (a.k.a. the "peers") who most supported him on the battlefield.

The land was still too big for the peers to control, so they divided up their lands into smaller tracts, awarding each section to their most loyal men, the Norman knights. The knights then became overlords of whatever populace lived in the area. The knights were not gods by any means, but they assumed the role of lord over the people.

The commoners, those at the bottom of this tiered system, could do only what they were told, and to disobey an overlord's command meant punishment. A major problem with feudalism became apparent during the Peasant's Revolt of 1381. Although the populace had many stressors at the time, including an outbreak of the plague and high taxes, one of the key dilemmas was this: the people didn't trust their leadership. Commoners called the men in charge "Lord", but it was only grudgingly; they didn't mean it in their hearts.

Now let's look back at Sarah. By calling Abraham, "Lord," she verbally acknowledged Abraham's authority over her. But what about her heart? Was it more than just a title she used to identify him? Let's look at her life:

In Genesis 12:10–20, Abraham deceives Pharaoh into thinking that he and Sarah are nothing more than siblings. In my mind, it makes it worse that this is not some last-ditch effort to save their lives. This is the plan going into Egypt before they encounter the first Egyptian! Scripture indicates that not only did Sarah comply with Abraham's request, but she did so without saying anything to anyone who would have told Pharaoh that Abraham wasn't telling the whole story.

In Genesis 18:6, Abraham gave Sarah instructions to drop everything she was doing and make bread for surprise visitors. The remaining verses do not tell us what she said or thought, but they give the indication that she did so and wasn't overly bothered by it.

Remember Abraham's dumb move in Genesis 12? Yep, he does it again. In Genesis 20, Abraham deceives the King of Gerar into thinking that he and Sarah are nothing more than siblings. Again, we're not told Sarah's thoughts, but Scripture indicates that Sarah complied without saying anything to the king.

FROM KATHY

The proof that Sarah's devotion to Abraham was deeply imbedded in her character is evidenced by these actions. The proof in our marriages of a surrendered heart must first begin in the evidence of our lives being given over to Christ. Everyone needs Christ as Savior. But few want a Lord over their lives. Fewer still will want to call themselves slaves to a master. But this is exactly the attitude of Sarah to Abraham. It was also the attitude of the early church to Christ. 1 Corinthians 7:22–23 says, "For the one who was a slave when called to faith in the Lord is the Lord's freed person; similarly, the one who was free when called is Christ's slave. You were bought at a price; do not become slaves of human beings."

According to Jesus, once He is Savior, He must become Lord. Matthew 10:39 states, "Whoever finds their life will lose it, and whoever loses their life for My sake will find it." The act of submitting your life to Christ is one in which you choose to lay down your life, your choices, and your sinful desires in exchange for following Christ as your master. Sometimes this is easier than others; sometimes it's a knockdown, dragout fight. But the reward, Jesus tells us in John 10:10, is abundant life! We must remember that we are submitting to the Creator of the universe, Who intimately knows us and jealously loves us.

Our lives and our marriages will never be what we long for, if we don't surrender them to the God who knows best what He designed them to be. He longs to be Lord of our life, and He won't share this role with anyone or anything else in your life. Learning to walk in obedience before God, as Christ exemplified through His complete surrender to the will of the Father, is the only true way to find the abundant life promised to us. It is the beginning steps to finding fulfillment in who you are and how you are supposed to function in all areas of your life, especially in your marriage.

So the question you must answer is this: Who really has control of your life: you or your Lord?

CHAPTER 3

KATHY'S STORY

Now have come the salvation and the power and the king-
dom of our God, and the authority of His Messiah. For the ac-
cuser of our brothers and sisters, who accuses them before our
God day and night, has been hurled down. They triumphed over
him by the blood of the Lamb and by the word of their testimony;
they did not love their lives so much as to shrink from death.

—Revelation 12:10–11

The power of our testimony. It is more than we know. In the life that your God calls you to walk is the very power He has given you to overcome the enemy. To overcome the darkness. To overcome the pain. To overcome the loneliness. To shut down the lies that you have already walked through and past into the beautiful light of truth when you embraced the blood of the Lamb.

When I read those verses from Revelation 12, it gives me a whole new perspective on why my life has looked like it has. When Jesus walked out His life, and gave His life, He paved a way for me to be covered from all unrighteousness and to embrace life abundant, which I could never know apart from Him. His blood covers all the sin, pain, and loneliness and allows me to look up from my filth and despair through the blood and see, not with empty promises of rose-colored glasses, but with eyes of truth that suddenly grasp reality unlike I ever perceived. The mess isn't ugly, but beautiful, like when you first catch sight of a newborn babe just from the womb. Covered in blood and mess, but screaming with life and energy and the hope of a future unknown, all before him. This is the blood of the Lamb. Truth. Life. This is our hope.

So I will share my testimony with you. I want to show you how this sweet Jesus covered me with His precious blood, demonstrating to me how to lay down my own life following His example, and where He has met me and how it had the most profound effects on not only me, but also on my marriage. His Word has been the unchangeable compass that has forever directed my path, even when I was unaware of it, and it protected me even in the haziest, darkest places of my walk. My prayer for you is that you find a new longing to press into the perfection of His Word and find His plans for you there. And that you will learn to embrace your own precious testimony as you see it through the eyes of Christ.

I come from a relatively small family, having only one younger brother. But both my parents came from large families, and family was very important in my life growing up. When I was born, I had eleven living grandparents and great-grandparents. I didn't lose the final one until I was thirty-nine years old, and several of them affected my life even into my adulthood. Not many people can testify to that many loving grandparents for so much of their lives. I have dozens of aunts, uncles, and cousins who have been vastly important to me in various seasons of my life, and I am so blessed to have them all.

My mother was saved while raising my brother and me, but my father was not. My father is saved now, and for that I am eternally grateful. But he did not come to Christ until after I had my third child; when I was a child, he was not a godly man. A good man, who loved my mother, brother, and me, but not a godly man. All I knew at that time was that my daddy and mommy loved each other and loved me. And I am still very grateful that they showed me this powerful truth. My mom always made sure we were in church with friends and family, even if, due to her full-time job as a nurse, she couldn't be there. I'm grateful for her persistence to make sure we were given that foundation. But in an unequal marriage, there were many gray areas in biblical truth presented with two very different belief systems.

My family instilled in me basic manners from a very early age. I learned to respect adults and their authority in all areas of my life. A token biblical model of morals was handed to me from all sides of my family, even the unsaved ones. Most of them had exposure to biblical truth even if they didn't embrace it, and they knew enough to know how to at least look the part of a good moral citizen, even though they weren't actually Christian. My family stressed the outward appearance of actions rather than the motive. This helped instruct me in my path of outward obedience without inward heart change.

I accepted Christ as my Savior when I was nine years old and followed through with water baptism at that time. I sincerely loved Jesus and wanted to be a good girl. I remember realizing then, for the first time, that my dad wasn't saved. I remember grieving for him, and wrestling with the fact he wouldn't go to church with us. I have journal entries from this time of my life, praying that my dad would get saved so he wouldn't go to hell. I began, for the first time, to notice differences in the belief systems of my parents.

Even in my Baptist church, a worldly faith walk was often acceptable. Now that certainly wasn't preached, but it was obviously emulated by the people whose lives I watched. For example, I was told we should always put God first and that the Bible was truth, but then I saw them clearly putting other things—such as jobs, relationships, and possessions—ahead of Christ, and very few read their Bibles or embraced the Word as absolute truth in their lives.

I recall reading my Bible before bed one night when I was twelve. I stumbled onto the passages in 1 Corinthians 12–14 that discuss the many gifts of the Spirit. I got so excited that I ran to my mom to show her. I knew when I read those chapters that I wanted to have all those gifts, which is just what Paul had said . . . to desire the greater gifts. I wanted to move in prophesy and healing. I wanted to lead, and have faith, and speak in tongues. When you are twelve, that all sounds so cool! That still sounds cool at forty-two!

But when I approached my mother excitedly, she was dumbfounded and didn't know what to say to me. She had never considered those gifts for our lives. I don't know if she believed that we, as good Baptists, could even have those gifts. She saw them there plainly in the Word and so wanted to tell me it was truth, but she didn't know how to justify telling me that, since these gifts clearly were not a part of our life of worship and doctrine. She told me she honestly didn't know what to say. She encouraged me to talk to my pastor to gain insight. So I did.

He told me God could choose to give those gifts, since after all He is God, but He simply didn't choose to do that anymore. It was something He did for a season in the early church to help them during their trials and to take the gospel forth.

My question was immediately, "But what about our trials, and aren't we supposed to still take the gospel forth?" I also questioned him about the fact that the New Testament was written for the church after Christ's resurrection, and weren't we still, in the present day, under the same title of *the church* until Christ's return, meaning that all the Scriptures were applicable to us?

He was rather dumbfounded with me as well. He proceeded to fumble about and tell me I was too young to grasp the full theological relevance of things, and began using large words (which I'm sure he learned in seminary) that shut me right up. He made me feel quite silly for questioning the Word as I did. He commended me for reading my Bible, but said I really shouldn't hope for those things as he really didn't think God would choose to operate that way today.

I didn't know it then, but the Holy Spirit was guiding all of that. God placed in me a great desire to read His Word, and to not just read it, but to study it. But I can also see that the enemy placed some serious webs of deception in my thinking. What I took from this experience was that God's Word was not true all the time. It was true only when it was relevant to a particular time period or season. It didn't necessarily apply to my life today.

So, I began to pick and choose from the Scripture what I would apply to my life. For example, I didn't mind the Scriptures about not making an idol. I wasn't about to go craft a golden calf, but surely my overt fascination with my clothing and appearance wasn't idolatry, was it? After all, this was the twentieth century, and no one back in New Testament times had to face the peer pressure and choices I had to face in middle school . . . right?

This shocking incident made me feel quite stupid for questioning someone with greater authority than me about the Word. Up to that point I had always believed, without question, my parents and authorities. My parents had never made me feel silly for asking questions. In fact, just the opposite. But now I began to question whether I could trust the authority figures in my life— or my own heart.

I spent the next several years wrestling within myself about what was right and true. I wanted to believe my parents, pastors, and teachers, but because I often got mixed messages from them, I also began to wonder whom I was supposed to believe. I often caved in my personal conviction because I was ashamed or afraid. But there were times when my pride rose up and I got angry, because I wanted to follow my heart and I either didn't think others cared or understood. I was a mixture of obedience and rebellion, all in one.

I still read my Bible, but I also often decided to skip the parts that would have illuminated the truth during this season. The result was that through the next few years I walked with one foot in the world and one in the Word. James 4:4–10 and 2 Timothy 4:3–4 talks about this kind of person. My friendship with the world would cause me to be double-minded and my desire to satisfy what my itching ears wanted to hear would keep me far from the truth, long into adulthood.

Through my teen years, I was an oxymoron of tendencies. I was a leader in my church youth group, but I didn't mind going to parties where drinking and smoking were commonplace among my friends. I actively read my Bible, but also regularly watched MTV and R-rated movies. I was an "A" student and well liked by most adults because I was responsible and well mannered. But in many ways, I had begun functioning in a way that I knew would please them and would ultimately gain me some acceptance or benefit. I behaved in peer groups similarly. By most of the world's standards, I simply skirted the boundaries of wild living. Thankfully, alcohol and drugs were never real temptations to me. Quite possibly because I had seen the effects of alcoholism on some of my extended family, and because it was out of my reach financially.

I met my husband, Sam, during driver's education class. He told me on our first date that he planned to join the military. He was sixteen years old, and he had a plan. My sixteenth birthday was the next day, and I had a plan for my life as well, which did not include being with someone going into the military. The thought had never occurred to me, so it wasn't in my plan. I teased him a little about having "a girl in every port," and he said he wasn't like that, that he wanted a wife and family to come home to after deployments. I was somewhat impressed that he was already contemplating his wife, because most boys I had met were only interested in the moment. Sam was the first guy I had met who was looking for not only marriage, but a family as well. Those things were in my plan, so I decided to go out with him again.

We went out several times over the next few months, and by that following summer we were inseparable. During my junior year—Sam's senior year—of high school we missed no less than 40 days of school: we skipped them just so we could spend the days together. Miraculously, we both still managed to pass our classes and avoid being caught, until the final nine weeks of school. My mother was the one to realize the truth when she went to the high school one day to question them about why her straight-A, honor-roll daughter hadn't been inducted into the National Honor Society. She had the eye opening experience of learning that I wasn't as honorable as I had led her to believe.

So my parents tried to rein me in. I finished the school year without another absence, and they began to take a more vested interest in how and where I spent my time, but I staunchly refused to bend on my relationship with Sam. My mother especially tried to make me end the relationship, but by this time, Sam and I knew we were going to marry. I began to be openly defiant to my parents, and refused to end the relationship.

At this point, my dad was unsaved, so my parents were still unequally yoked in their marriage. My dad, although disappointed with my deceit, wasn't as against us being together as my mom was, so I became a very good manipulator and would speak to whichever parent I thought would give me the answer I wanted to hear in any given situation. This caused more stress in my home than I can begin to tell you. Stress between myself and my parents, but also, I think, stress in my parent's marriage. I can see now how God used the stress they were going through to stretch them both into new levels of dying to self. My mother learned much about dying to self in her faith walk during those years. My father just had his heart broken and got angry, until eventually he came to see that he needed a Savior to heal his heart. So in all of this season of my walk, although I am not thankful for the ugliness of it, I can clearly see the beauty Christ brought forth from it in my parents. For Sam and me, the beauty was to come, but it would take more mess and more time before we would bend to that dying to self and resurrection power.

Sam graduated school and left for Ft. Benning, Georgia. I went with his mother to see him in the fall when he graduated from basic training, and he gave me my engagement ring. He was able to come home for Christmas after getting his jump wings, and then promptly left for Germany for two years.

My parents were not in support of my engagement. They wanted me to finish college and have a career before finding my husband and settling down to start a family. Education meant a great deal to them both. They were the first ones in each of their families to graduate from high school and go on to get college degrees. They pushed to instill in me, at least at that time, that education was the one factor that would set you apart from everyone else, and it meant security and success for your life. I remember when I came home with the engagement ring, my dad said to me that he didn't mind if I married Sam. He just stressed it was critical that I got my education so, if the marriage failed, I would be able to take care of myself.

I know now they were so concerned because many of my parents' siblings walked through serious marital issues and divorce. My grandparents all stayed married, and I thank God that legacy passed to my parents, but, sadly, for so many others in our life, marriage was transient, not permanent. My parents feared I would not be able to provide for myself and any future children if I didn't have a degree and a career firmly established. Education and a career were to become pillars in my life: pillars on which I would base much of my worth and value.

Don't misunderstand me. I see education as a God-given blessing, and it should be embraced for what it is meant to be. And certainly, I would never see a career as sinful for anyone. But I made both of these things an unhealthy measure of my worth. Because I was successful academically and had a promising future ahead of me, I held a great deal of pride in those areas, as well as a false notion that a career would solidify my success in life. God would later show me just how different His perspective was about my value and from where I was to draw my worth.

I did go to college while Sam was in Germany, but when he returned for three weeks' leave after being gone almost a year, we eloped. We didn't tell anyone. He wanted to tell the world and take me back to Germany, but disappointing everyone by not finishing school was not something I was willing to do. I believed the lie that school was my measure of personal success, so to let that go was to become a failure. My pride was too great for that. I didn't want to lose Sam, my family, or my own personal success. I wanted to have it all: The American Dream. It was easy for me to cover up the truth at this point, though, since I had been practicing telling lies for years. I convinced Sam to keep the news quiet, and he left to go back to Germany alone while I went to school. (And worked three jobs to pay our phone bill!)

I justified my deceit by convincing myself that I was doing everyone a big favor. After all, I wasn't hurting anyone, was I? After all the pain I'd caused my parents through the lies in high school, I reasoned that they would be better off not knowing. And Sam would be a better man if he had a better woman, which I would be once I got a degree and could earn a good living to help support us. So I fell again into deceit.

I even tried to convince myself that getting married was just a legality to justify what we had already consummated. I wanted it to be legal, because in my heart I knew that being with Sam physically while not married was a sin, and I was eaten up with guilt. So I reasoned within myself that if we just got married, then this heavy weight of sin would lift, and I would be free. But I just exchanged one sin for another. My insecurities and pride all mingled with the many decisions that followed, and soon I was swallowed up with the tangled webs of deception I found myself weaving constantly with my family and friends.

While I was busy with work and school, I also spent time reading my Bible. I had an idea in my head of what I wanted my marriage and life to look like. I wanted a man who loved me more than anything else. I wanted a couple of children. I wanted a successful career. I wanted a great relationship with my extended family. I wanted to raise my kids in church as I had been raised.

But unlike with my parents, I wanted my husband to be in church, too. I desired to have God in my marriage. I had felt His tug on my heart for years, and had heard the whispers of the Lord in my mind. After almost a year of being married and having seen Sam only once when I flew to Germany for a week's visit, I remember one day driving to work and praying to God to bless my marriage. I clearly heard the Lord say, "I am Truth. Only that which is founded in truth can I build upon."

My heart sank. I knew we were lying to everyone. Now I knew I couldn't live with that lie anymore. Sam was due back from Germany in a few short months. He had come to the States, passed the Special Forces selection process, and was due to begin the SF (Special Forces) qualification course at Fort Bragg, North Carolina, upon his PCS (Permanent Change of Station) from Germany. I would be leaving my parent's home to join him as soon as he returned, and they didn't even know we were married. I had to tell them the truth. This was the most difficult thing I had ever done.

When I told my parents, they were emotionally crushed and angry. As was my brother. Then I had to go and confront my grandparents. Amazingly, although everyone else in my world was furious with me, my grandparents all handled it extremely well. I remember my granddad just hugged me and told me he loved me. My other grandpa and grandma each wrapped their arms around me and began praying for me, my young husband, and our life together. My grandma even smiled through tears and said, "I always did think he was a nice boy. You'll get along just fine, sweetie. He'll be a good man. Just remember to keep loving Jesus."

What love. What forgiveness. What hope and peace that was given to me by those who had lived enough to know life is hard, but tomorrow is a new day full of mercy. They had all made similar mistakes in their own lives. They had created their own messes and made their own mistakes, but they knew life would still go on. They knew God was bigger than this present dark situation I found myself in. And they loved me. It would take time for my parents to forgive me, but God used even this as a time for revealing truth in their lives. I praise our Lord that He wastes nothing in our lives. Especially our mistakes.

Sam came home, and I was eager to begin a new life based on truth with him. I was experiencing a new rush of hope in the Lord and it strengthened me for the things ahead. I had already gone to North Carolina by myself and arranged an apartment and the utilities. Having never even done my own grocery shopping or laundry, now I had left home to join with a man I hadn't spent time with in more than two years. I would need all the guidance and protection God could give me.

Two weeks into our new life together, we found out I was pregnant. We were using birth control when this happened, so it was definitely a surprise. I was terrified. I barely knew the man I was living with, and now we were going to have to get used to the idea of being parents and sharing our life with someone else!

Sam, remarkably, wasn't nearly as scared about us having a baby, which would prove to be true throughout our lives. It seemed with each new child God always rattled my trust, but Sam embraced the idea of being a father. That amazed me, because

Sam never had a father in his life, only his mom, who raised six children alone. Sam was the youngest of his family.

Sam had not grown closer to the Lord during our time apart. As a child, Sam had been invited to church by an older gentleman. The old fella would regularly pick up Sam and one of his sisters to take them to church. Sam found a love in that church that he didn't have in his home. His mother ended up joining them in church after some time, and when Sam was nine years old, he received salvation and was baptized in a river, along with his mother and sister, one cold, spring, Sunday morning in West Virginia. For a few short years, before junior high, he attempted to press into the Lord and grow in faith. But, even with the professed faith from his mother, she continued to live a rough lifestyle and several of her life choices ended up causing her and her children to struggle. Sam had very little accountability in his life from about the age of thirteen.

During his time in Germany, he had a roommate who was a professed Satan worshipper. With no understanding of how the spirit realm operates, Sam was being affected greatly by the influence of darkness that was so near his life. Like the slow creeping of fire across a piece of paper, the enemy began to burn into Sam's thoughts and choices, destroying the good that the Lord had for him. Through the music he listened to, the people he chose to engage with, and even the clothes he wore, a darkness was evident in Sam by the time he returned to the U.S. Where prior to high school graduation he had never cursed, his speech now would have made a sailor blush.

I wanted to find a good Baptist church to attend when we re-united, but Sam wouldn't even discuss it. I eventually guilted him into attending with me on a couple of different Sundays through the course of our first year, but I was easily persuaded into skip-ping church and spending our Sundays together, as it was our only day to see each other. Sam was busy with his training and school, and I was enrolled in school full-time, plus working at a local restaurant nearly full-time. And so again, I knew I was hear-ing the Lord's voice, but I chose to disobey by continuing to place Sam as an idol ahead of my God.

I was still up to my old tricks of justifying my sin. I told myself I needed to foster a good marriage by following my husband's lead. We needed to get to know each other all over again, I thought, and quickly, before our son arrived in nine months! Choosing time with Sam seemed like the right course of action if we were to build a strong relationship.

During those months, I was still praying, but I slowly gave up reading my Bible. So, I had little input into my life that resounded with truth. I was struggling to feel loved by Sam. He told me he loved me, and he was affectionate, but when you are trying to fill the God-sized hole in your heart with someone or something other than God, you will always be left feeling hollow. So there was emptiness in the love I felt from Sam, because I was unknow-ingly expecting Sam to fill the place that was meant for only God.

We experienced other issues as well. Sam struggled with an ad-diction to pornography that he was able to keep hidden from me, but somewhere in my heart I knew it was there. I confronted him, and we fought several times, but he always denied everything and said I was just insecure and it was my problem, not his. I suspected he was having an affair, but I acknowledged to him that I was growing increasingly more suspicious of everything in our life. I always ended up begging him to forgive me at the end of our fights, because I was mistrusting him even though he had given me no reason to not trust him.

Another problem we had was that I had no idea of the long-term effects that premarital sex would have on a marriage, and on a woman, in particular. We will elaborate on this later in the book, but what I didn't know was that deep in the heart of every woman is a hard-wiring by God with a need to be covered and protected. When a woman is not cherished and valued through purity, and when she doesn't hold that sacred virginity until her marriage bed, she will always wonder if she is valuable enough for the man to want to stick around. After all, she will think: if she was cheaply gained, how valuable could she be?

So, I had self-esteem issues and insecurities permeating throughout my thoughts and emotions.

Plus, I was still walking with idolatry and lingering deception in my life. I was terrified to let Sam see who I wanted to be. I wanted to go to church. I wanted to follow God, but I was so afraid of losing Sam that I began to do as I thought he wanted. I was back to my old tricks of putting out there what I thought others wanted to see in me because I was too afraid to be who I knew I was called to be.

I was also disappointed with how little time we had to be together. I was becoming increasingly aware of the frustrations of being an Army wife. Sam would have to report at a certain time of day, and, since we had only one car, I would have to drive him there. That meant me waking up and heading to base sometimes as early as 4:30 a.m. That was hard, but not nearly as hard as being told to pick him up at 5:00 p.m.—only to arrive and wait until 8:30 p.m. because someone lost something that day in training and no one was allowed to go home until the item was recovered. Even if they knew who had lost it. So I was missing classes, arriving late to work, and losing sleep all because of the Army rigamarole. I could not understand the foolishness of so many people who were supposed to be leaders. Clearly, they had no idea how to run things efficiently!

And so many weeks were still spent apart. The military life-style was not conducive to us making plans of any sort. We would plan a weekend trip to head home to see family or to go to the beach, only to be told at the last minute that he couldn't go be-cause he was now on alert and had to stay in town, or he had to go to the field. I was not pleased with any of this. I knew it wasn't Sam's fault, but I still got angry, and as he was the only person standing in front of me, he usually caught the full brunt of my frustration and anger. I tried not to make him feel worse, but oc-casionally, he actually seemed excited about the trips and training, and then I would get furious with him. How dare he choose to enjoy work over time with me? I began to wonder if he even loved me as much as I loved him. I was quite selfish in this manner, and adjusting to the military lifestyle was not easy to do with so many insecurities and selfish tendencies in my life. Add pregnancy hor-mones into the mix, and I was a mess.

We were slowly spiraling down together in our personal and collective sins. But in all our failings, good was happening also. I was doing well in school. Sam was too. We were sharing our first pregnancy, and we both grew increasingly excited to see our first child. We really did love each other. Despite all our sins, we were trying to give of our best to one another. The foolishness of youth often affected our decisions, but we were trying to love even in our selfishness. Sam and I were trying in our own strength to offer each other our best. And for a short while, it seemed like it might be enough.

We had our first baby, Jedidiah Gunner (we call him Gunner), but Sam nearly missed the birth. He got home while I was in labor, and only five days later he left for six weeks. He got home and finished up with graduation, got his green beret, and began language school. He was assigned French. That meant we were going to be stationed with 3rd Group, keeping us at Ft. Bragg once he got to his unit. I kept working, taking houses to clean so I could take our son with me in a pack-n-play, and I continued to work on my degree. We were incredibly busy in our own separate goals, along with raising a baby and living on a very meager income. Money was tight, sleep was scarce, and our relationship was in a constant roller coaster of ups and downs. Our son was probably the best thing we shared at that time.

When Gunner was sixteen months old, we bought our first home, in a small town called Parkton. We moved away from Fayetteville and many of the unhealthy relationships we had developed there. Our first week in our new home, Sam actually suggested that we try going to the Baptist church in town. I felt like we were being given a new start.

When we began going to church, I rejoiced. As our son had gotten older, I knew I was supposed to have him in church. I often thought of how my mom had made sure to get my brother and me to church when we were children. But I was such a coward. I wouldn't leave Sam's side in order to do what was best for our son—what I knew God was calling me to do.

I think with the purchase of the house, Sam also wanted to start fresh on our marriage and life together. He began to look forward to attending church. We made some friends there and joined the couples' Sunday school class, where we met about half a dozen other young couples all our age and in similar life circumstances. Sam and I both were opening up to Christ in a way we never had before.

We decided to try to get pregnant with a second baby. We both agreed we wanted at least one more child, and we didn't want them more than three years apart. We tried for nine months to conceive, with no success. This was surprising to us both, considering we had gotten pregnant with our son while using birth control.

Despite our inability to have a baby, we were much happier in our marriage than we had ever been. We had a beautiful healthy son. I was almost done with school—so a promising career with better income was ahead of us. And we placed God back into our life on Sundays. I was more fulfilled than I had been in years.

My relationship with my parents and family was also nearly restored, due to the birth of our son. My parents were proving to be doting grandparents, and my mother was finally able to stop nagging me about why I wasn't going to church. Also, I stopped being so distrustful of Sam. I still had nagging doubts about him, and us, but he was putting much more effort into loving me.

Yes, life was aligning perfectly in my best plan. I began to live with a confidence I hadn't experienced since high school. I found success in all I set my hands to. Relationships were smooth, and life was good.

I honestly thought that where we were was as good as it could get. My limited brain couldn't conceive of more than we had. We were completely unaware that powerful storms were about to hit us.

I am so very glad that God didn't give me only what I asked for. It says in Romans chapter 2 that God's kindness leads us to repentance. It says later in the same chapter that God will judge men's secrets through Jesus Christ. What that meant in our life was that God loved us too much to let us sit in the mess we had made and pretend it wasn't there. He didn't want my husband's secret sins to have any hold on his heart. He loved Sam too much for him to have anything less than true freedom. God loved me too much to let me find my worth in my husband's approval of me or my success at school and work. I could never earn my blessing from the Lord by keeping up appearances. My life finally looked good to anyone looking through our window; the outside of our cup was clean. But what about the inside? I was so conditioned to a depraved way of thinking and moving in my life, that truth was something I could catch only glimpses of, and usually in others, not in myself.

The young pastor who began to mentor Sam in that small Baptist church was a shining example of real love. He held the Word of God as his absolute authority on life. I loved what he would say when he would open up the Scriptures. A hunger that had long lain, sleeping and starved, in the recesses of my mind began to awaken within me—I wanted more truth. As I began to tentatively step out and ask God for more of Himself in my life, I had no idea the power and love I was about to lose in my world. For those who seek Him will find Him. And make no mistake, He is seeking us. He had never once, in all those years, let go of me. He had never once forgotten that He had placed in me a hunger for truth in His Word and that He had giftings lined up for me from before the foundation of the earth.

Quite frankly, if at that very moment God had opened a crack into the door of heaven and given me a glimpse of what lay ahead of me, I believe I may have run screaming for the hills. I don't know that I would have eagerly raised my hand as Isaiah did and said, "Here am I. Pick me!" (Isaiah 6:8). But in my ignorance of faith, I tentatively placed my big toe out of my comfort zone and whispered to God that I thought maybe there was more to life, and I would like to see if that was true. God answered my prayer.

I got pregnant. Two days later I found pornography in our home. Sam was with me when I stumbled upon it. It was as much a shock to him as to me because he thought he had finally gotten rid of all the evidence. I felt like someone had punched me in the gut. I didn't even know how to react. I got up, left the room . . . and vomited. Sam didn't even try to follow me. The shame at having been caught was more than he could bear. He had tried to hide his addiction and put it behind him.

I was exposed to pornography at a very young age in different situations. In many ways, the safety of growing up in a small town and being near all our family lured my parents into a false sense of safety for us. Or maybe neither of them were in a place to know that Satan was really out to steal, kill, and destroy (John 10:10), but either way, I was exposed to far more as a child than I should have been. I didn't just see magazines. Hard-core porn videos had crossed my path on more than one occasion before the age of ten. I never discussed this with my parents, because dark things have a natural bent to stay in darkness. The enemy likes it that way: keep things hidden.

In many ways, this exposure to sex as being something dirty and something that needed to stay a secret in dark places helped to pave the path for Sam's and my future sins together. But I had always hated porn. I felt dirty enough in my own heart without bringing smut into our life. Sam had never even suggested we have porn in our life together. He, too, knew it's dark hold, and he had lived alone in that secret place of bondage a very long time.

When I saw the evidence of what I had suspected for three years, I was angry. I felt betrayed on so many levels. What else could he have done to deceive me? Were there other women? My mind whirled with the gravity of it all. There I was, pregnant, and suddenly having to question everything I had placed my faith in. My self-esteem went through the floor. After all, if he needed to look at pornography, I reasoned, I must not have been enough to satisfy him. And then I remembered all the times he had told me I was crazy and insecure and the one with the problem. I wanted to hate him. He had purposefully made me feel like a jerk, and I had begged *him* to forgive *me* for doubting his faithfulness.

My house of cards was crashing hard and fast. We barely spoke for two days, and I cringed when he got near me. He tried to give me space, and he ended up begging me to forgive him, as he was reduced to tears for the first time in our five-year relationship. I was so broken and hurt. I wanted to believe him, but I was so wounded and raw. I told him I would try to forgive him and we would try to move forward.

The very next day he was told he was being emergency-deployed to Haiti for an invasion. It was September 1994, and Jimmy Carter was sent as an ambassador to run interference in the escalating situation, but thousands of troops were sent with a 48-hour notice to invade. Sam was to go with his team in Third Group and would be one of the first to go in on choppers for a ground assault.

I was terrified. For the first time in our marriage, I was suddenly faced with the possibility that Sam might die. He had never been sent to Iraq during Desert Storm in 1990–1991; he had simply been on alert status. But now he was actually going to go fight. I was overwhelmed with the thought of losing Sam. I was pregnant. I had a two-year-old son. My heart was still raw from the fresh betrayal, and yet it still belonged to this man. In fact, more of it belonged to him than my jealous God wanted to allow. For this reason, I believe God allowed my whole world to topple. He allowed me to lose my grip on all I had held onto for so many years. He wanted to show me a better way. Himself.

God wanted me to hold onto and trust in Him. To allow *Him* to minister to my broken heart, not Sam. He wanted me to know my worth. He wanted Sam to know freedom. He wanted both of us to see ourselves as He saw us. To see ourselves beyond our messed up thinking and beyond where we were right at that moment, but what we *could* be if we would surrender ourselves to Him. But we had to let go of ourselves and each other in order to do that. God helped us, by causing us to face the very real possibility of living life without each other.

Sam left. Two weeks later I had a miscarriage. I plummeted even further into a dark abyss of pain and fear. One of my two reasons for holding onto the marriage was now gone. I wasn't sure I had the strength within me to go forward. I wanted so much more out of life for Gunner. I had always sworn to myself that I wouldn't divorce, as I had seen the pain and suffering divorce had caused to so many in my family. I wanted more. I had believed for more. But I was out of resources; I was out of strength.

All my pillars of emotional support were gone. I didn't have Sam. I didn't believe in myself. I had just lost a child. And I began to believe the whispers of the enemy that God had taken that baby because I was an awful mother, and it was better for that baby to not grow up through a divorce because that was where I was headed. I was utterly alone. I couldn't even share the loss of our child with Sam. I wasn't sure I would ever share anything with Sam again. I was sinking so quickly into darkness.

Sam was able to call me for a few seconds from Cuba about 10 days following the miscarriage. The conversation went as follows:

"Hey Kath, I love you. How are you feeling? Do you have morning sickness?"

"There is no baby. I lost it. There probably isn't even a marriage at this point. I don't know what to say to you."

Silence.

"I'm sorry. I don't know what to say either. I love you."

"I love you too. I'm not sure that will be enough anymore."

He proceeded to tell me they were leaving Cuba and heading into Haiti within the next couple of days. The evening news had just indicated that Carter had managed to negotiate some sort of treaty and so we would be occupying Haiti instead of invading. Everyone expected there to be some insurgents, though, so we would have to gain control of the rebellion upon our initial entry. Sam was still going in first.

I was scared. And for the first time in our life together, Sam could not pull me out of the despair I was sinking into. No promise he could say was going to help me. No hope for a future together was going to mend the brokenness of my shattered heart. And Sam knew it too. So for the first time in Sam's life, he faced the realization that he might be losing me. He too was lost and broken. All that we had built our hope on and gained our strength from was now collapsed and broken.

Sam and I had very little contact over the next several months. Sam's team went into Haiti fully armed. Thankfully, there were no major threats to their arrival. But there were also no phones where he stayed in Haiti after occupation, so over the next five months I got only about five radio/phone calls. He was able to send me a few letters, through people heading back to the States with the supply planes. I tried to write to him and send him packages sporadically with the resupply planes when we were allowed.

For you younger folks reading this, you probably don't remember a world without Internet and cell phones. But this was before any of those glorious modern conveniences. We had to rely on letters and radio communications. Since I was not a ham operator, we were dependent on those who were. Sam would radio out of Haiti and find someone in the U.S. listening on the same frequency as him. When he found someone willing to make a call for him, they would call me on the telephone and hook their radio up to it so I could communicate through this mediator. I had to use the same words the radio operators used, so they would know when to hand the call over to Sam on his end, for him to speak. I had to start everything I said with *Roger that* and end everything I said with *Over,* knowing that a stranger was listening to every word we shared.

When your marriage is in such a desperate place as ours was and there is so very much that needs to be said, this is not the most helpful means of communication. The calls were usually very brief, with little information exchanged, and even less emotion and affection due to the impersonal disjointedness of the whole thing. It made our lives seem more separate and lonely than ever.

I was still going to school full time, when I bothered to go to classes. Gunner was two-years old and deserved so much better than I gave him at that time. I trained the child to work the VCR and get his own pop-tarts to eat so I could sleep half the day on the couch. I would go days without showering and rarely ate. I honestly contemplated suicide for a brief time, but because I couldn't imagine how that would affect my son's future, I refused to linger there in my thoughts. As selfish as I was, I praise God He still showed His love for me, His child, by reminding me of my love for my own child. And so I pressed on in darkness.

I didn't want anyone to know what I was going through. Keeping up appearances was *still* hanging in my twisted thoughts. I know my parents were worried because I had just suffered a miscarriage and my husband was away, but they had no idea the state of my marriage, and I wasn't about to let them see what a lousy mother I was turning out to be. I had a new acquaintance in my life at the time whose husband was in Haiti with Sam, and her friendship would prove to be one of the greatest gifts God has ever brought me. But she too was kept at arms length from my heart struggles.

I would occasionally drag myself to school, because it was one of the last fragile pillars I had built my hopes and worth on that had yet to topple. I unknowingly allowed myself to walk right into the hands of the enemy of my soul, who was so eager to devour me completely in my now weakened mental, emotional, and spiritual state. Two things helped me stumble into the pit I was to fall into next.

The first was that Sam had taken very little interest in my education up to this point. He valued it very little, and even suggested that I might not be able to complete my degree due to our financial stresses. He wanted me to quit school and go to work more to alleviate the immediate financial pressures we were under. But I had convinced him that if I stayed in school I had a plan to make much more money with my career and it would be worth it in the end. He agreed, but other than the financial gain it would ultimately bring us, he had no real interest in the things I was learning.

I think he was just too busy with his career. But Sam's lack of interest in my goals left me feeling as if he didn't care about me. Remember, so much of my worth was falsely tied to my educational success. I felt that me being the one left to pay the bills, clean the house, raise our child, and face the stresses of our home—all alone—were all that Sam was entitled to as my show of support for his career. By comparison, he offered me little to no support with my goals. In my young, foolish mind, I felt like I was being short-changed by him. My own apparent lack of interest and support of his job at this point didn't affect my thinking or cause me to realize my own selfishness.

The second thing that helped me open the door to the enemy of my life in a profound way was that I had an immense amount of pride and arrogance; this was about to usher in a great fall. I reasoned in my foolish heart that Sam couldn't truly love me, since he had fallen into sin with pornography and deception. I was convinced at this point that Sam had been involved in at least one affair, even though he denied it; I didn't trust him at all. I had placed Sam on such a pedestal of idolatry in my heart until then, that I believed I could never cheat on him and betray him as he had done to me. I even told him this: I would never tell someone I loved them and then treat them that way. He didn't love me as much as I loved him, I said. I reasoned that I was a better person than he was. In my foolish arrogance, I was about to learn a very valuable lesson. Never say never.

During a Shakespeare class one day (I bothered to show up, in sweat pants and with unwashed hair in a ponytail), I answered some questions brought up in class discussion. When class was over, I was approached by a guy whom I shared several classes with. He too was an English Literature major. He was very kind to me and said that he always enjoyed my comments. He thought my insights were engaging, and said he always looked forward to the stimulating discussion I brought to the class.

The door was opened. My rock-bottom self-esteem had its first encouragement in months; someone was finding worth in the only thing of value I felt I had left in my life. This man's compliments began to stroke my ego and make me hungry for more of the same to satisfy my starved, lonely heart. He saw me as smart. He liked what I had to say. He was *listening* to what I had to say. Nothing is more attractive to someone who feels worthless than a person who tells them they have worth. Even if they are lying. And I was so good at believing the lies of the enemy, I thought the only thing of value I had left was my success in academics. It was easy to believe and embrace that this person saw my value in that as well.

My already dark journey was now on a slippery slope. The more I shared with this man, the more I rationalized that he was good for me. I felt like he was bringing me out of my emotional pit. He was encouraging me to move forward in my school and career. He told me what a great mom I was to be caring alone for my son. He was always complimenting my abilities to handle everything so well. The enemy was using every word he spoke to continue to stroke my fragile ego.

I was torn in my spirit unlike any other time in my life. My best description of myself during this brief season is that I was like Dr. Jekyll and Mr. Hyde. Falling into this relationship the enemy had laid out to ensnare me, sinking quickly into a dark ocean of sin, I was also walking in a new friendship with the military wife whom God had laid out for me as a lifeline.

This new friend was a Christian. She began joining me in our small church, and she forced accountability in my life, by persuading me to continue to attend church, when on my own I would have fallen away. She also held the unique position of having her husband posted with Sam. This forced me to keep up appearances with her so my marriage would not seem to be in shambles, and to hide the fact that I was becoming an adulterous wife. I genuinely liked this woman, and it caused me great grief to, once again, be continually lying to someone I cared about. It seemed I was born to lie to everyone in my world. I was soon to discover that I had become so adept at the skill that the one I had lied to the most was me.

My new Christian friend and I had gotten in the habit of hanging out every Saturday night. The holidays were approaching and we were getting Christmas packages ready for our husbands. In front of her, I was playing the role of being such a good wife. I managed to get my house picked up on her visits and had my son bathed and cared for those days, too. I was quite convincing due to my years of practice. But the thing I never expected was her genuine faith.

I had never met anyone like this woman. She was honest in her true love for Jesus. She didn't just want to talk about Him on Sunday. She wanted to talk about Him all the time. She started bringing her Bible to my house on Saturday evenings, and we began to look to the Word to study the different things we would talk about. The hunger I had always had regarding God's Word was aroused, and I found myself reading my Bible between our visits so I would be able to discuss with her more readily, and because I had a newfound yearning for truth.

The more I read my Bible, the more I longed for the promises within it. I knew I was a mess. I knew I was wrong. I knew He was the answer. I knew He was the Way, the Truth, and the Life, and I wanted to follow. But I had no idea how to do that. I only knew going to church. I only knew trying to be good and look good. And I had proven, most soundly, that I couldn't do either.

One night, after realizing the treachery of my own heart, I was holding empty hands to heaven, crying out in total desperation for Jesus to show up and fix me. Not just fix the situation I was in, but fix *me*. I had fallen into the same condemning sin as my husband, and I felt powerless to affect any change in my world. For the first time in my life, I was finally broken enough to see that in His great mercy, my God was the only one who could lead me. I begged Him to show Himself to me.

The next day, my girlfriend and I attended a Christmas church program. After the program, I drove her home, and we sat talking in her driveway for a few minutes. I dropped my guard for the first time ever with her and admitted to struggling with my own faith and belief that God was the only Way, Truth, and Life, because I had so little proof in my life. She immediately said that she had been waiting for me to admit that. She pulled out a list of Scriptures from her Bible that she had written down weeks before and had been carrying around, waiting for God's timing to give to me. She then proceeded to tell me I needed the power of God's hand in my life and I needed to be baptized in the Spirit.

I didn't know what she was talking about, and said immediately that I had been baptized at the age of nine. She said that wasn't the same thing. My heart started pounding and I whispered, "Are you talking about getting gifts, like speaking in tongues?"

This was almost sacrilege, after having been raised a good Baptist. But deep in my heart, I felt she was speaking a truth to me which had been buried under a lifetime of lies, and I yearned to believe her and grab hold of what she was saying. I had just challenged God the night before to show up, and now I felt light-headed, as if I might pass out. The power of the Holy Spirit was filling me and the car, and God was leading me, like never before, into truth. He was taking me back to the very root of the lies that had sidetracked me so many years before regarding His Word.

I took those Scriptures and read them. And I believed them. In fact, I believed the Bible was true from Genesis to Revelation. My friend came the next evening and asked me if I was ready to surrender everything to God and make him Lord of my life. Was I ready to receive all He had planned and the many gifts He had for me?

Shaking and terrified, but with an anticipation for a new life unlike anything I had ever experienced, I let her pray over me, and I was overcome by the power of the Holy Spirit. I was truly "slain." After she left, I stayed up most of the night devouring the Scriptures; I felt as if God Himself was speaking them to me. There was no picking and choosing. I knew it was truth. And I knew it was the only way I could ever walk if I wanted life. And I wanted life. Jesus met me there, and I understood for the first time that the Word was with God, and the Word was God (John 1:1). And in Him was life, and that life was the light of men (John 1:4).

I went to my final exams the following Monday and immediately broke off the relationship with the other man. In fact, I went so far as to tell him that he needed Jesus, and he needed to go straight home and work on his marriage. Then I turned and left.

My heart was free and full. My life was beautiful. My God had picked me up in my bloody mess and loved me right there.

I prayed for Sam. I prayed for my marriage. But I wasn't worried about either. I was so filled with new faith and hope in Christ that I knew God would find a way to fix it—anyway, I had no idea how to do it! Recognizing my own inability to control my life became my liberty. I truly turned into an overnight Jesus freak.

Two weeks later, I took Gunner and we went to West Virginia to spend Christmas with our family, since Sam was still deployed. Sam and I had not had any contact during this time. While I was in West Virginia, someone broke into our home in North Carolina and robbed us of many of our things, but also did a lot of damage to our house. I contacted Red Cross just to get a message to Sam about what had happened. I had no other way to notify him.

Although I was nervous about the break-in, I was still on a honeymoon high with the Lord and was confident, even in this new mess in our life, that God would work it out for our good. And He did. Within a week of hearing about the break-in, Sam was allowed to come home. This was more than a month ahead of his team, and they didn't ask him to rejoin them there. So when he got back, he had nearly a month to just be at home with Gunner and me.

Want to hear the most amazing part? While I was being slain in the Spirit in December, Sam was on a mountain in Haiti crying out to God too! He was sure that he had lost me and Gunner, and he was crying out to God in desperation, just like I was. And our great, merciful, and mighty God met Sam on that mountain. He too was slain in the Spirit. We have never been able to confirm it was the exact same night, but God was definitely breaking down the walls of deception in both of our hearts so He could become Lord in both of our lives at the same time. Sam feared our marriage was over, but he knew God could fix it, because he knew he couldn't. Sam and I both were freshly committed to our marriage and each other, without either of us knowing *anything* about what had happened to the other.

When Sam came home, there was a lot of confession which had to take place on both our parts. Besides the pornography, he had been in two adulterous relationships. But I had to confess my own sin to him in this area as well. This was fairly easily confessed in the beginning, but the next couple of years would prove to be difficult for us both, but especially me, in overcoming trust issues between us.

God was good during all this time, but it was only after a couple of years of ups and downs, and some relapses in our old patterns of sin, that we finally agreed to get some counseling; through this we made significant headway in our healing. Lies we have believed for a long time can be easily fitted back into our pattern of worldly thinking, but, as followers of Jesus, we must be transformed by the renewing of our minds (Romans 12:2). The more Sam and I pressed into the Word, the more the lies we had believed in our lives were replaced by truth.

We got pregnant with our daughter, Hannah Grace, within two months of Sam's return from Haiti. After Hannah was born, God showed me two things to comfort my heart about the miscarriage of the earlier baby. First, that if we had carried that child, we wouldn't have Hannah, as I would have only been about seven months pregnant with the other child when I conceived our precious Hannah. And we can't imagine our lives without her.

But second, and even more profound, the Lord impressed upon me that of all my children, the lost child was the only one who had already completely fulfilled their purpose before the Lord and had heard, "Well done, good and faithful servant!" This is all that I could ultimately pray for all of my children. So I am doubly blessed by the grace of God in this knowledge. That precious little one did much to help bring his mama to the great mercy of a mighty God. I thank God for the truth that He does "work all things together for the good of those that love Him and are called according to His purpose" (Romans 8:28).

About two months into my pregnancy with Hannah, I completed my student teaching and earned my degree. I graduated with honors and was eager to begin my career, which I unknowingly still hung a lot of my value on. It would take God asking me two years later to give that up, for me to realize the lie and replace it with the truth that I am valuable simply because God says I am.

My mother-in-law was diagnosed with cancer when Hannah was born. So I moved back to West Virginia with Gunner, then age three, and Hannah, two weeks, and began a nine-month stretch of living between my parents' and my sister-in-law's homes, helping to care for Sam's mom. She passed into heaven after losing the battle to that wretched disease. And as hard as it was, I wouldn't trade a moment of that season. I watched her strengthen in her faith, as did I, while her body weakened. She passed from this life with a peace and a surrender that was sweet to behold after many years of seeing her fight her Lord. It was a privilege to witness that blessing.

On many levels, Sam's family grew closer and stronger during this time as well, where before, all of his siblings had been very disconnected. It was another blessing from our Lord in our time of sorrow. The unity and fellowship with his siblings has continued as an ongoing blessing for the past eighteen years.

The very week I returned to North Carolina, I began my first teaching job. Gunner started preschool at the Christian school where I taught junior high English, and Hannah went to a sitter daily. She was an awesome babysitter and actually became a dear lifelong friend. She was one of the first shining examples in whom I saw the joy of being a stay-at-home mom and wife, and this would help me later.

I am very grateful for that year, on many levels. God taught me much about grace and mercy in teaching. But the personal gain I received from teaching was not worth the loss I felt that my children suffered. When I finished the school year, I was unexpectedly pregnant with another baby. That was not our timing, or at least not my timing. But God still had things He wanted to teach me about trust.

While pregnant with our third child, Sam deployed for several months. One of the routine maternity tests, the AFP (Alpha-fetoprotein), came back positive for Down's Syndrome. I was quite startled upon hearing the news, but I pressed into Jesus immediately. I didn't want to pray for the child *not* to have Down's, because if that was what God willed for us then I wanted to embrace that call and that child. But no parent *wants* to have their children struggle with health or mental issues of any sort, so obviously I was conflicted with this knowledge.

My dear friend who had helped lead me into truth earlier was still my greatest confidant, after my husband, and she stood by my side again while I faced this great trial. She went with me to the doctor for additional tests to confirm or deny the validity of the first test results.

To my shock and horror, a doctor at the military hospital counseled me, prior to receiving any further testing, that it was to my advantage to terminate this pregnancy. I was appalled. I knew, no matter what, that this baby was sent by God and we would embrace whoever she was! I insisted they run the tests, but also affirmed that no matter the results, we would not entertain such an idea. The test results came back perfectly normal and our healthy baby girl, McKayla Faith, was born five months later. The enemy would not have our child or my trust!

During that same pregnancy and deployment, both Gunner and Hannah contracted chicken pox. I had to miss weeks of work in order to care for them, and I still ended up working some days when they were not feeling well. It was an incredibly hard deployment, with me both working full time and pregnant, the stress involved with the health of the unborn baby, caring for our two little ones (four years and eighteen months), and trying to run our home with Sam gone.

By the school year's end, Hannah, then nineteen months, was a disciplinary handful because of her lack of consistent training by me. Between the time in West Virginia and then my commitment to a full-time job, she had fallen lower on my priority list than I should have allowed.

Don't misunderstand: I loved her very much. But I knew in my heart she deserved more of me. God wanted me to be unselfish and put my kids before myself. He had a totally different plan than I had for me, and I had a hard time stepping into it. I had to wrestle through many of my worldly precepts: that my worth was caught up in my career success, or that by offering more financially to my family I was offering them the better part of me.

I needed more transformation with the renewing of my mind. I knew motherhood was valuable, and I knew my kids were valuable, but being a stay-at-home mom seemed like such a waste of my education, on many levels. And the financial hardships we would willingly put ourselves into by me coming home would prove extremely difficult. We had quickly adjusted to our new level of income and had foolishly incurred debt beyond our means with the anticipation of years of money to come. Oh, how God would change my perspective!

First of all, we did struggle for nearly two years due to our foolish financial decisions during the one year I taught. But God, in His mercy, always managed to give us what we needed. Not always what we wanted, but every *need* was met during that humbling time. We learned to trust God with the whole tithe and God blessed us in ways that were astounding to Sam and me. God showed me a level of creativity I didn't know possible in the area of grocery shopping and budgeting. He began to speak directly to me about being frugal in ways I had never considered. The challenges of making ends meet was a monthly issue, and one in which God stretched both my faith and my respect for myself (in my newly discovered talent for being a successful mother and homemaker).

It was also during this time that God spoke to me about home-schooling and began whispering to Sam and me both about trusting Him with the size of our family. Sam had no trouble with this. I, on the other hand, was quite nervous about surrendering control of my womb and the number of children we might birth into God's hands. That might sound silly to some of you, but you must remember, we already had three children, and I came from a family of only two children. We were already a big family in my book. But, at Sam's insistence, we opted to not use birth control after I weaned McKayla around her first birthday. Within a month we were pregnant with baby number four.

When Cora Abigail was born, Gunner had just turned seven, Hannah was three, and McKayla was almost two years old. I began homeschooling for my second year, and Sam was gone roughly six months that year.

Our marriage was now much better, but I was finding myself becoming more and more discontent on many levels. Part of it was the process God had me in during that time with finding my worth in being at home. That was a huge process for me, and it took me several years to fully take hold of the weight of what God was blessing me with by bringing me home to work. Also, surrendering the size of our family was throwing me for some nasty curves at times, too. Having four small children and being asked to step into homeschooling was a lot, since—between constant pregnancies and nursing—I had been running on very little sleep for about three and a half years straight.

I had a hard time finding joy in being weary and alone so much. I loved my babies and I loved Sam, but I didn't love me or my life a whole lot. I was walking in obedience to what I heard the Lord telling me, but I was not very cheerful. I struggled in that spot for several years. I began blaming Sam and his Christian walk, or lapses in his walk, for my struggles. I also blamed him for my discontent because he was never home to help me. Even when he wasn't deployed, the military life of an SF unit meant that he was never home frequently or consistently.

Sam had shifted from Third Group into another Special Operations group during my pregnancy with Hannah a couple of years prior. And although he had gone to that unit as a support guy, he was transitioning and getting ready to go to their selection so he could serve on a team. He had been exceptionally busy, traveling on several shorter deployments (two month stretches at a time) and with a lot of training both in and out of the States.

I had grown increasingly more agitated with Sam about his career. He was quite successful in his career and so was traveling all the time. He often worked with women, and that caused me no end of frustration and fear, as I would often slip into my old insecurities. It worried me more with each new pregnancy and the way my body was changing shape constantly. I am one of the only people I know who has spent her entire adult life adding fifty pounds one year, only to work like a fiend to lose that same fifty pounds all over again the next year. The cycle has been perpetual for me for nearly twenty years, through nine children!

With the pregnancy of our fifth baby in 2001, I continued wrestling with the Lord about our family size. By the pregnancy's end, though, I had finally totally surrendered that fight to God. I would love to tell you that I graciously surrendered, but I am so stubborn that God had to wrestle with me for nearly three years, almost like He had to wrestle with Jacob (see Genesis 32:22–32). I felt like Jacob, fighting and demanding a blessing all at once. God was trying to bless me all along, but because it didn't look like I wanted it to look, I refused to accept it.

When I was holding our precious son, Josiah Gabriel, I couldn't remember why I had tried to tell God I didn't want this. If God would entrust us to raise one of his precious children, who was I to turn away that amazing blessing?

Also during 2001, my fight with God and Sam about his career reached a climactic point and in many ways God had to wrestle me again into surrender mode. When Tuesday, September 11, 2001, happened, my world, along with every other military wife's world, was forever changed.

I had given Sam an ultimatum just two days before. He would either choose me and his children, or he would choose his job in the military. I was convinced that my unhappiness stemmed from his lack of leading me and the children. I was certain that

God had not intended for us to have all these kids only for them to be raised by only one parent. That could not be God's best plan for a family, I was certain. Sam was simply not listening to God like I was. He needed to make a drastic change in order to support us and love us as a godly man should.

One of the things I remember laying down in my ultimatum was that Sam could request a transfer from his unit and probably get anything he requested, due to his good status and reputation there. I suggested he get a job pushing a pencil at the Pentagon until his enlistment was up. Two days later the Pentagon blew up . . . along with all of my arguments.

Within a few weeks of the attacks, Sam was with the very first troops to go in for a ground and air attack in Afghanistan. I was once again terrified. I was pregnant with our fifth child. I was back to where my heart was in Haiti. God had a new level of idolatry to show me in my life. Only this time it wasn't Sam. It was me. It was me wanting control of my life. I was so afraid I would lose Sam that I remember crying out and asking God, "What will I *do* if You take him from me?"

God's response was simple, "What *will* you do if I take him from you?"

No! No! No! That was not the response I wanted! I wanted God to whisper to me that He loved me beyond measure, and that He had a great plan, and that I would not be alone to raise my children. I wanted to be in control of my life. I wanted to be in control of my husband's life. I wanted my husband with me, and I wasn't going to be satisfied until I had him my way.

That was the truth God showed me: I did not trust my God. I loved God. I was obedient to God. But I didn't trust Him. I forever trying to tell God what my life should look like, rather than ask Him what my life should look like and embracing the peace that comes in that place of surrender.

By proxy, my poor Sam had a wife who was forever telling him what his life should look like, instead of having a wife who would ask her headship what she could do to serve him and help him in his life's work and calling. My call was to be Sam's help-meet. But that meant surrendering my life to a man who was rarely there and who might not even notice or appreciate what I was offering to sacrifice!

But my God noticed and appreciated it. And once I began to be willing to die to my own fear, my selfish expectations, and my agendas, God amazed me by having my husband be more atten-tive, more appreciative, and more tender than ever before. But first I had to die to *me*. I had to die to my own dreams and allow God to give me *His* dreams. He would give me the desires of my heart . . . after I allowed Him to take my selfishness and lack of trust—in exchange for the desires He would bestow upon me in His infinite wisdom for my life (see Psalm 37:4).

So in the end, I did receive all the things I wanted. God did whisper to me that He loved me beyond measure. He did have a great plan. He would never leave me alone to raise my children, for He would always be there, whether Sam was or not. Mercifully, it has meant sharing life with my precious man. But it has had to be God's plan. I must trust Him regardless of what it looks like. Trust has been the best plan for me, for Sam, and for our kids.

In the twelve years since that time, we have had four more amazing children and survived more than a dozen deployments, adding up to Sam being absent for at least six of those twelve years. And I, my children, and my marriage are more beautiful for it. God has done more through the amazing giftings in my husband and through his career than I could ever know, this side of heaven.

The prince of darkness has been overthrown on the physical as well as the spiritual battlefield, because Sam was willing to fight the fight few others would go to war for. Many of our children have become and are becoming amazing adults who reflect their trust for God in their lives, despite the circumstances they are in. They value family and each moment God blesses us with as a true gift to be celebrated. They understand much of this due to only having shared precious, often limited, seasons with their dad. And although there is so much more I could share with you about my life, family, church, and ministries, it is enough to say that I am a blessed woman who has more joy than I can contain. My God is great. His strength is great.

We are standing now on the threshold of retirement. Our oldest two children are in college and our youngest is potty training. I am currently teaching six different grade levels in our homeschool. Sam and I help lead a vital military ministry at our church, and we both stand in awe of how beautiful our life is. Neither of us is exactly sure what God holds for us in our future, but we are "confident in this, that he who began a good work in us will carry it on to completion until the day of Christ Jesus" (Philippians 1:6).

This is where we begin anew and, like a newborn baby, become completely dependent on the God who holds us in His hands. We surrender because we can't do anything for ourselves or fix our messy lives any more than the newborn babe can clean itself at birth. And as you allow your God to bathe you, dress you in righteousness, and place a crown of beauty upon your precious brow, please know, dear sister, that your life and your testimony will become the very thing which will draw others into this God of life and love. He means for you to not only draw others with your life, but for you to draw strength through that testimony every time you share it.

You will overcome through the work of your Jesus, but make no mistake: the verse also says there is power in your testimony. Every time you share what Jesus has done for you, you overcome the accuser who would continue to whisper that you aren't clean or worthy. He is a liar.

You are clean. Jesus's blood is more than adequate, and Satan knows it. He is already defeated. He is already hurled down. Down to where? To our doorstep. We must learn to recognize his lies and learn to overcome them by remembering who Jesus is and what He accomplished. Then look at what Jesus did in you and what you have accomplished through Him!

And if you are still in unbearable pain and don't feel like you have accomplished much, dear sister, hold onto truth. Hold onto His Word. You are born again. You are a precious fresh creature who was worthy of our Lord paying the ultimate price. You are so valuable. Your life is one that God wants to use. He wants to make you an overcomer.

Are you willing to believe that Jesus is enough? Are you willing to share with the world that you believe it? Are you willing to surrender whatever He is asking of you today? In your heart, in your marriage, in your children? Then you are an overcomer!

And if you are frightened, then be encouraged that if God can take the mess of my life, and the mess of Carrie's life, and use us for Kingdom work, then sweet sister, He can use you. Your testimony is powerful. And the messier it is, the more glory it will bring God! Don't fear the mess. Embrace the blood! And overcome.

Tis so sweet to trust in Jesus, and to take him at his word;
Just to rest upon His promise, and to know, "Thus saith the Lord."
Jesus, Jesus, how I trust him! How I've proved Him o'er and o'er!
Jesus, Jesus, precious Jesus! O for grace to trust Him more!
—written by Louisa M.R. Stead in 1882

CHAPTER 4

CARRIE'S STORY

*Now to Him who is able to do immeasurably more than all
we ask or imagine, according to His power that is at work within
us, to Him be glory in the church and in Christ Jesus throughout
all generations, for ever and ever! Amen.*
—Ephesians 3:20–21

Ordinary. If I had to pick one word that summarized myself,
that would be it. I've always thought of myself as average. I'm not
athletic, graceful, or coordinated. I'm always confident that someone in the room is better at what I'm doing, and my deficiencies
are at the forefront of my thoughts, even in skills in which I've
proven myself very capable. Deep down, I just believe that I am
nothing special.

My first breaths came on a military base in Virginia. And
although Dad retired from active duty when I was five, you
wouldn't know it looking at my long list of previous addresses.
My first move came when I was about three years old, then

another about two years later, and the third three years after that. I've lived in eight states, four of those twice, and more houses than I care to remember.

I surprised the family. The previous child was twelve when I was born, so while I have a brother and a sister, both had moved out of the house before I turned six. I remember almost nothing of my sister living at home, even less of my brother, and they both moved to other states when they moved out, so I was rarely around them. I grew up more like an only child than the baby of the family.

The first event to have a major impact on my life happened just weeks before Dad retired from the US Air Force. Mom had undergone routine surgery, and when she went back for her follow-up appointment, the doctor had bad news. Cancer. With a capital C. A rare, aggressive form, with a 100% mortality rate.

At the time, we lived on Elmendorf Air Force Base in Anchorage, Alaska. Mom was medically evacuated by airplane to Wilford Hall, still the USAF's premier medical education and research hospital, located on Lackland Air Force Base in San Antonio, Texas. While she began treatments, Dad finished his out processing and the necessary preparations before TMO (Travel Management Office) came to pack us out and send our household goods to Kentucky.

I cannot imagine the great stress my father was under during those weeks. In addition to Mom's illness, a cross-country move, and a change in careers, his dad lay dying in West Virginia. However my father dealt with all these issues, I don't remember it affecting me. Perhaps it was because I'd already experienced the loss of one family member when my brother left for college.

Perhaps my five-year-old brain simply didn't comprehend the seriousness of what was happening around me. Perhaps it just all blended in with the turmoil of another move.

All I really remember from those days are family stories, knowledge of the prayers of friends and family as Mom underwent radical therapies, and pictures of the aunt and uncle who flew up to Alaska to see us and used our truck camper to drive my sister and me back to their house in Ohio.

I can imagine my mom's fears of the future: not seeing what her husband would become now that the Department of Defense had released its hold on him, not watching any of her babies get married, and not meeting (at least in this world) any of her grandchildren. With her family foremost on her mind, she told me that she prayed for a very practical thing: that God would grant her the time to raise me.

At different points in history, the Israelites built markers to remind them from where they had come, through what they had lived, and from what God had saved them (e.g., Genesis 28:110–22, Exodus 17:14–16, Joshua 3:14–4:9). That simple desire uttered by my mom through countless prayers is a spiritual marker to me, a reminder of how much she loved us, how much she loved God, and how much God loved us—for He gave her the desire of her heart. Not only did my mom survive, but she saw all of her children marry and met all seven of her grandchildren. She is now watching her grandchildren marry and is meeting her great-grandchildren.

As Mom recovered from chemotherapy and radiation treatments, life went on. The next several years were fairly quiet. Immediately following her release from the hospital, Mom and

I lived with relatives for a short time before joining my dad and sister in Kentucky, where Dad was attending the Southern Baptist Theological Seminary. It was here that I remember my first best friend. She was a little younger than me, but we shared many interests and spent a lot of time together.

Dad graduated from seminary and we moved to Ohio. For the first time in my life, we were living near family. This felt odd, but I enjoyed it for the most part, despite the fact that none of them had any children my age. A couple of moves later we ended up back in Ohio and again close to family. Within a few years, I would meet the boy who would become my husband.

I don't want you to think, because I'm not giving you a lot of details, that my life growing up was easy. On the other hand, I'm certainly not telling you that my childhood was rough. My parents stayed together through the different challenges that life brought them. I grew up mostly in hand-me-downs and thrift-store finds, sometimes out of necessity and sometimes out of choice. My brother and sister kept in contact with us, and I have good memories of visits over the years. I know that many children would love to have the option of growing up in such an environment. I was very blessed and I know it.

But tragedy wasn't unfamiliar. Among other things, I don't remember my paternal grandparents at all. Dad's mom died long before I was born, and his father died when I was five. My mother's mom died shortly after my mom was born, so the only woman I knew as Grandma was my mom's stepmother. Mom's dad died just before my twelfth birthday, and although we lived near him at the time, we hadn't done so for much of my life, so my list of memories of him is short.

I didn't realize how much I missed the influence of older generations in my life until my early 30s. The lack of close, extended family in my youth, my natural proclivity toward being an introvert, and the constant moving drove me into myself. I became very contemplative, and learned to love books more than people. At every place we lived I always made a friend or two, but I preferred the ease of being alone over the work involved in forming and maintaining relationships. This tendency would play a major role in a crisis later in my life.

My husband, Brian, and I had known each other for several years through our church youth group before we got married. We dated for a little over two years, and, just ten months after our wedding, our daughter came along. Brian worked at an entry-level position with an up-and-coming company, while I worked part-time in the office of a small construction company that allowed me to bring our baby with me. We thought life was good, and we dared to dream into the future.

Then a series of calamities hit. Brian lost his job: largely due, I felt, to a personality conflict between him and his direct boss. It took several weeks before he found another position—and it paid less and had far fewer benefits. The weeks without his income had hurt; the lower pay and lack of medical benefits for well-baby checkups left us sinking into debt. And I was pregnant with our second child.

One day we left our daughter with Brian's mother and went for a motorcycle ride. As we reached a red light, he half-turned back to me and asked, "What do you think about me joining the Air Force?" The light turned green, and he took off down the road.

This statement was a lot to process, coming from the man who in high school had run from military recruiters. I had only recently adjusted my thinking to the idea of living in the same town with family for all of our lives, so this was a huge curve ball. As we talked, he revealed that he thought God was directing him to join the Air Force, not that he was excited about it. But it would provide the medical benefits and regular paycheck we desperately needed.

As I listened to him, an excitement built within me. I hadn't realized how much I wanted to explore the world, one duty station at a time. I knew military life would be an adjustment, but I looked forward to it. Major obstacles, such as selling our home, were downgraded in my mind to inconveniences. Moving was familiar, even comfortable. His family, however, had limited experience with the military life and I feared they would take it hard, his mom in particular.

But as we talked with a recruiter and began the paperwork, it became clearer to us that this was the path God wanted for us. A signing bonus in his career field of choice relieved some of the pressure from the debt, and financial paperwork that normally would have caused a red flag processed through the channels without a hitch. In October 1998, Brian left for Basic Training in San Antonio, Texas.

His first phone call came one week later. It was wonderful to hear his voice, but I could tell he was fighting emotions. I was caught off guard when he said he could tell me only that he was fine and give me his address. The TI (Training Instructor) standing nearby would end the call if we tried to say more. As I frantically wrote the precious postal address down, I fought back tears so I could say something he would remember, something to help him during those long days of training.

I anxiously flew down for graduation while my parents took care of our daughter and pets. The weekend was wonderful, but bittersweet. Leaving Brian at the dorms on his final night of liberty was tough. I felt like I was leaving half of myself behind. When I returned to the hotel room, I found an urgent message from my Mom. I immediately called home, fearing something had happened to our daughter. My parents let me know that my precious dog had died. The one that helped me corral our toddler. The support beam that helped me heave my pregnant belly out of our waterbed each morning. My constant companion while Brian was away.

I sat in a hotel room in a strange city, unable to reach out to the one person I wanted. Feelings of sadness for the pet I loved mixed with intense feelings of loneliness and abandonment. The man who was supposed to be my support was locked behind doors I could not open. I wondered how many times I would have to face such crises alone.

On the plane ride back home, I began preparing myself for Thanksgiving. Until my aunt and uncle had retired, Thanksgiving was always a huge holiday at their house that I looked forward to, complete with family and friends, too much food, and special desserts. With my husband stuck 1,300 miles away, our daughter too young to care about traditions, and no one planning to host a big meal, the holiday looked bleak.

And then, on the Wednesday night before Thanksgiving, came a great surprise: Brian called. He had just been informed that the previous 400-mile limit on travel for the holiday weekend had been lifted. He could come home for Thanksgiving! We had no money for a last-minute plane ticket, but I did have an airline ticket to visit him in January when he graduated from Technical School (Tech School). He wondered what I thought about switching the ticket to him, then driving down with my parents, who spent the winter each year in southern Texas. Our daughter and I could live with my parents during the week, and drive up each weekend to see him at school.

First, I had to clear this plan with my parents. Under normal circumstances, I knew they wouldn't mind us moving in with them for the ten remaining weeks of training, but during their winters in Texas they lived in a fifth-wheel trailer. An additional adult plus a toddler would be a significant adjustment for all of us.

When they agreed to the plan, I frantically called the airlines and asked about switching the ticket to Brian and somehow delivering it to him in San Antonio. I was told that the only way to possibly do this was to ask a ticket agent at the airport. The offices were closed for the night, but they would open at 6:00 a.m.

I was up and moving early Thanksgiving morning, full of hope that the airlines would somehow make the day bright. Brian had caught a ride to the airport near him the night before, sleeping there in the hopes that I would be able to switch the ticket.

The airport was largely deserted, with one lone gentleman at the counter. He listened patiently as I explained the situation, adding that my husband had been gone with the military for two months. But he had a problem. Because the ticket was purchased with frequent flyer miles, I had to call the airline directly and have the miles added back into our account, so they could then be removed again for the new flight plan.

I dutifully went to the nearest phones and called the airline, explaining everything to the person who answered the phone. She kindly explained that we could certainly exchange the ticket, but she had a problem. Everyone who worked with the mileage program was off for the holiday, and no one would be there until the next day. I'm certain she heard the disappointment in my voice because she added, "If anyone can help you, it's the ticket agent at the counter."

I quietly hung up. Struggling to hold back tears, I made my way back to the gentleman at the ticket counter. He looked at me and asked what I was told. As calmly as I could with eyes full of questioning hope, I simply told him, "She said that if anyone could help us, you could." He looked at me for just the briefest moment, then asked to see my ticket. After a few keystrokes, he handed the ticket back to me and told me that my husband should be able to pick up his ticket at the counter in San Antonio at any time. It was the first time in my life I'd ever wanted to hug a stranger!

During the Thanksgiving holiday, we talked with my parents and finalized our plans for the next few weeks. Our house was going up for sale and most of our belongings were packed and placed in storage. Brian spent as much time with his family as he could before we left for the long drive back to Texas. I then dropped him off at school in San Antonio before meeting my parents further south.

Each Friday, our daughter and I faithfully drove four hours north to pick Brian up at the dorms, and each Sunday I would drop him back off and head south again. After graduation, with orders in hand, we drove to Ohio to watch movers crate our belongings. We then said goodbye to the family there, drove west to St. Louis, Missouri, to drop the car off for shipping, and boarded a plane to our first duty station: Elmendorf AFB in Anchorage, Alaska. I was 38-weeks pregnant.

That was the most uncomfortable plane ride I've ever endured, but thankfully none of the stewardesses questioned me on the pregnancy. Our vehicle was still at least two weeks from arriving, but the temporary housing was nice and within walking distance of the commissary.

One week after our arrival, the city got the worst snowfall of the season. We woke up that March morning to snow in the yard almost as deep as our toddler was tall! My mom flew in the next day so she could take care of our daughter while I was in the hospital having our son, and I still remember her struggling to push my daughter in an umbrella stroller through the snow-covered sidewalks while I fought the metal shopping cart laden with groceries.

Our son arrived, and a couple of weeks later, our car. We moved into an apartment while waiting for military housing to open up, and our strained finances continued stretching ever thinner. Our house in Ohio still had not sold and when the lady who rented it for a short time moved out, we discovered that she had destroyed the bathroom. It had to be gutted and redone. On a young airman's salary, we were paying a $675 mortgage, a $923 rent payment, and had less than $100 in savings. We were sinking into deep debt.

Our church situation wasn't much better. Prone to shyness and still avoiding relationships, I did not make friends easily, and after five months of training in Texas, Brian was out of the habit of going to services. I tried everything I could think of to get him to go, flagrantly ignoring the Apostle Peter's advice to win our husbands through our life example (1 Peter 3:1–6). After nine months of attending services in our new town, though, I couldn't name more than a small number of people, and I'm not sure I knew any of their phone numbers or addresses. I spent most of my time at home alone with our two children.

Two weeks before Christmas and five days after we moved into our house on base, Brian left for his first tour in Saudi Arabia. We chose to open presents before he left. While I've never regretted allowing him the gift of seeing his children enjoy the holiday, it made December 25th the longest day I can remember. It seemed that everyone around me had family to enjoy, and I felt left out. I was too self-absorbed to care what my husband was going through on the other side of the world, much less the families of those he left with that lived near me on the base. I felt like I was the only one alone that Christmas.

Even though the separation was difficult, my husband and I grew closer during his time at Prince Sultan Air Base. We emailed as often as the system was functioning, and talked about almost everything. The little bit of extra pay for hazardous duty and family separation was nice, but it certainly didn't come close to covering the mortgage in Ohio. Emotionally, I dealt with most of his tour fine, as long as he didn't talk too much about crawling under cars in his cotton jumpsuit to look for bombs or the interesting items he confiscated from locals coming on base.

Shortly after Brian returned, we received a surprise bill from the Department of Defense. Our move north had been overweight and we owed them over $1,900. On top of our other money problems, we simply could not afford the $50 payments they told us they were going to siphon off each paycheck. Brian applied for a reprieve, and we received the one-time forgiveness. We absolutely could not go over weight on another move.

Our financial issues were becoming a larger problem. With an inconsistent work schedule, Brian's prospects for a second job were nil and, with two young children, day care fees would cost us more than I would likely make in a typical job. I signed up to deliver papers for the Anchorage Daily News, but this still was not enough income to cover the mortgage. We finally decided to ask the state for help. I took the kids downtown and applied for public assistance.

The lady I spoke with was very nice. She looked at everything and quickly saw that the house in Ohio was creating the mess that was dragging us down. However, the law was set up to work against us. Because the house was in our name, she had to count it as an asset, which meant we owned too much to receive assistance. The state's position was that we should sell the house. She understood my frustration because she knew the house had been on the market for months, but there was nothing she could do.

The only other solution we could think of was home day care. I like children, and doing day care in our home would allow me to make money while caring for our own two children. I knew a lady at church was expecting a child soon, and although I didn't know much about her or her family, I knew she and her husband both worked and would need some day care for her baby. I approached her with my idea and she agreed to let me care for her infant.

At the time, Brian worked the 2:00 p.m. to 10:00 p.m. swing shift. I was up by 4:00 a.m. to pick up newspapers and get them delivered, sometimes with one or both kids in the car. I rushed home to make sure the sidewalks were shoveled as the base required, so I could open my door for my friend to drop off her baby at 6:15 a.m. We had to play quietly all morning so my husband could sleep, while also meeting the other base requirements, such as a minimum of fifteen minutes of outside play in the morning and monthly fire drills, sometimes during naptime.

Shortly after Brian left for work about 1 p.m, we would all get into the car to go pick up another child from school who I kept until her mom got off work about dinnertime. Once everyone went home, I had to sanitize toys, clean and mop the kitchen, and vacuum the living room. By the time I got our two into bed, I barely stayed awake long enough to say hello to my husband when he got home from work around 11 p.m. As exhausting as this schedule was, life was about to get more complicated.

Brian received orders for his rotation back to Saudi Arabia. Trying to keep up with everything while he was gone was tough, but at least I didn't have to worry about keeping kids quiet during the day. Soon after he left, the mother of my school-aged day care child stayed one afternoon to talk. Her job was going well, even though she had been newly assigned to the second shift. The problem was that her husband, freshly returned from a twelve-month remote tour, was already being sent out on a three-month TDY. His mom was able to come up for the first month to help, and her mom would be available the third month, but she needed help for the four weeks in the middle. It would mean picking up their son from the base day care center before 6 p.m. each day and keeping both him and the girl I already picked up from school until about 10:30 each night through the week. This would be a huge task, but since they had been such great parents, how could I tell her no?

Thankfully I'd already quit the newspaper job, so I had the day only care to worry about. For three very long weeks, I signed in my first child at 6:15 a.m. and signed out my last child at 10:30 p.m. with no break in-between. I went to bed exhausted every night and looked forward to weekends when I could sleep in a little and go to bed early.

And then one morning, everything changed. I was home with my two children and the infant, ages three, two, and nine months, respectively. The baby began to get a little fussy, signaling her need for food, so I stood up from the couch and walked toward the kitchen to get her bottle. The next thing I knew, I was lying on the ground having a minor seizure. When I regained control, I sat up. My shoulder ached from where I had hit a doorframe when I fell. I remembered nothing after taking a few steps toward the kitchen.

Seizures were new to me and I had never blacked out before, so I wasn't sure what to think of it. Perhaps I was just overly tired. Uncertain what else to do, I called the moms and canceled day care for a few days while I figured out what was going on.

A trip to the hospital emergency room found everything normal, so I went home with my kids to rest. After so many weeks of having anywhere from three to five kids running around, it was odd only having my two, but the quiet was a nice change. For the next few days, I rested a lot during the day, slept longer at night, and tried to eat healthy foods. Everything seemed fine.

Until it happened again. Once again, I had been sitting on the couch. When I stood and began walking toward the stairs, my vision started going black. I felt light-headed, and I barely managed to sit down on the first step before I fell down. As my vision and center of balance returned to normal, the phone rang. A friend was calling to check on me and when she heard what had just happened, she came over immediately to take me to the ER.

Once again, nothing seemed out of place. Pregnancy tests came back negative, no drugs in my system, hormones all within normal ranges. My blood pressure was fine, my heart looked good, my breathing was normal. I was a medical mystery, and the ER doctor wasn't happy. Considering my husband was TDY and I had two small children, the doctor wanted me to have a friend move in with us to monitor me, recommended that I didn't drive, and wrote in my file that I was to follow-up with a licensed medical doctor. I went home, made my follow-up appointment, and packed bags for us and our dog to stay with a friend.

In the meantime, Brian was stuck in Asia. We knew nothing except that I was blacking out. He desperately wanted to come home and his Commander overseas agreed that he should return, but until my doctor revoked my driving privileges, he had to stay put. So we waited. I felt like a trapped rat, not living in my own place and not really supposed to be driving anywhere.

After a few days of nothing happening, I moved back home. The episodes only seemed to happen when I was standing, so I felt confident that if I stayed sitting, everything would be fine. Still, as others speculated about what could be wrong, my imagination feared the worst.

Finally the day came for my appointment. The doctor quietly read over my records and said the good news was that I didn't have a tumor or diabetes. In fact, nothing major was wrong with me. He said he had never told any patient this before, but he wanted me to take my dinner plate and sprinkle it liberally with salt. I'm sure my face showed disbelief. I had too little salt in my diet?

He went on to explain that I had low blood pressure. When I'm sitting or standing, it stabilizes and is fine, but when I am changing from a sitting to standing position, my heart simply cannot get the blood to my brain fast enough, so my body reacts by forcing me down so it can get the blood to my head. Eating salt would help raise my blood pressure enough to keep the blood moving at a good rate. I joyously left the doctor's office and began spreading the news.

When my husband returned home at the end of his TDY, preparations to leave Alaska began. We planned to drive to our next duty station, so we needed to be prepared to leave as soon as possible so we could maneuver the mountain passes in the best possible weather. Our scheduled departure date: September 14, 2001.

Everything was going smoothly. Anxious to make our weight limit this time, I cleaned out everything we didn't need or didn't want to move, then allowed the packers to take over the rest. We spent the last couple of nights in town with friends. On September 10, 2001, we went to bed, expecting to clear housing in the morning.

About 5:20 a.m., our friend woke us up. A church family who had moved to Virginia about two months earlier had called our pastor to alert us to the chaos unfolding in New York City, four time zones away. I knelt on the floor of their bedroom in shock as we watched the Twin Towers burning. Our eyes met, and Brian and I knew we needed to get to the base.

Grabbing our children, now four and two years old, we got on the road as quickly as possible. The drive that normally took about twenty minutes stretched longer, and came to a screeching halt about a mile-and-a-half outside the base gate. When it was finally our turn to pass, Brian asked the guard on duty, an airman from my husband's squadron, if recalls had been issued yet. We were told that the night shift, still on duty two hours past their normal end time, had no idea when they would be relieved, but the Commander hadn't yet issued a recall.

We went to our empty house and waited. The neighbors with whom we shared an entry opened their door to us so the kids could play and we could watch events unfold on their television. Our entire move was now in question. As the borders were secured, we didn't know if Canada would let us in, and if they did, if the U.S. would let us back across the border into Montana. Most of our belongings were already on a ship headed south, so we would have very little if we were forced to stay in Alaska. And, as all the inspectors were civilians, we didn't know when they would be allowed on base, which meant we couldn't finish out processing to leave anyway. Questions circled through our minds, and we could do nothing but sit in an empty house and wait.

At long last, the inspector showed up and passed us through housing. Brian checked in with his First Sergeant and found out that no one really knew what was going to happen. PCS assignments hadn't been stopped, though, so we should proceed to our new duty station: Malmstrom AFB, Montana. The only advice anyone could give us about traveling through Canada was to try it and see.

We arrived at the Canadian border on September 15th and proceeded through without a problem, and three days after that, we passed through the U.S. border without incident. Instead of stopping at our new base, though, we continued on to South Dakota to drop off our dog with friends until we gained housing, then onto Kentucky and Ohio to visit family. We finally arrived back in Montana over a month later.

Housing opened up very quickly, and we got our belongings out of storage and arranged for our friends to bring us our dog. The more I found out about Brian's new job, the less thrilled I was about it, but at least he wouldn't be going TDY out of the country, facing the dangers that the new War on Terror was bringing to so many other military families. He would be guarding the U.S. nuclear missile supply, and it meant he would be in the field for five days, train for three days, one day of Commander's discretion, and one day off before the cycle started over again. We wouldn't see much of him.

To add stress to our situation, I was pregnant again and not doing well emotionally. After my first pregnancy, I'd experienced a brief period of post-partum depression, but this was considerably worse. I remember crying out to God, desperate for relief from my situation. My husband was rarely home, and when he was, he was irritable and didn't want to interact with us. I was exhausted from keeping up with a four-year-old morning person and a two-year-old night owl. Not to mention trying to keep up with all the base regulations, such as cleaning up daily after our dog and shoveling within 24 hours of it snowing. I tried calling credit consolidation companies for help with our finances, but they all told me the same thing: I had better rates on our credit cards then they could give me.

I was reaching the end of myself and I wanted out. Not divorce and not abandonment—I was too weak to consider living on my own. I wanted to die. I wouldn't hurt the baby in my womb, though, so I felt stuck between a rock and a hard place, and I continued on a downward spiral. Still bound in my shyness, I had no one to reach out to in our town, even though I'd been attending church faithfully for several weeks.

Friends stationed at Ellsworth AFB, 550 miles away in South Dakota, were very worried, and they checked on me regularly through email and phone calls, offering what support and encouragement they could. During one of Brian's rotations in the field, I finally admitted to them where I was at, and they arranged to meet me about halfway between our homes. They took our children for a week to relieve some pressure from me and give me uninterrupted time to talk to Brian. With the pressure of the kids gone, I went home and cried. I knew I couldn't verbally speak all the things in my heart, so I wrote a letter.

My husband reacted quickly, giving me everything he could. He tried to spend more time with us, although he was in the early stages of his own medical issues that would soon cause other problems. He encouraged me to get more involved at church, and he took me to our friends' home in South Dakota or invited them to our home frequently. It was enough to get me through the last months of pregnancy and emotionally stabilized afterward.

He also stopped in to see a financial expert on base, reportedly the best in his field in our area. After looking through everything, the expert advised us to do something he rarely recommended to anyone: bankruptcy. He confirmed for us that we were not trying to find some extra room in our budget. We were trying to find a mortgage payment, and it simply was not there. He believed he might be able to help us trim a little here and there, but the truth was that we already had things pretty tight. Brian thanked him and brought the news home to me. I was not pleased.

I've never heard anyone say anything positive about bankruptcy. While I think many people get into financial crises by making bad choices or having poor management, I also know that sometimes bankruptcy just comes from life. Sure, we had made some bad choices, but ultimately we still had a house that no one wanted to buy that was costing us a significant percentage of our income. At the time, I believed that all our financial troubles were the house's fault and if someone would just buy it then we could climb out of the mess we were in. I wouldn't admit it to myself then, but the truth was that I was furious at God. If He truly cared, He would have brought a buyer months ago.

After a short time of fighting my husband, I grudgingly acquiesced, and we began the paperwork to file bankruptcy. We talked to a lawyer, stopped paying the bills we knew we could not afford, and reaffirmed our commitment to pay those we could. I felt horribly guilty. Few people knew what we were doing and some of those who did were encouraging, reminding us that God allowed a period of time in the Old Testament law when debts were written off. However, one person I told innocently said, "I thought debt was a sin for the Christian." That comment fed into my shame, and I went deeper into myself, sharing even less of my life with those around me.

As we waited for the courts to decide our case, I began homeschooling our daughter. This was not something I jumped into with great joy, but I knew that God had called us to it. Brian fully supported me, but I was overwhelmed with all the options, money was still largely not available, and homeschooling in our area seemed non-existent. I felt very alone, like I was being set apart again—not for some grand purpose, but left behind; unchosen, like the kid no one wants to pick for their team.

To compound things, Brian was doing worse. His irritability was increasing and sleep evaded him. By the time he sought medical help, he was sleeping only every other night. His doctor ordered a series of tests including a sleep study; the results were overwhelming. He was diagnosed with insomnia, restless leg syndrome, and sleep apnea. The sleep apnea could be helped with a machine that provided continuous positive air pressure (CPAP), but that irritated his insomnia. And all the medicines used to treat insomnia would put him on a profile—removing him from his job protecting the country's nuclear arsenal.

The doctor wanted six months to stabilize my husband's sleeping pattern through the use of meds and new routines, so Brian temporarily lost his worldwide qualifications and clearance to carry a weapon. Not only did his commander not take this news well, he didn't believe the diagnosis. My husband was a cop, on a base that was roughly eighty percent cops, and he wasn't allowed to carry a gun. What was he supposed to do?

After working a short time managing a couple of the dormitories on base, Brian was assigned to work at the base jail. It was small, but able to hold several prisoners in varying stages of court proceedings or short-term confinements. As guards are not allowed to carry weapons, their demeanor is often the best method of maintaining control. The longer he worked at the jail, the more angry and pessimistic my husband became.

In an attempt to convince his Commander that he was serious about working in the field as he was originally assigned, Brian opted for surgery. Among other things, his tonsils, uvula, and part of his soft pallet were removed. Recovery was painful, and he had to learn to purposefully swallow his food. Yet we discovered that his Commander still didn't believe him. In fact, the Commander began paperwork to administratively discharge him from the Air Force. And that was before we found out the surgery had made Brian's medical problems worse. Additionally, his condition required a medical board be called to determine if he should re-main on active duty, and his post-surgery diagnosis required the permanent suspension of his worldwide qualifications and ability to carry a weapon.

We weren't sure what else to do, so we prayed for God's guid-ance. After a lot of talking, we decided we should fight to stay in the Air Force. Brian completed the necessary paperwork and we waited. After weeks of uncertainty, trying to hope for the best and prepare for the worst, the news came back. The med board had ruled in our favor; we could stay in.

Again, the Commander was not happy. I'm sure in his view Brian was a useless troop, but that didn't help our situation. We again prayed about our options. Brian finally admitted that when he had enlisted it had been on his own terms, because he wasn't happy about God pushing him into the military. Now, he was ready to do whatever job God asked of him, so we asked for a change of MOS (Military Occupation Specialty).

The request went through with minimal drama. Brian was changing to the IT (information technology) field and would be assigned to Tech School at Keesler AFB in Mississippi. Because it was only a three-month-long school, we were not permitted a PCS, so the kids and I couldn't stay with him. We decided that if his follow-on base was anything east of the Mississippi River, the kids and I would move in with my parents in Kentucky while he went to school. Otherwise, we would stay put in Montana and wait for him.

We prayed and waited. And waited. And waited. A mere five days before he was scheduled to leave for his follow-on school, orders finally came down: Pope AFB, North Carolina. A couple at church teased that we were going to "No Hope Pope," but I couldn't begin to consider what this meant, as I had only five days to prepare for a cross-country move with a six-year-old, a five-year-old, a two-year-old, a dog, and a cat. Five days to consider all we would need for the four to five months we would be without our household belongings. And my husband had to convince TMO that they had no choice but to pack us out in two days, because we had to clear housing before he left.

It was a whirlwind, but we got everything done, said goodbye to friends, and got on the road. Brian dropped us off in Kentucky and then arrived at Keesler only to find that they had no on-base housing for him. He spent his training living out of a hotel just outside the gates. Assigned to the second shift of classes, with every other Friday off, he traveled the 650 miles north to see us every other weekend.

The kids and I tried to fit ourselves into my parents' lives with the least possible intrusion. Although I know my parents cherished the time we got with them, it was again an adjustment for all of us. At least this time they were living in a house! Even our dog, a seventy-five-pound shepherd/husky mix used to living inside with us, had to adapt to being an outside pup. But she faithfully followed my dad wherever he walked on their seventeen acres of land in the middle of nowhere, thankfully only surprising a skunk once. Soon it was time to move to North Carolina.

Our introduction to North Carolina was impressive. The towering pines were beautiful, and I marveled at them from the large picture windows in our temporary lodging on Pope. Within just a

day or two of our arrival, as I sat relaxing in the living room reading through an impressive pile of information about the base, I
watched airmen arrive in the grassy area around the quarters. They
worked in teams of two, picking up the metal picnic tables and
chaining them to the pine trees. I'd never seen such a thing. Soon
I would learn more than I wanted to know about hurricane season.

Not dramatically different from the earthquake preparedness
I'd learn in Alaska, our first month in North Carolina introduced
us to hurricane preparedness as we sat through Tropical Storm
Bonnie, Hurricane Charley, Hurricane Frances, and Hurricane
Gaston. At least living in Montana had prepared us for the winds!

In between storms, God brought us a fantastic realtor who
tirelessly showed us home after home on our pathetic post-bank-
ruptcy budget, even bringing a birthday present for our daughter
to lighten the lack of festivities in our small, constantly changing quarters. Pope's temporary housing could not keep us long
term, so we moved out every few days to a local hotel until the
much more economical lodging on base had room for us again.
Eventually we found a hotel that would accept pets at a reason-
able rate so we could get our pets with us and end the kenneling
fees. Every couple of days, we all had to leave the room for the
maid to clean, but the kids and dog made the best of it. The cat
tolerated it.

Ten weeks later, we finally moved in to our new home. It was
a foreclosed modular home, dirty from lack of care, and considerably smaller than our home in Montana had been, but it was
ours. I could paint the walls if I wanted to, replace flooring if I so

desired, and not shovel the snow if I didn't feel like it. If this part of North Carolina ever got any snow. I expected life to level out.

Instead, my husband's health continued to go downhill. In addition to the sleeping issues, he'd injured his back, and his arms would sometimes go to sleep in the middle of the night. Swollen legs, pain radiating from everywhere, and other symptoms began showing themselves with greater frequency. He endured more medical tests than I can remember, yet the doctors couldn't figure out the problem. Many tests came back *normal*, but even the ones that didn't were not very helpful. Yes, they could see a small problem in his back, but it was too small to be causing the amount of pain he experienced. Yes, they could see a small tumor on his pituitary, but many people live with similar benign tumors and the size was too small to be causing his symptoms.

Physical therapy, occupational therapy, chiropractors, neurologists, endocrinologists, urologists, psychiatrists, pain management clinics. Truthfully, I've lost track of the many different types of doctors Brian's seen over the years and the medications he's tried. And while we have concrete explanations for some of what's going on in his body, much of it is unexplained and therefore dumped into the category of fibromyalgia.

We finally came to the realization that my husband might not live a long life. So his thoughts turned to protecting his family and deciding what he needed to do in case he ever got to the point where he could no longer work. We opted for a medical board, asking for medical retirement. The board ruled in our favor, granting a temporary medical retirement that would be re-evaluated annually for up to five years.

Brian started looking for a civilian job, but hiring managers wouldn't consider him without his official release from the military. So the job search couldn't begin in earnest until his DD–214 was in hand. It was tough because he was dealing with so much more than just changing careers. His health problems loomed before us, forcing us to look at reality. It felt like dreams ending, as if I could no longer expect a full and vital marriage. His diseases took so much from him, and I wondered if he'd see his children grow up, walk his daughter down the aisle, teach his boys basic automobile maintenance. So many emotions. And he was home—all the time.

Finally, after four and a half months, a job with the civil service came through. He'd be working for the Army on Fort Bragg, so we didn't have to move. That was a moment of relief in the midst of all the other turmoil in my heart.

Emotions were bubbling to the surface as I dealt with my husband's mortality, and I began seriously dealing with emotional pain from my past. As a child, I'd been molested. As a pre-teen, I'd taken the pain of that to God. I'd heard a sermon, by some well-known preacher I've since forgotten the identity of, who said that some pain is so big that we can never forgive it—only God can forgive it through us. That resonated with me. I wouldn't even consider forgiving the perpetrator. I didn't *want* to forgive him. But I also didn't want to live tied to the anger I felt forever. It had to go. So I asked God to forgive him through me and help me release the anger.

It was a huge step on the journey to forgiveness, one that slowly, over many years, gently led me from hating that man to loving him as Christ commands us to love others. But it was during this time that my husband transitioned into the Army world that I again felt like I had unfinished business. I went to my pastor, a licensed family and marriage counselor, to talk about it. I discovered that the issue I was having didn't have anything to do with the molestation itself. I was struggling with the bigger question of "why?": Why did God allow this?

My pastor gave me some practical advice, prayed with me, and sent me home with homework: deal with God. If I was going to fully trust this Supreme Authority, I needed to know that He truly was in control, even in ugly circumstances. If He couldn't control situations like this, then what else could He not do? Was He even aware of what had happened to me? Had He been present? Did He care?

As I prayed and asked for answers to these questions, God gave me a picture of the room where the incident had happened so long ago. As I looked around for evidence of Him, I saw Jesus, standing in a corner, tears running down His face. Not only had He been there; He cared. A lot. It was all the proof I needed to be able to release my other questions into the categories of *free will* and *everyone sins*.

As you read this, it may come across as a quick process, like TV sitcoms that solve all the family's problems in one thirty-minute show. Let me assure you that this was not quick. In fact, some of its remnants continue to rear their ugly face from time to time. The difference is that now I see it more clearly for what it is: the enemy's attack on my life. I know that my enemy wants to "steal, kill, and destroy" (John 10:10), and many times with me it was no more difficult for him than providing an emotional distraction.

But I don't want to live distracted. I want to grab hold of the abundant life promised to me (see John 10:7–10). I want to encourage you—healing from past hurts is possible! It is hard work. It is painful, particularly at first. But with God's help and guidance, it is worth it! On the other side of the pain and fear I have found great freedom—freedom that makes every battle worth the fight.

And that's where I want to leave you. I'll talk more about living with a husband with medical issues later in this book, but right now I want you to see great hope for yourself (Jeremiah 29:11). Hope that things don't have to be perfect for God to work. Hope that God really does transform pain into something beautiful (Isaiah 61:1–4). Hope that He really loves you and is seeking you out.

Reach for Him. He's waiting.

CHAPTER 5

THE CALLING OF THE WARRIOR

Greater love has no one than this: to lay down one's life for one's friends.

—John 15:13

FROM CARRIE

Before I say anything else, I want to be clear that I am not some spiritual giant with everything under control. In fact, here's a secret from the dark part of my heart: sometimes, I did not like being the spouse of an active duty airman.

Don't get me wrong. I love the United States of America and its military. I enjoyed the opportunity we had to travel the country, meet great people, and learn new cultures. And I am so thankful that we get to continue to support our military directly through my husband's civilian job.

But I struggled with the knowledge that my husband belonged to the government. Sometimes I outright hated that they could call and interrupt our plans. Frustration would build when I planned a special night or one of my children's birthday parties, knowing that he might (and frequently did) miss it.

At times, the words of people who didn't understand, or perhaps didn't care about, the sacrifices we made as a family hurt me deeply. Occasionally I'd get discouraged that my husband endured things I knew I didn't want to do for ideals and freedoms that other people took for granted. And I can't forget about the anger that would overwhelm me in rare moments when someone, either ill-informed or unaware, would spout off at how much America paid its military to sit in schools, go camping, and travel the world.

The bottom line, though, is none of that matters. None of my feelings change the calling God gave my husband. He is still a military man. He's still called to sacrifice for his country, even now as a civilian. How I deal with that reality is part of what we'll talk about in the next chapter, but it starts by fully grasping what God is asking of my husband, and thereby of our family.

When is the last time you spent some time reading the book of Judges? In chapters six through eight, we get a glimpse of an amazing transformation, and I encourage you to read it with fresh eyes after finishing this section.

Chapter 6 lays the scene before us. The Israelites aren't following God, so He allows an invasion. It gets so bad that they are hiding out in mountain caves. Verse five says that the enemy "came up with their livestock and their tents like swarms of locusts. It was impossible to count them or their camels."

It was worse than those verses indicate, though. The Bible says, "they camped on the land and ruined the crops all the way to Gaza and did not spare a living thing for Israel, neither sheep nor cattle nor donkeys" (v. 4).

When Israel is so impoverished that they can't take any more, they cry out to God. And He answers them by saying, "I rescued you from the hand of the Egyptians. And I delivered you from the hand of all your oppressors; I drove them out before you and gave you their land. I said to you, 'I am the Lord your God; do not worship the gods of the Amorites, in whose land you live.' But you have not listened to Me" (verses 9–10).

Under these circumstances, most of us would not blame Gideon one bit for hiding out. The Bible tells us he was threshing his wheat at night inside a winepress. Threshing is simply the way the Israelites separated wheat from its outer shell, or chaff. Normally, the wheat was beaten in a large open area or on a hill. Then the farmers would throw it up so the wind could blow the light chaff away, leaving only the grain behind. Instead of using nature to help him, Gideon worked in a pit under the cover of night, hoping both would offer him protection from his enemies. Let's jump into the scene as the Bible records it in Judges 6:12–15.

> When the angel of the Lord appeared to Gideon, he said, "The Lord is with you, mighty warrior."
>
> "Pardon me, my lord," Gideon replied, "but if the Lord is with us, why has all this happened to us? Where are all

his wonders that our ancestors told us about when they said, 'Did not the Lord bring us up out of Egypt?' But now the Lord has abandoned us and given us into the hand of Midian."

The Lord turned to him and said, "Go in the strength you have and save Israel out of Midian's hand. Am I not sending you?"

"Pardon me, my lord," Gideon replied, "but how can I save Israel? My clan is the weakest in Manasseh, and I am the least in my family."

I love Gideon's response here, because it sounds like something I would say! "Who, me? You've got to be kidding!" Can't you just picture the expression on this man's face!

Although Gideon started cautiously, he did obey. When the Midianites, Amalekites, and other enemies joined forces to cross the Jordan, God's Spirit came upon Gideon. In the span of a few short days, he was changed from a cowering farmer to an army leader! With God's help, Gideon trimmed his forces from 32,000 volunteers to a mere 300 brave men. Imagine: 300 men fighting a coalition force too numerous to count! Yet the battle was easily won. What a difference God makes!

It is critical for the military spouse to understand at least two things from this story. First, God calls our men to military service. This is a hard calling. I won't pretend otherwise. But it is a necessary duty of our times. Until Jesus returns, we need people who are willing to stand between us and evil. Your husband has the high calling to go forth and protect your family, my family, our country, and God's people (see Deuteronomy 9:2–4).

As part of the calling to serve and protect, God allows you a front row seat to witness a grand Kingdom purpose come to fruition in your husband. Have you ever thought about your man fulfilling Kingdom purposes? Perhaps even more significant is that the Kingdom purpose is one not many are willing to live out in daily practice.

In John 15, Jesus says, "My command is this: Love each other as I have loved you. Greater love has no one than this: to lay down one's life for one's friends" (verses 12–13). How many careers can you name that meet this ideal of love? Police officers, firemen, and the military are the only ones that come to my mind.

Few men are willing to lay down their lives for another, even less for those who boldly stand against their mission under the protection of free speech or opinion entitlement. Your man may never be called to lay down his life, but he is called to be willing to do so. And you must understand that this calling is not from the US military, the Department of Defense, or the current Commander in Chief. It is from the Lord God Almighty, and it is an honorable, noble calling.

Second, Gideon helps us understand that God strengthens those He calls. The angel told Gideon, "Go in the strength you have and save Israel out of Midian's hand" (Judges 6:14). After Gideon stepped out in timid obedience, "the Spirit of the LORD came upon Gideon" (Judges 6:34). God will always provide everything your man needs when he needs it. You may not see a brave warrior in your husband today, but in the heat of battle, God will provide. It is imperative that you believe this and encourage your husband with it.

Our husbands need to fight because they believe in their calling to fight. They must understand that the battle is over more than oil or the right to democracy. The battle is really darkness fighting truth, evil fighting good, Satan fighting God. Our husbands need to fight this darkness with every weapon God provides. Sometimes it should be through simple candy given in love to children who have never seen chocolate. Sometimes it will be through firing weapons against those who mercilessly kill their own people.

You are a key component of this battle. You can strengthen your husband and help him to believe that his calling is good and important. Or you can whine about how it affects you and help him doubt. That's harsh, I know. But it's truth that I wish someone had imparted to me early in our military journey.

THE JUST WAR DOCTRINE

Perhaps your battle is not so much over the sacrifices your husband is called to make as it is over war itself. I know I struggled to reconcile the God of the New Testament who sent Jesus to die for everyone with the God of the Old Testament who frequently sent the Israelites into battle. I would look at our very fallible leaders in Washington, DC, and wonder how they knew the time was right to declare war. In my mind, men who commit atrocities like Hitler did make the decision clear. But when does a leader cross a line that makes war right?

Enter the Just War doctrine. Although it has its origins with the Romans, many great minds have weighed in on this topic over the last 2,000 years, discussing the circumstances under which the suffering of war becomes justified. Saint Augustine, a Christian theologian born in 354 AD, believed that God accorded government the divine authority to protect its people, by force if necessary. In his classic book *City of God*, Augustine writes several chapters concerning the sixth Commandment: *You shall not murder*.

Early on in the book, he points out that the Bible's command to not murder cannot be a blanket statement to never kill anyone or anything. He argues how ludicrous this would be if taken to its logical conclusion. If nothing could be killed then what would you eat? After all, even plants live and die.

As he continues, he keeps his readers focused on biblical principles and turns to the question of when killing is justified.

> These exceptions are of two kinds, being justified either by a general law, or by a special commission granted for a time to some individual. And in this latter case, he to whom authority is delegated, and who is but the sword in the hand of him who uses it, is not himself responsible for the death he deals. And, accordingly, they who have waged war in obedience to the divine command, or in conformity with His laws, have represented in their persons the public justice or the wisdom of government, and in this capacity have put to death wicked men; such persons have by no means violated the commandment, "Thou shalt not kill."[3]

3 Augustine of Hippo, *City of God* (England: Penguin, reprinted 2003, original print edition 1467), 33.

Augustine goes on to give examples from the Bible. He first mentions the time when Abraham was prepared to sacrifice his own son on an altar (Genesis 22:1–18). He notes that not only do we exonerate Abraham from all judgments of cruelty, but we hold him up as an example of righteousness. Next, Augustine mentions Jephthah, who killed his daughter, following through on a vow he spoke to God, probably without thinking through the implications of his words (Judges 11). And finally he talks about Samson's justification when he killed himself and his enemies after God renewed his strength (Judges 16).

Augustine saw within the Bible the precept that those who act under authority are not the ones responsible for their actions. While a soldier who kills will have to deal within his own heart and mind with having caused the death of another, God lays the responsibility for the act upon the one who issued the order. Which leads us back to the question: When is war justified?

The Just War doctrine differs slightly depending upon whom you ask, but essentially, these are the basic premises upon which it operates:

- Just Cause/Right Intentions. War is never justified to simply take something from another or punish someone who has done wrong. Governments who strive to follow the Just War doctrine look to see if innocent life is in imminent danger, and they go to war to protect life.

- Competent Authority. Whenever I hear this stipulation, I think of Proverbs 11:14: "For lack of guidance a nation falls, but victory is won through many advisers." A declaration of war is only justified if it comes through a legitimate authority within a government system. This does not include dictatorships or military regimes.

- Probability of Success/Proportionality. War is not justified if a positive outcome is not likely; the amount of force used must be proportional to the expected harms.

- Last Resort. Other viable methods must be attempted before war can be declared.

MAKING THE DIFFERENCE

While all this is sound theory, we must remember it is being carried out by fallible humans. And these humans affect your husband's military career and the time he gets with you. So let's talk about what you can do to make the most of it.

First, pray. A lot. Pray for your husband to boldly represent Christ in all he does and to have a heart that seeks God above all else. Pray for every leader in your husband's Chain of Command, all the way up to the Commander in Chief. Pray that they will be wise in their decisions, have full and accurate information to make those decisions, and will be able to negotiate before military action is deemed necessary.

Secondly, ask God to work within your heart to accept and love your husband's calling within the US military. Look for evidence of where God is working in your husband's life, and purposely encourage him to stand tall, stand firm, and persevere. Ask

God for grace to handle long training sessions, short notice TDYs, and insensitive commands.

Thirdly, cultivate an environment of honor and respect for soldiers within your home. Children and other visitors can sense whether or not you are happy about your husband's job. Working toward respecting his decision to enlist and honoring his determination to follow God's leading will go a long way to soothing your own heart in the uncertainty of military life.

FROM KATHY

> *The LORD is a warrior; the LORD is His name.*
> —Exodus 15:3

> *It is GOD who arms me with strength and keeps my*
> *way secure. . . .*
> *He trains my hands for battle.*
> —Psalm 18:32, 34a

Those verses tell us some powerful truths we need to learn and begin to believe if we are to understand the call on our husband's lives, and ultimately our own lives as their wives. First of all, God is a warrior. Second, being created in His image (Genesis 1:27), we were created for battle. *Webster's* dictionary defines a warrior as "a man who is engaged in or experienced in battle."[4] God,

---

4 *Webster's Comprehensive Dictionary*. 1987 international ed. (print), s.v. "warrior."

being a warrior, is experienced in battle, and it says in His Word that He will train us for the battles we will fight.

God was the first one to fight for truth and justice. War began long before the creation of man. There was a great battle in heaven that was set into motion because God's premiere angel wanted the only thing God had not granted him: the ability to be God. The glory of God can be shared with no one. But Lucifer, who was given all authority and gifts in heaven, was also given free will, and so he devised in himself the desire to attain the only thing forbidden him. And a great war broke forth in which God fought his once highest honored servant and cast him from heaven (see Revelation 12:4, Isaiah 14:12–15 and 46:8–13, Ezekiel 28:13–18).

That war, which began in the spirit realm in unknown times and space, is still continuing today. And we are now a part of it. God has a great plan to restore full revelation of truth and to fully show His glory to all creation, both in heaven and on earth. And that plan includes us.

He created man in His own image and astounded the angels of heaven at how much He could do with such a feeble race. You see, God could have just ended Satan and could have destroyed him anyway He chose. But He elected to do it through the most un-likely manner imaginable to all of His creation. He chose men. He knew Adam and Eve would fall to Satan before He created them. He is omniscient. Hebrews 4:13 says "Nothing in all creation is hid-den from God's sight." So why even create Satan? Why create man and so be forced to clean up a mess that He knew would happen?

The very essence of our God is love. He displayed His amaz-ing glory by showing the objects of His wrath how great His love was for them, as it says in Ephesians 2:2–10. He walked in humility, the one thing Satan would never do. He showed sacrifice for another as the most beautiful display of love that could ever be seen. Jesus humbled Himself to become a man. He then further humbled Himself to an unjust, undeserved death on a cross, just to spare us and show His overwhelming love for us. Where Satan has never bent to the authority of our creator God, we are given the amazing opportunity to do something that causes all creation to stand in awe. We receive grace, mercy, and forgiveness when we, as lesser creations (Psalm 8:4–5), surrender ourselves before our mighty God (Philippians 2:5–11).

The purpose of all mankind is to be a display of the Lord's splendor, as mentioned in Isaiah 66. When we talk about mankind as a whole, we share a common purpose. How that purpose is to be played out in our lives is done with the unique calls upon each of our personal walks of faith with our God. Each man and woman will have a divine, unique call upon their life to best be able to display God's glory upon this earth and in heaven. Serving in the military is one of those calls.

CREATED IN HIS IMAGE

Allow me to expound on our being created in the image of our God; this should help us in understanding our call. The triune nature of God is difficult to comprehend. (You can find some sources for study on the doctrine of the Trinity in the appendix.) The leading of the Father, the sacrificial Son who came in the flesh, and the indwelling Spirit who guides us each have their own job descriptions, yet somehow the three are always in perfect harmony.

Going back to the truth of Genesis 1:27, we can draw parallels to this triune nature from within our own creation. Almighty God formed us of three key components. We are flesh, soul, and spirit, 1 Thessalonians 5:23 tells us.

The flesh is the most obvious component, just as when Jesus walked the earth, He was the most obvious aspect of God. It is the part we all see. It is the part that desires comfort and satisfaction above all else. We observe this from the beginnings of infancy. Our flesh longs for hunger to be satisfied. We long to be warm and comforted. Our flesh dislikes discomfort from wet, soiled diapers and from noises and lights that disrupt our rest. We long to be comfortable above all else. This remains true for the remainder of our lives.

We learn, though, as we grow from babies to children and then into adulthood, to withstand increasing levels of discomfort and varying levels of pain, but rarely is that what we want. We always seek to satisfy our basic needs, such as food, rest, and sexual gratification. These are all tied together and eventually, even when patiently put aside, they will ultimately rise to the point that satisfaction of these needs must be met or, in some cases, death will occur. Death is painful. And we avoid pain. We are physically geared to meet those needs to avoid pain and gain comfort and satisfaction. Yet if we are walking in the image of our God, we must learn to walk as Jesus did, who gave us the ultimate example of overcoming pain and mastering the flesh with all its desires (see Hebrews 4:14–15, 1 Peter 2:20–25).

The soul within us is the next portion of our being that makes us like our God. It is the part that governs our thoughts and feelings, where our loves and longings reside. It is our soul that drives us in this life. It is here the Holy Spirit is represented, as He longs to lead us in this place filled with varying emotions. When our thoughts are full of grocery lists, raising kids, doing school and work, or figuring out how to love our husbands, it is this level of our being that is affected.

The soul is more easily masked. You can't know exactly what someone else is thinking or feeling. They may share those things with you verbally or with their body language, but it requires more effort to see this part of them. It even requires more effort to discover things about yourself at this level than it does within your flesh. When your flesh is dissatisfied, you can usually determine what need must be met to satisfy that desire. Food satisfies hunger. Sleep satisfies the body's need for rest. It is much more difficult to reveal why you are feeling discontented in your soul.

Pinpointing dissatisfaction within the soul can be hard. We wonder why we are lonely even though we have people around us. We wonder why we can't feel loved even with a loving family. We wonder why we find ourselves angry with people or situations when we can't find a justifiable reason for such an emotion.

The soul is often difficult to understand, but it is often the part of us that drives and compels us to particular choices more than the other two aspects of our being. It guides our lives through our intellect and rationale and through our constant emotional changes. When we allow the Holy Spirit to lead us, we can be guided into all truth in this area. We can live by the Spirit, as Galatians 5:16–25 discusses. We must renew our minds with the watering of the Word. This allows the Spirit to bring all things to our remembrance and help us navigate the uncertainty of this world and of our own emotions and thoughts (Romans 12:2).

The final aspect of who we are is the most mysterious. It is the spirit man within us. This is who we were before the foundations of the earth. It is the part of us that was created to be connected with our creator God. The one facet of us that can be truly united with the Holy Spirit, once we have entered into salvation through Christ. Within our spirit is the very nature of God, manifested into His creation for the purpose of reflecting Him. This is the center of our being and purpose.

The spirit man within us is never fully alive until united with God through Christ and the indwelling of the Holy Spirit. Until this time we are spiritually dead. At the moment of salvation, though, we truly come to life and see truth and begin to understand that our purpose is to bring God glory and be a reflection of Him (Ephesians 1:11–14). Our purpose is to be one with God, regardless of our circumstances. Regardless of our thoughts or feelings. Regardless of the pain or needs of the flesh.

We become one with our husbands in the flesh, and sometimes on the soul level we share intimacy. But oneness in the Spirit doesn't happen until we are united to Christ. And then we are united to the church as a whole, not just our spouse. This is the great mystery spoken of in Scripture. This is the reason marriage is a beautiful picture of the love of Christ for His bride, the church. It is a picture of oneness and unity we can only begin to understand dimly. I don't feel we are going to experience full oneness with God until we are in His manifest presence in heaven. Then we will all be united to the holiness of our Creator in a way that this fallen flesh and crippled soul can never understand. For this reason, we are called to renew our minds with the watering of the Word. We are called to have new minds. To have new souls. But not until heaven will we truly have a new flesh, and the fullness of who we are created to be can be united to the fullness of God.

ENCOURAGING YOUR MAN'S CALL

So how does all this relate to being a warrior bride and assisting in our husband's call? We are called to war. Ephesians 6:12 says, "For our struggle is not against flesh and blood, but against the rulers, against the authorities, against the powers of this dark world and against the spiritual forces of evil in the heavenly realms." So we are each charged with going to battle. And it is God who arms us with strength for that battle. But, as was stated earlier, there is a God-given call to the military to protect peoples and nations from the encroachment and empowering of evil within our world.

God ordained military might. He was the first warrior. In the beginning of the Israelite nation, it was God Himself who went to war for them with the Egyptians. He fought the first battle at the Red Sea in Exodus 14–15, completely obliterating the opposition. God always intended to lead them—with a pillar of fire and a cloud of smoke. In fact, He made it quite clear that He wanted to do the fighting for them! He never wanted them to lose their lives in battle.

But so often, they ignored Him and went in their own strength. We see this throughout Scripture. When the Israelites went with God before them, they always won. When they ignored His commands, they were destroyed. Military forces are one aspect of the governing bodies that God put into place to protect man from the evil with which Satan would overwhelm this world. The military is a very practical as well as a spiritual means for God to protect mankind from the terrible results of our own sins. Just as God wars on our behalf, since we are made in His likeness we must war on men's behalf as well.

When our military husbands enter the earthly battlefield, they take all three aspects of themselves into the war. This is true of all mankind in whatever spiritual battles they may fight, but in all respects, our men truly lay all of their being on the front line. They put their flesh on the line, not just their soul and spirit. Their very life is at risk at every moment. They could physically die.

As wives, we worry the most about this aspect. But this is a childish view. Not insignificant or unimportant, but that is just one aspect of our men on the line. We, as the wives of these valiant men, often fear the loss of their lives, or flesh as we see it, as the greatest of these three aspects.

But do we ever consider that our men are equally dying a slow death if they are to lose either of the other two parts of themselves while on the battlefield? A child worries only about their fleshly needs, not their emotional or spiritual ones, but we must begin to mature. We must begin to see and pray over the other two critical aspects of our men's lives. We should be praying for their minds and emotions. We should be covering their inner man in prayer that they might begin to understand in their depths that they are called to their life. They serve with purpose. That purpose can find fulfillment and satisfaction, especially when they have a wife supporting them in prayer, words, and actions.

I'm not suggesting that we don't pray for our troop's physical protection and safety. God commands that we follow the example of Christ, who taught us how valuable prayer is in our daily walk with Him. Prayer moves mountains (Mark 11:23). I know of two separate incidents where God laid my husband heavily on my heart at particular moments of time, and I prayed in the spirit until the burden was lifted. I found out later that in each of these two cases, my husband narrowly escaped death. Prayer is vital to our helping our husbands thwart the enemy on the battlefield.

However, we can never control when or if our men will lose their lives on the battlefield. We constantly plead with the Almighty in fear. We don't trust that He will work out all things together for our good with regards to life and death. But can we trust that what He calls good is really the best plan for us, even if it doesn't *feel* good or look like we want?

When we pray, we must always pray trusting that God's will is the perfect plan for our life and the life of our beloved man. I believe too many women move in fear, not trust, when they pray. God alone numbers each of our days (Psalm 139:16). We can, and must, pray for our men on and off the battlefield. However, we must always remember that their life's breath is in God's hands alone.

Salvation also belongs to the Lord alone. I pray that you are blessed with an equally yoked marriage. But many of you may not be. Do not doubt that, if your husband is not serving God, it is His great desire to pursue your man and bring him to salvation (2 Peter 3:9). You can rest in knowing that however much you want your husband to have life and life abundant, your God wants it even more.

God's Spirit alone can bring salvation and determine the length of days your husband will live, but we have a huge opportunity to influence whether our men are champions within their souls and their spirits. In fact, I believe your support in aiding victory in these two arenas is the greatest gift you can give to your husband as his precious bride; it is a huge part of your God-given calling. Your choice to speak encouragement and to offer your husband support in his job is monumental in helping him to rise to the potential God sees in him. Your respect of his position, both as head of your family and as a warrior called by God, can propel your husband into new levels of victory.

In 1 Corinthians 7:12–16, Paul addresses the power we have in our marriages, especially if our spouse is not saved. God has called us to live in peace and to stay in the marriage to bring sanctification to our spouse and children. In an unequally yoked marriage, God will view your family as holy because you stand on His Word and promises. Paul suggests that you—more than any other person in your husband's life—have the power to show salvation and usher it into your home.

Peter says something similar in 1 Peter 3:1–2: "Wives, in the same way submit yourselves to your own husbands so that, if any of them do not believe the word, they may be won over without words by the behavior of their wives, when they see the purity and reverence of your lives." The way you choose to surrender to God and submit to that man will have the greatest effect on whether or not he will ever turn his own heart over to Christ.

I recently heard Mark Driscoll, pastor of Mars Hill Church, make a comment that struck me hard. He said his wife had recently caused him to be convicted about an area in his life. She had invited him to examine himself—by *not* causing him to feel that he had to defend himself. Let that sink in for a moment. How often do we try to play the Holy Spirit for our husbands and guilt them into seeing Christ? Surrender, by definition, has to be chosen. No amount of manipulation or condemnation will ever bring surrender. It will only cause a man to become bitter and defensive. If we aren't careful as wives, we can end up pushing our men in the opposite direction from God when it is our heart to draw them closer.

Men are called to lead and love their wives. This is part of the amazing responsibility and blessing that God ordains for them. My guess, though, is that most American men have absolutely no idea how to do this. Very few men that I know—or women either—have ever had godly manhood modeled for them. And so we all, men and women, often have false perceptions of what godly manhood should look like. In our society, there are so many deceptions about what the roles and responsibilities are for men and women that are counter to the Bible. Armed with this knowledge, I come to two conclusions.

One is that I should have an abundance of grace for my husband as he struggles to figure out how to be a man at all, much less a godly man. I need to encourage him and give him room to make mistakes. The other thing I can conclude is that if a woman was never meant to lead a man, she was never meant to show a man how to be a man. I am incapable and unequipped to show my husband how to lead or love me.

Proverbs is full of verses about the negative effects of nagging. It is also full of the amazing power of the tongue, and how wonderful our words can be to encourage healing and growth in others. God means for you to be the greatest helper He has in drawing your husband to Him. But you must do it His way. Sometimes that means getting yourself out of the way. Our husbands don't need us to show them how to lead. That is still us trying to lead them.

Trust that God is big enough to hold your husband and cover you and your children. Trust God through trusting your man, especially if he isn't saved. You will be showing him true biblical respect and causing him to be elevated to the positional authority God intends him to embrace. God is calling him forward, and you must be following him so you don't get in between him and his Creator.

We have great power to affect how our men will begin to trust God for their lives and their calls. Make no mistake: they are called. Their lives and their life's work are vital to God and to Kingdom advancement. They are part of a much bigger plan then they may ever see, this side of heaven. They are valiant men, who do what so many will never have the courage to do. They will struggle, and they will doubt, but it is God who will arm them with strength and keep their way secure. They are warriors. They are made in the image of Almighty God, and they are honorable and worthy of honor. Embrace your husband and his calling, and give him the honor due him, and let God lead him to embrace his calling and purpose within Christ.

CHAPTER 6

THE CALLING OF THE WARRIOR'S BRIDE

You are My witnesses, declares the Lord, and My servant whom I have chosen, so that you may know and believe Me and understand that I am He.

—Isaiah 43:10

FROM CARRIE

Perhaps I should warn you right now that as we continue to dig into our hearts, this will get harder. Learning that I was to die to myself as a wife and let my husband lead me was tough, but at least the one I was striving to follow loved me in return. As I began to realize that I needed to have this same attitude toward the US government, to let the government have control of my family's life and to humbly accept whatever came our way—well, . . . it didn't go over smoothly.

I knew the promises of the Bible, the verses that tell me God is in control and has great plans for me, such as Romans 13:1–7 and Jeremiah 29:11. But when a command would come down that disrupted my day, I would get angry. Frustration would build because I knew that we had no recourse. We couldn't make an appeal to work longer hours tomorrow instead of today. This wasn't even a job we could walk away from if we didn't like it!

Oh sure, we could get out when the time for re-enlistment came, but in my moments of calm, I wanted what God planned for us. Those verses of blessing (Psalm 40:4–5, Psalm 92:12–15) would return to me, and I would know that God's way was best. I desired to follow His path no matter what, and that path included my husband's military service. Until the next command came down that interrupted my plans.

This vicious cycle continued, and now I can see the turmoil I caused myself, my husband, and my marriage. Ultimately, I was fighting for control—control I knew that I didn't really want. But I struggled to give it all over to God and leave it there. I was taking my problem to the cross, but then returning home with it still firmly in my grasp. Until the day I reconciled myself to the fact that if I am married to a man called to be a warrior, then I am called to be a warrior's bride, complete with all the baggage of the US military.

Now I know some of you are wondering if maybe your husband made a mistake, and that you were never meant to be a military spouse. You think that maybe your husband chose the wrong career; perhaps he should be in a different MOS (Military

Occupation Specialty), or maybe he shouldn't be in the military to begin with.

You need to stop that thinking right now. You aren't going to like this, but the reality is that it doesn't matter. Your job is not to tell your husband what career to choose. Your job is to support your husband and follow his lead. God will help him determine the proper future for you and your family, but you need to stay out of God's way.

Or perhaps you think you married a different man than the one God originally planned for you. Maybe. But the bottom line is that it no longer matters. Your choice was not a surprise to God, and your act of free will does not change the reality that you vowed your life to that man in uniform. Regardless of how or why you got married, the moment you said, "I do," you aligned yourself with him and his calling. You are now his warrior bride.

Please understand, I am not talking to the person with an abusive spouse. If you fear your spouse, seek counsel. But for the rest of us, take a moment to process your thoughts about being aligned with your husband's calling. If you are frustrated, it's probably for one of three reasons:

You don't like it because you didn't marry a warrior. Maybe, like my husband, he joined up after you were married, so you didn't know what you were signing up for when you said your vows.

You don't like it because it means someone else is in control of your life. The story of the cross is beautiful to you, but God being in total control of every decision of your life is the problem. Boy, can I relate to that!

You don't like it because you had little experience with the military lifestyle and didn't understand what you'd be dealing with.

Sweet one, let's call these what they are: excuses for bad attitudes and temper tantrums. It's my belief that anyone could use any of these rationalizations about something in their lives. And truthfully, prior understanding has little to do with follow through. You either determine to finish what you started, or you walk away and deal with the consequences.

Ultimately, that's what you must decide: determine to finish what you started or else walk away and deal with the consequences.

The book of Ephesians comes to mind when I want to walk away from something, particularly if I think God wants me to do that which is frustrating me. The Apostle Paul is a prisoner in Rome when he writes to the church in Ephesus to encourage them and to help them understand what the church should look like. Take a look at the first seven verses of chapter 4:

> As a prisoner for the Lord, then, I urge you to live a life worthy of the calling you have received. Be completely humble and gentle; be patient, bearing with one another in love. Make every effort to keep the unity of the Spirit through the bond of peace. There is one body and one Spirit, just as you were called to one hope when you were called; one Lord, one faith, one baptism; one God and Father of all, who is over all and through all and in all.
>
> But to each one of us grace has been given as Christ apportioned it.

This passage contains so much truth for the wife struggling with contentment. I imagine Paul, with passion flowing, reaching out to this church and begging them to live a life worthy of their calling. Live a life worthy of what they have received freely from God. Live a life worthy of their inheritance waiting in Heaven.

Just in case the church is uncertain, Paul adds exactly what it means to live worthy: to be completely humble, gentle, and patient, showing love and unity. I don't know about you, but those are a tall order for me, especially when I am disappointed that my husband is going to miss yet another special event. But they are possible. Verse 7 says it so beautifully: "grace has been given."

And that's the secret to your primary calling. We aren't going to tell you that you can't work outside the home, when or if you should have children, whether you should return to your family when he deploys, or any other specifics about your life. Those are between you, your husband, and God.

But what we desperately want you to understand is that your primary focus after God is your husband. And to serve him well, there will be times when you will need every drop of grace God offers. Because gentleness, patience, love, and unity are not within the human heart's natural capabilities (Jeremiah 17:9, Romans 3:9–12): they are gifts of the Spirit (Galatians 5:22).

And this is where everything in your life comes full circle. The gifts of the Spirit come from God after salvation. And as you allow Christ to become Lord of your life, these gifts grow and overflow onto others around you. The encouragement of seeing God's grace cover you and be passed onto others helps you to step out in greater faith, trusting Jesus to be Lord of even more of your life.

But it is a process that takes patience, because we don't change overnight. It takes faith, because we are trusting biblical promises for future results that we can't see clearly. And it takes determination, because your enemy Satan seeks to distract you from what's important, diminish what God is doing through you, and negate what God is doing in you.

Just as you need to keep your attention on Jesus as you walk through your daily life, you must keep your calling to your husband in focus before you, so you don't stray from God's plan for you and your marriage. Knowing that your calling is to God first and then to your husband will help calm your heart's turmoil when the military swoops in and changes your plans.

FROM KATHY

> Who among you fears the Lord and obeys the word of His
> servant? Let the one who walks in the dark, who has no light,
> trust in the name of the Lord and rely on their God. But now, all
> you who light fires and provide yourselves with flaming torches,
> go, walk in the light of your fires and of the torches you have set
> ablaze. This is what you shall receive from my hand: You will lie
> down in torment.
>
> —Isaiah 50:10–11

There was a season in my marriage where I wanted nothing more than for my husband to get out of the military. I blamed his job for all of the discontent and unhappiness in my life. I believed that if my husband were to just leave the service, he would focus more on our family and he would focus more on the Lord and about how to lead us. I was absolutely convinced that my unhappiness was due to his poor leadership and lack of involvement with myself and our children, because of his choice of career. To me, the solution was simple: find a new career.

You can imagine my surprise when God revealed to me that it was me, and not Sam or Sam's career, who was making me so miserable. One of the key ways God showed me this was in the verses above. You see, I was walking in a dark place with no light. I couldn't see or understand why the military was our life's call. I was scared. I was lonely. And, often, I was angry.

In that place, I didn't trust in the Lord or rely on my God. I was trying to rely on Sam for my source of contentment and happiness. And so I began to light my own fires and torches to see out of my darkness. I tried to take control of my situation by taking control of my husband and his career choice. But God's Word is always true. And I was in torment.

God showed me that, by not trusting the call He had laid on my husband's life, I was not trusting Him. He showed me the high calling of my husband. He revealed to me that the military was God-ordained. It wasn't just a career choice my husband had made and could now unmake. God had placed in the heart of my man the ability and willingness to go and do what few could do. God needed godly men who could endure great hardship to lead in that place. It was a high and difficult calling: not for the faint of heart or weak-spirited.

Then God showed me the truth about my position in my marriage. Just as in the military there can't be success in a mission unless everyone does their part, we can't have success in military families and marriages unless everyone understands their role and how to persevere in their jobs. We can't all be generals! We have got to understand that our roles as women are to submit to our husbands.

Submission is so hard for us, not just because of our sin nature, which Eve first set us up to struggle with, but because we have to fight the cultural mindset we have as American women. Did you know that it was a requirement for all young men of the Israelite nation to serve in their army once they reached manhood? There was a constant draft in progress. And no one even considered trying to dodge it. It was a part of their men. It was a part of the call of their nation to take hold of their promised land and hold it, with God's grace and oversight. All men went to war. Therefore, all wives sent their men to war. All Hebrew women understood this reality. I believe it is harder for American military wives than it was for the wives of the Hebrews to understand and walk in this command.

But God knew then and He knows now how difficult that is on a family, especially on a wife. In Scripture, God speaks directly about His heart for you, a military wife. Deuteronomy 24:5 says, "If a man has recently married, he must not be sent to war or have any other duty laid on him. For one year he is to be free to stay at home and bring happiness to the wife he has married."

God knew we would need and want our husbands to be home. He knew we would want them near us to make us happy, especially as young brides. But He never wants anything or anyone else to be our source of happiness. Only He can be that. By trying to place my will above God's, and in hoping that Sam could fill the gaps of longing in my heart, I was sinning. Learning to love the Lord our God with all our heart, with all our soul, and with all our strength, as stated in Deuteronomy 6:5, is our caution to keep from falling into this trap. The New Testament adds that we should also love Him with all our minds.

God designed women's minds different from men's. Men tend to compartmentalize, but we women have balls of wire for brains. We think one thing, and it sends us into many different thought processes. God wants us to take *all* thoughts captive to Him. We must fight battles in our thought lives as we learn to surrender our way of thinking to God's way of thinking.

God says in Isaiah 55:9: "As the heavens are higher than the earth, so are My ways higher than your ways and My thoughts than your thoughts." In order to know the thoughts of God, we need to be in communication with Him through prayer and the reading of His Word. I submit to each of you that when you are not communicating with God, you are trying to figure out all of your life on your own. You wrestle within your own thoughts, ways to love and communicate with your husband, raise your children, run your home, and live this life as a military wife, often all alone. You are lighting your own torches. Please, dear sister, don't lie down in torment.

God doesn't want us to *endure* this call on our lives to be military wives, but to *embrace* it. He doesn't just want you to *survive* in this marriage, but to *succeed* in it! You are called to live a life

of abundance with our God and with your husband. He desperately wants to bless you with all good gifts. Surrendering to His
thoughts and designs for your life will bring this blessing.

So what did God mean when He issued that law for the young
Hebrew soldiers to be home for a year? What happiness did He
mean to impart to those young military brides? Well, for one, He
wanted them to get to know each other and simply enjoy the honeymoon of life. Many of their marriages were arranged, and so,
more or less, they often were marrying strangers. I'm sure God
wanted them to begin to unite as one, not just in flesh, but on a
much deeper level that would include their emotions and hearts.

But I think there was a much more practical reason as well.
He wanted to give them time to conceive and birth a child. Birth
control was unheard of then, and the fruit of the womb was a
great blessing to be embraced quickly in married life. I think this
offered a two-fold purpose for those young Hebrew couples.

One, it ensured that the name of that man was already passed
on to the next generation. These young men were going to war.
The real possibility of them never returning was always looming.
The idea of passing a man's name on to his son was so critical in
their culture that when no son was found for a man who had
died, his brother would actually take his widow and marry her so
that he could give his brother's name to a son born to him. This
male relative was called a Kinsman Redeemer. We witness this in
the book of Ruth, when Boaz marries Ruth and their first child,
Obed, is laid upon Naomi's knee and she calls the child her son
(Ruth chapter 4).

The second reason I think God would have sent them a child was for the benefit of the wife. Nothing will keep a woman busier than having a baby. Nothing can bring more comfort to her lonely arms than to be rocking a new baby. A new child would have kept that mommy's life so full that there wouldn't have been time for her to have sorrow over her husband's departure. She would have been busy about her home, which was what was good and acceptable for a woman of that culture.

Please do not misconstrue what I just said, as if I am saying that only when you have a baby can God give you comfort in your husband's deployments and TDYs. That isn't true. God brings comfort to us in many ways. But, putting the verse into the context of the Hebrew culture at the time it was laid forth, I think that was why God issued the order for men to stay home for a year: to unify the marriage and to bring forth a child.

In our culture, it is quite different. First of all, I don't know an American military wife who wouldn't do backflips for joy if a law was written that said during the first year of marriage your husband was to be given no other duty but to stay home and bring you happiness! Can you imagine that?

Humor me, however, just a moment to consider that we, as Americans, don't understand the model of a Christian home as God designed it to look. We believe that we, as women, are equal to men. And according to the Word, there is no difference between men, women, Greek, Hebrew, slave, or freeman (Galatians 3:26). But that verse is talking about our relationship to God and our ability to stand before the cross. It means that God loves each of us the same unconditionally. It does not mean (as we modern

Americans often assume) that we all have the same rights and responsibilities. Men were designed to rule and subdue the earth. Women were designed to help men. Period. That is a hard concept for our American minds to wrap around, but it is biblical.

But just because God designed women to be a helpmeet to their husband doesn't mean that we all must fall into the model of a Hebrew wife of 3,000 years ago! Heavens, no! Each marriage will look different. You each come from your own backgrounds and your own upbringings. Each of you was uniquely fitted for the man you married, and you were ordained by God Himself to help your husband succeed in all he is called to do. That is your greatest success . . . to help him succeed. You see, when your man succeeds in his call from God, you will reap all the benefits and rewards of having a godly man lead you. You will be blessed beyond measure. Your life and home will be more blessed than through anything you could ever do in your strength to try to make that happen.

That result, though, will look as different for each family as each couple is different. Some will be called to have children. Some will not. Some women will have careers. Some will stay home. Your actual job and day-to-day tasks will be whatever best suits your family and benefits your husband's calling. You do what best helps him succeed.

Too often, however, we are selfish. We can agree that children should obey parents. We agree that husbands should lay down their lives for us. But we really fight on that whole submission thing. But there is no room for selfish ambition in marriage—for either partner.

Philippians 2:3–4 says, "Do nothing out of selfish ambition or vain conceit. Rather, in humility value others above yourselves, not looking to your own interests but each of you to the interests of others." Please, dear one, let nothing be done in selfish ambition, especially in your marriage.

> What causes fights and quarrels among you? Don't they come from your desires that battle within you? You desire but do not have, so you kill. You covet but you cannot get what you want, so you quarrel and fight. You do not have because you do not ask God. When you ask, you do not receive, because you ask with wrong motives, that you may spend what you get on your pleasures.
>
> You adulterous people, don't you know that friendship with the world means enmity against God? Therefore, anyone who chooses to be a friend of the world becomes an enemy of God. Or do you think Scripture says without reason that He jealously longs for the spirit He has caused to dwell in us? But He gives us more grace. That is why Scripture says: "God opposes the proud but shows favor to the humble."
>
> Submit yourselves, then, to God. Resist the devil, and he will flee from you. Come near to God and He will come near to you. Wash your hands, you sinners, and purify your hearts, you double-minded.
>
> —James 4:1–8

We must ask ourselves if we are friends with the world. Are we more comfortable with our culture and our upbringing than we are with the Word of God? God has laid out a beautiful plan for a successful marriage. What drives your thinking and decisions? What are your motives in asking God for help with your marriage? Do you want God to change your *husband* so your marriage will change? Do you want your husband to agree with you? Do you want him to love you? Do you want him to support and minister to you? What if we were to pray according to Philippians 4:4–7?

> Rejoice in the Lord always. I will say it again: Rejoice! Let your gentleness be evident to all. The Lord is near. Do not be anxious about anything, but in every situation, by prayer and petition, with thanksgiving, present your requests to God. And the peace of God, which transcends all understanding, will guard your hearts and your minds in Christ Jesus.

Could your motives then be changed? Could you dare to ask God to change *you* so that your marriage would change? Could you learn to agree with your husband? Could you learn to respect him? Could you learn to support and minister to him and his call?

God has given you power in your marriage to help your husband. You can either learn to submit to that man and seek his greatest good, by seeking what God has for him, or you can seek to manipulate your husband to suit your selfishness. If you don't want him in the military, you likely have the ability to make your husband miserable enough to change his plans and get out of the service eventually. You might get your way, but you will have lost a great part of your marriage in the process. If God called your husband to this life, or any life, your job is to help him be as successful as he can be where he is called. He may not be called to the service for a full career. This may just be a stepping stone to what God has next for you. But as long as you are here, your job is to bless and support your man. I know it is tough. But if you undermine what God has placed in the heart of your husband, you are destroying the heart of your man. And you are being disobedient to God.

God knows how hard it is to be a military wife. He desires your happiness and longs to give you contentment. He is magnified when your marriage is glorified. God alone can bring glory to it, but he seeks to do that through you. You have the mighty privilege of trusting in a mighty God. And you have the amazing challenge of doing that through trusting your husband in whatever job he happens to be doing.

This is the high and difficult calling of a military wife. It is not for the faint of heart or the weak spirited. But if you were meant for that man, and that man is in the military, then you were meant for this greatness. Dear sister, begin to lay down your agendas and your torches. Learn to fear the Lord and obey His Word, for there is where you will find great joy and peace. Allow God to help you, as you learn to be a helper to your man in this amazing call on your life: his warrior bride.

CHAPTER 7

THE WORK OF A MASTER CRAFTSMAN

Accept one another, then, just as Christ accepted you, in order to bring praise to God.

—Romans 15:7

THE FOUR PERSONALITIES

FROM CARRIE

It doesn't take much study in nature to see the remarkable workmanship of our Heavenly Father. I am in awe of the complex systems that He put into place on this earth and marvel at their interdependencies. The water cycle, photosynthesis, the web of life. All of it would break down if any one part stopped doing its job.

Our bodies are the same. Scientists labor to understand the brain, yet it needs the eye to see, the ear to hear, and the skin to touch. It would die without the circulatory or respiratory systems.

Watch anyone with a digestive issue, nerve problem, or even a broken bone struggle to function like a person with a healthy body.

Like it or not, just as God formed both the earth and our bodies to be interdependent, He also created us as people to need each other (Psalm 133:1, 1 Corinthians 12). Does that discourage you? Take heart!

I am not a people person; I would label myself an introvert. I like alone time, activities that rely on no one but myself, and quiet. To me, dealing with people requires great energy, and the bigger the crowd, the more exhausted I am when it's time to go home.

But that's not something I have to feel guilty about. Now, I can't go off and live on an island by myself, no matter how tempting that may be at times. However, in the midst of living my life with other people, I can take time to be alone. It's the way God chose to make me. And it's good.

Each one of us has a personality that greatly influences how we react in various situations. Perhaps you are like me and find people draining. Or maybe you are like many of my friends who thrive off other people and live for social occasions. We know in our heads that God created us differently, and we long for others to accept us as we are, yet often we struggle to extend to others the same courtesy.

For example, I love my husband dearly, but he simply cannot tell a short story. He must tell you every detail, turning a three-minute event into a fifteen-minute monologue. Always entertaining to those listening, they walk away knowing exactly what happened through the eyes of my spouse. When I tell a story to friends, he usually takes over for me because he thinks I leave out too much.

I remember being incensed with him more than once over this. I have memories of thinking that he was ruining a good movie for someone because he was telling them everything but the last ten minutes of the film. Or being furious when he'd interrupt my story with my friends so he could finish it his way. Why couldn't he just communicate more succinctly? Or let me tell my own stories?

What I didn't understand was that I was fighting the very character God designed in him. My attitude changed dramatically when someone finally introduced us to the four personality types. Suddenly, I understood that he wasn't intending to be rude or inconsiderate: he was simply dealing with the nature God gave him! The one God chose for him. The one God deemed best.

Now please understand that this is not an excuse for bad behavior. Yes, I could use my introverted nature to avoid every party for the rest of my life. Or my spouse could take over every conversation, never allowing me to add anything to the discussion. But that would be living at the extreme, which is not what God wants. Typically, spousal personalities offer some balance and opportunities for growth; ultimately we want to become like Jesus, who perfectly balanced the four types.

Over the years, different names have been used and some experts expanded them further, but as you look closely, all personalities boil down to four main categories: sanguine, choleric, melancholy, and phlegmatic. As we look at the characteristics of each, I want you to do two things.

First, consider Psalm 139:23: "Search me, O God, and know my heart; test me and know my anxious thoughts." Take an honest look at yourself and see which one or two of the personalities best describe you, then make sure you are operating within your God-given strengths and not simply lounging in your weaknesses.

Next pray about Romans 12:10: "Be devoted to one another in love. Honor one another above yourselves." Prayerfully look at your spouse to see how God created him. Do you honor him by allowing him to function within his personality type? Can you accept the strengths that God put into him, even if they are the opposite of yours?

I'd encourage you to begin to consider others around you: your children, your parents, and your closest friends. Understanding how God designed each of them can truly make a difference in how you view the most important people in your life. Now, let's start with the extroverts.

THE EXTROVERTS: SANGUINES AND CHOLERICS

How can some people make friends with a store cashier? They never meet outside the shopping experience, but as goods are processed through the checkout, these strangers carry on a conversation like they've known each other for years. Why must other people always be in charge of everything? One woman in my past with a controlling personality refused to be part of a group unless she could lead it. Such is life with *sanguines* and *cholerics*.

Sanguines and *cholerics* are the active, outgoing people in life, the ones who must be busy doing something. They rarely sit on the sidelines. Instead, they are the ones keeping life moving in the fast lane.

The sanguine person is the popular one, the one who loves social events and parties. They want to be happy and have a good time, and they want you to be happy and have a good time, too. Sanguines are talkers. One well-known sanguine says that she can talk about anything, anytime, anywhere, with little-to-no information. They never let facts get in the way of a good story. To the rest of us, they can seem unorganized, scatterbrained, and forgetful. This is merely because God created them with a love for people. Relationships control sanguines, not details.

Cholerics, on the other hand, are powerful people. They simply must find someone or something to lead. While they often come across as bossy or arrogant, they simply want to shape everyone up, make sure tasks are done—and, by the way, have everyone do everything their way! Cholerics love to work, and while they are not overly emotional people, if they think they can't win, they may enter the race simply to prove they can. Very strong-willed, they can have a deep desire for change. They are goal-oriented, can run almost anything, live independently, and exude confidence.

When you think of sanguines, think of Tigger, the lovable tiger from Winnie the Pooh, or Snoopy from the Peanuts cartoon. Emotionally, they are frequently like children who never grow up. They need attention and acceptance. If they don't get uncompromised approval, they will not try something again. Sanguines are the only group of people who will not grow and mature by applying negative consequences for undesirable behavior; they absolutely rely on positive reinforcement. Most importantly, they measure their self-worth by how many people love them.

In stark contrast, cholerics are so controlling of their own emotions that their emotional lives are frequently underdeveloped. Think of Rabbit from Winnie the Pooh, or Lucy from Peanuts. Emotionally, they need people to obey them, and they need a lot of credit for every good deed they attempt. They thrive on opposition and excel in emergencies, but they can be possessive, domineering, impetuous, and have little patience with mistakes. Cholerics measure their self-worth by how much work they accomplish.

THE INTROVERTS: MELANCHOLICS AND PHLEGMATICS

Melancholics and *phlegmatics* are the introverted, restful people, the ones who are totally content to sit. With a great tendency toward passiveness, they enjoy the sidelines, watching the sanguines and cholerics rush about life.

God blessed me with a melancholy nature. I am detailed and scheduled. In addition to my endless lists, I like to plan and research. I want every job analyzed so a task can be done perfectly the first time. Melancholics tend to be artistic or musical and can spend hours in silence, thinking deeply. And we rarely answer questions with a simple yes or no.

Phlegmatics are the ones Jesus may have been thinking of when He said, "Blessed are the peacemakers" (Matthew 5:9). Phlegmatics want peace, and they will cheerfully sacrifice personal desires in favor of letting the cholerics make the decisions, just so there is no arguing. They are easy-going people who like to sit and rest. While they prefer things calm, cool, and collected, they will go out of their way not to make problems for anyone.

When you think of melancholics, think of Owl from Winnie the Pooh, or Linus from Peanuts. Emotionally they are very mature; they recognize the difference between similar emotions, such as anger and fury. They make friends very cautiously but become fiercely loyal. They need someone in their life who is willing to be patient and drag out the information they've so carefully thought through, but they absolutely must have space. They tend to be both self-sacrificing and idealistic, combining the reality of problems with the optimistic hope that others will change. Melancholics tend to measure their self-worth by how well they complete a task. That is, not by the speed or quantity of work done, but by its quality.

Phlegmatics, on the other hand, keep their emotions hidden. Think of Christopher Robin or the piano-playing Schroeder. They tend to be sympathetic, good listeners and do not get upset very easily. They have many friends, are pleasant, enjoyable, and generally unconcerned about things that go wrong. More than anything else, they need to know they have value.

Between God's design and our environment growing up, we tend to reach adulthood with a pretty good blend of two or three of the personalities. For example, I am a melancholic-phlegmatic, with a lot of choleric tendencies (and almost no sanguine). I prefer to be alone or with a small group of close friends and will avoid conflict at the expense of my personal desires. I prefer someone else be in charge; however, if they seem inadequate to the task, I have no problem taking over.

My husband is a sanguine-choleric, with a lot of melancholy. He loves to tell a good story and delegate tasks—unless he doesn't think it will be done perfectly, in which case he'll just do it himself. Choleric melancholy is a tough blend, as the need to be right blends with the need to be perfect; however, when combined with true humility, this blend of right and perfect makes incredible leaders.

DEALING WITH THE BLENDS

Now that we've gone over many of the characteristics of each personality, what do we do? First of all, we must realize that each personality is designed and given by God, which means that each one is also a precious gift to us from Him. Do my husband's sanguine tendencies drive me, the melancholic, crazy? Yes, sometimes they do. But, God designed him as a sanguine for a specific purpose, and I need to recognize that and offer my husband grace.

Let's think about it this way. A verse common to wedding ceremonies says, "That is why a man leaves his father and mother and is united to his wife, and they become one flesh" (Genesis 2:24). Many husbands and wives are opposites: sanguines who love to talk often marry melancholics who prefer silence; cholerics who love to work marry phlegmatics who prefer to sit back and relax.

Do you see how perfectly this can blend us together, if we let it? Typically, our weaknesses are our spouse's strengths, so when we work together, we become one person with the strengths of all the personality types.

What does this mean for those who did not marry an opposite personality? You keep working together within God's plan for your marriage! Even those of us who married perfect opposites struggle to blend personalities, so don't feel like you are left out of this command from God.

We can also take a look at our children and help them understand what is going on around them. When she was younger, my daughter loved to play with one particular girl at church, but they were also constantly at odds with each other. As we began to look at their personalities, we saw that both girls had strong choleric tendencies. They both wanted to be in charge. Once my daughter understood this, she recognized that this precious girl was not out to purposely hurt her feelings, they were both simply trying to dictate playtime. Armed with this knowledge, my girl more easily showed this friend grace and more quickly offered a compromise when they hit an impasse.

One thing we must guard against, though, is not relaxing into our weaknesses. Jesus clearly showed the strengths from all four personalities. He was popular and social, He led various-sized groups during His entire ministry, He planned and thought deeply, and He is the giver of peace.

To best follow His example, we also must choose to operate in the strengths of our personality and not languish in our weaknesses. Sanguines can be forgetful, disorganized, and undisciplined, while cholerics can be demanding, domineering, and tactless. Melancholics can be unforgiving, withdrawn, and overly meticulous, while phlegmatics can be lazy, selfish, and indecisive.

None of those traits were exemplified in Jesus and therefore should be guarded against in our lives. Working together with friends of different strengths is a great way to not only make progress toward becoming more like Jesus, but to step toward the interdependency God desires in us.

The sanguine could ask a melancholy friend to help with organization. The phlegmatic could ask the choleric to help him with decision-making. The melancholy could ask the sanguine to be sure that she doesn't hibernate without social interaction. And the choleric could ask the phlegmatic to help him relax and enjoy an evening with no schedule.

Remember, we were not made to live or grow alone, and one personality type is not better than another.

> Now if the foot should say, "Because I am not a hand, I do not belong to the body," it would not for that reason stop being part of the body. And if the ear should say, "Because I am not an eye, I do not belong to the body," it would not for that reason stop being part of the body. If the whole body were an eye, where would the sense of hearing be? If the whole body were an ear, where would the sense of smell be? But in fact God has placed the parts in the body, every one of them, just as He wanted them to be. If they were all one part, where would the body be? As it is, there are many parts, but one body.

The eye cannot say to the hand, "I don't need you!" And the head cannot say to the feet, "I don't need you!" On the contrary, those parts of the body that seem to be weaker are indispensable, and the parts that we think are less honorable we treat with special honor. And the parts that are unpresentable are treated with special modesty, while our presentable parts need no special treatment. But God has put the body together, giving greater honor to the parts that lacked it, so that there should be no division in the body, but that its parts should have equal concern for each other. If one part suffers, every part suffers with it; if one part is honored, every part rejoices with it.

—1 Corinthians 12:15–26

THE FIVE LOVE LANGUAGES

FROM KATHY

The Lord said, "If as one people speaking the same language they have begun to do this, then nothing they plan to do will be impossible for them. Come, let Us go down and confuse their language so they will not understand each other."

—Genesis 11:6–7

[Jesus prayed:] I have given them the glory that You gave Me, that they may be one as We are one—I in them and You in Me—so that they may be brought to complete unity. Then the

world will know that You sent Me and have loved them even as
You have loved Me.

—John 17:22–23

Have you ever had an encounter with someone from a foreign country and tried to communicate with them? It can be very frustrating if you don't speak one another's language. Once, I was flying from the US to Germany to see Sam while he was stationed there, and I had to catch a connecting flight from Frankfurt to Berlin. The flight I had arrived on was delayed due to a winter snowstorm. I had only five minutes from the time we landed to run across the entire airport to catch my departing flight. I was nervous before landing, knowing how short my time would be to quickly navigate to my next flight in an unfamiliar airport. But I was sure someone would be able to assist me.

What I wasn't counting on was that everyone there spoke German, not English! And every sign in that airport was written in German as well! I was completely at a loss as to how to get where I needed to go. Fortunately, I saw a young American girl darting through the crowd, and I just began to follow her asking if she could help me. She never stopped moving, but she spoke very clearly, "I'm going to Berlin. If you want to go, you better keep up."

Needless to say, I kept up. I was terrified to lose sight of that girl. She was the one person in that entire airport who could help me, because she understood me and I understood her. I felt total relief in that knowledge, and I was willing to follow her and trust that she could get me to where I needed to go simply because I understood her.

Have you ever felt like you and your husband speak totally different languages? Have you ever tried to follow him as he is leading you through the channels of your life, but you don't understand why he is leading you down a particular path? Sometimes it is difficult to understand why our husbands react or behave certain ways. There can be such a disconnect in communication that you may have trouble trusting his decisions. At times, you may even begin to struggle to believe that he still loves you. This can be very frightening and discouraging as you seek to understand and follow him.

God gave different languages at the tower of Babel for the reason indicated in the opening verses of Genesis 11. He knew that if mankind could all communicate effectively, and they had evil intentions in their heart, they could unite together and nothing would be impossible for them. And throughout human history we have seen dictatorships and strong regimes arise using exactly this principle. God made man with the potential to have great power when they were unified. By causing them to have confusion in their communication, He knew He would undermine their ability to be united against Him.

But God's first and best intention was for men to be able to unite under Him, for His glory and our benefit. He only implemented the different languages to offset evil. When we choose to come together under God's authority and leading, we are meant to find incredible freedom in our communication with one another. He actually longs for us to unite together as one body with one mindset. Jesus prayed for this unity so that we might walk in the fullness of the love that God gave us through Christ for the advancement of His kingdom. He knew that if we came together in like-minded purpose and power, there would be nothing impossible for us to accomplish.

So if we actually speak the same language as our husband, why do we misunderstand each other so often? Why do we sometimes feel unloved and disconnected from each other, if God means for us to be otherwise? The reason is a very simple one. We speak different love languages.

Love Language is a term that was coined by author and speaker Gary Chapman. He had worked as a Christian marriage counselor for many years when he began discovering common patterns to problems within marriage. One of the key things that separated couples was their inability to communicate their love for one another effectively. He slowly began to recognize that different people, often different personality types as Carrie discussed, will express and receive love in different ways. He narrowed these ways down to five specific expressions of love, or "languages" of love, as he called them.

Dr. Chapman noted that when people were not feeling loved by their spouse, their hearts would begin to feel empty. But when they could begin to express and receive love from one another their hearts would feel full. He calls this, *filling your love tank.* When you are being loved in a way that you need to feel loved, your tank gets full. When you aren't receiving love in a language you understand, your tank gets empty.

Because we all express our love in different languages, we may not always be communicating with one another in the same love language. This can cause as much frustration as I felt when I was standing in that foreign airport with no one to understand what I needed. When someone came along who spoke my language, I was quick to follow and to trust her to know the direction—because she communicated to me where we were going!

Once we begin to recognize these five different love languages, we can begin to speak them with purpose and practice. One of the key things to remember in this language-learning process is that love is a choice. Jesus chose to come here and die on a cross for us. He didn't enjoy the cross. But "for the joy set before Him, He endured the cross" so that He could best communicate His amazing love for you and me (Hebrews 12:2).

We must choose to love our husbands. Real love is much more than the heart-palpitating, palm-sweating, butterflies–in-the-tummy that we felt when we first met them. Those feelings were not false, but it is unrealistic to believe that we can stay in a constant state of newness and exciting romance in our marriages.

For one, as we begin to share life together in marriage, we must face life—with all of its responsibilities and work. Sometimes that is exhausting and not exciting. We have to work to pay bills. We have to do laundry and clean toilet lids (that are often left up). We will of course have love and romance in the first year or so of marriage, but that is also usually when the kids start to show up, and this often tosses romance right out the door with the trash full of dirty diapers and formula bottles.

Another thing that can cause us to feel less love as our marriages progress is that we begin to see each other's flaws, which were often masked by the great qualities that stood out so strongly when we met. We must learn to not only live together, but also offer grace to each other. Forgiveness is not a feeling; it is a commitment. Just like love, it is a choice. We must learn to exercise mercy in our marriages and not hold onto offenses that our spouse may have committed. Again, Jesus on the cross fully exemplifies better than anyone else this commitment to loving us through forgiveness. We must look to Him as we learn to love and forgive each other in our marriages.

I'm not suggesting that love in our life should be all work and suffering. I'm also not implying we throw in the towel now and give up hope for romance in our marriages. In fact, I'm hoping that, through the eye-opening lessons within this book, you can learn to better communicate with your spouse so that together you can rekindle romance and love—like never before! But you must purpose in your heart to learn how to love your husband.

Just like you would have to purpose to learn a foreign language in order to communicate with someone of that language, you must purpose to learn your husband's love language if you are going to be able to effectively communicate love to him. I know you want him to love you. And I hope that once you begin speaking his language, you can communicate your needs to him in a way he can understand. But for now, I want you to focus on learning to love him in his language.

Carrie and I highly recommend that you read Dr. Chapman's book on this subject, *The Five Love Languages* (see appendix). It revolutionized our marriages. The entire book is well worth reading and gives lots of valuable insights, but I'll summarize it here for your convenience. Hopefully you can begin to implement loving your man in such a way that he can begin to see and feel your love for him in a powerful way.

The first of the love languages that Dr. Chapman discovered was Words of Affirmation. If you are a person who speaks this language, loving words are very important in order for your heart to feel loved. You thrive on compliments and words of encouragement from people. When someone speaks kindly to you or writes you a note, you immediately feel like that person loves and appreciates you. But when anyone speaks harshly toward you or is unkind or degrading in their comments, you can feel crushed. Often you can feel hurt just because your spouse fails to notice and acknowledge you with their words. Words of Affirmation people have to be careful not to place too much emphasis on the opinions of others in their lives.

This love language is exemplified by the many verses in Proverbs that address the power of our tongue. Our words can bring either life and healing, or death and cursing.

The second language is Quality Time. The key to this language is togetherness. People who operate in this language need full, focused attention from their spouse. They need to spend time with someone they love in order to be satisfied and feel loved. Quality Time people need to have time set aside just for the building of the relationship. This can be through quality conversation or sharing an activity. It doesn't necessarily have to be a large quantity of time, but the more time you can give them, the more full their love tank will be. Becoming a good listener is vital to giving focused attention to a Quality Time spouse. Trying to listen while reading the paper, watching TV, or talking over the

children's heads is the surest way to tell them that you aren't interested in spending time with them. And to them, that says that
you don't love them.

The third language is Receiving Gifts. This one seems rather
self-explanatory, but the key here isn't the gift itself, necessarily.
The key is that gifts are visual symbols of love. The gift is the
tangible object that a person can hold that represents the love that
someone has for them. The cost of the gift is typically immaterial.
In fact, they would probably be more excited to receive a home-
made gift that they knew required more effort on your part to
produce, thus showing even more love for them. Flowers picked
in the yard can be as special as the $120 bouquet of roses. Gifts
that will speak in this language can vary from physical things to
giving the gift of yourself through your time and presence.

The next love language is Acts of Service. A person who speaks
this language is going to have the heart of a servant. They are
eager to help you in practical ways. This spouse will fix your car,
take out the trash, and help bathe the kids. This is the lady who
always takes meals to the new mommies or offers to babysit for
people. People who love in this language are willing to serve, and
so they greatly appreciate service to them. If your husband is Acts
of Service motivated, he may not want you to tell him how proud
you are of him and give him surprise gifts expressing your affection. He probably just wants a hot meal and a clean house when
he comes home at night. Acts of Service people can be very diligent workers, but often they forget to stop long enough to listen
to what work others really need. Biblically, Martha is an example
of this type of person. She wanted to eagerly serve the Lord, but

in that moment, Jesus wanted her to simply listen to Him and receive what He had for her (Luke 10:38–41).

The final love language that Dr. Chapman outlines is the one entitled Physical Touch. Many people may assume this is just talking about sexual touch, but that is not true. To the person who operates and receives love in the Physical Touch category, any physical touch that is intentional is welcomed and fills their love tank. They want to sit right next to you, their legs touching yours, while watching TV. They want to hold hands or rest their arm on your shoulder. A hug can speak volumes to them. By the same token, so can withholding touch. If a Physical Touch person does not receive regular reminders of your love through physical interaction, they struggle. This can be especially hard for military couples when we face months of separation through deployments. And if this person is undergoing a crisis of any sort, it is imperative that they be held in order to receive comfort through touch during these times.

Many of you may have recognized your or your spouse's love language immediately while reading. Some of you may not yet be sure about yourself or your spouse. To help you discern your love language, think about the things that make you feel most loved, or the things you frequently request from your spouse. Also, the way you want to be loved is how you will most naturally offer love to others, so consider what you most frequently do for others to show them that you care about them. Again, we highly recommend that you get a copy of Gary Chapman's book in order to recognize and understand these ways of communicating love even more clearly.

It is unlikely that your spouse speaks your love language as their primary love language, so you need to begin to notice the ways they are trying to express their love to you.

When Sam and I first married, we had no concept of how to communicate effectively. We knew we had fallen in love, but the longer we were together the more frustrated we became in trying to express our love to one another. On top of our inability to give and receive love, we also had issues of unforgiveness and distrust. We both started serving the Lord and we knew God had more for us, but we each often ended up frustrated and confused as we tried moving forward in our marriage.

Recognizing that love and forgiveness are choices, not feelings, was very helpful. But even after realizing this, we still struggled. I would continually tell Sam how much I loved him. I was always trying to sit with him and get him to talk to me and tell me where his heart was. I was even very affectionate and I reached out physically. This was often hard for me to do, due to being pregnant, nursing, and exhausted. And although Sam would accept the sexual advances, he would often just roll over after lovemaking without a word and go straight to sleep, leaving me feeling alone and unfulfilled.

Sam was working very hard at his career. He would leave at 5:00 a.m. and not get home until after 7:00 in the evening. Often he wouldn't even see the children for days, because he left before they were up in the morning and didn't get home until they were down for the night. There were times he was frustrated with work and the dictates of the team or the command. When he would get home, he would often start cleaning the children's dirty dinner dishes before he would even sit and eat himself. He would be quiet, sullen, and exhausted.

It seemed no matter what I did, Sam withdrew even more. When we discovered the five love languages, it was like a massive light bulb going off in both of our brains at once. I suddenly realized that Sam's main language was Acts of Service. Every time he left our home to go to work, he was telling me he loved me. Each time he came home late, he still helped me by cleaning the house. It was also a natural response for him to fall into these habits in order to avoid his frustrations from work. He wanted to escape the trials there by pressing into what felt natural to him. All of my words and longing to spend time with him just caused him to feel pulled in multiple directions and overwhelmed.

You've likely already realized that my main languages are Words of Affirmation and Quality Time. When Sam was working hard, especially in the evenings, I felt that he was trying to avoid spending time with me and talking to me. I was jealous of his job, which consumed so much of his time and energy. I felt that he loved it more than me! The harder he worked at his job to show me he loved me, the more resentful I became. This cycle of misunderstanding went on for nearly two years, with us fumbling along before we realized the truth of our love for each other.

Once we learned about love languages and personalities, we were then able to move forward and begin to make a concerted effort to love in each other's different languages and have grace for each other's different personalities. We began to value each other more, and our efforts began to have huge results in our marriage. Suddenly, our "love tanks" were full again!

I started cleaning the house more, and I learned to be more organized in my home. I made sure that Sam came home to a hot meal with no dishes in the sink. He could then just sit and enjoy his meal without feeling obligated to do something else. I started rising in the early morning just long enough to pack him a lunch. Sometimes that meant getting up at 4:30, when I had already been up at 1:00 and 3:00 a.m. nursing an infant, so it required a lot of effort on my part. But I wanted that man to know I loved him. And my diligence paid off.

Sam began speaking to me more. He made concerted efforts to listen when I was filling him in on my days with our children. He would speak positively to me and the kids, and he regularly began affirming me in the work I did around the house and with schooling our children. My heart began to feel full. And the more full my heart felt, the more love I was able to pour into him.

At times, I can still get hurt and feel unloved by Sam's actions or inactions. But then I have to remember how he shows his love to me. We can get complacent or lazy in our efforts. When this happens and I start to feel a little empty, I can just talk to Sam, and he is usually quick to respond. But sometimes I just have to extend grace to him. I choose to not only love him as he needs to be loved, but to receive love in the manners he is able to give it. I remind myself how glad I am that he works so hard. That he takes out the trash and helps keep my car's oil changed regularly. This is easier to do when I think of the months he's been gone in deployments, and then I really do value those simple daily acts that he freely and naturally gives me. And I double my efforts to serve him, when all I really want is to sit and talk! But God has given me a smart man who responds to me and he usually remembers, eventually, that being fluent in several love languages is very beneficial to our marriage.

God gave us not only verbal language, but love languages and personalities, all with the express purpose of communicating His personal qualities and abilities of love to us. He longs for us to be united in love through the very differences He created in us. When we can learn to love in complete unity, we not only have stronger marriages, but we are able to show the world the beauty of God's love through us. The ramifications within this dying world of seeing a healthy, thriving marriage and family is extremely powerful. When we can walk out the beauty of love in our homes, people see that and they want it. Everyone wants to be loved. God made us capable of following Christ's example and modeling true love through sacrifice and forgiveness. We can learn from Him how to communicate love in unity, and in that place, nothing is impossible for us (Philippians 4:13).

CHAP

WHEN THE TWO BECOME THREE

Start children off on the way they should go, and even when they are old they will not turn from it.

—Proverbs 22:6

FROM CARRIE

Popular bumper stickers in AAFES Exchange stores tout that the hardest job in the military is that of the wife. And I'll agree that offering grace, swallowing pride, and placing my husband's desires above my own (Philippians 2:3) was frequently challenging. In fact, God continues to use my marriage to show me things within my heart that He wants to change. Yet becoming a mom offered additional chances for the Lord to get my attention.

A civilian once said to me that he thought spouses of deployed soldiers were essentially just single parents. Well, yes. And no. While the weight of parenting often seems to lie completely

oulders of the non-military spouse, she must never
t she needs to maintain her marriage as well. Those of
at home must learn to share the parenting with our spouses,
en when they are not physically present.

Aside from schools and trainings, my husband has deployed
twice for roughly 100 days each. Not nearly the twelve-to-fifteen
month deployments many Army spouses endured or the shorter
but more frequent deployments of many units within the Special
Operations realm, but long enough for me to feel his absence
from the home front. Even more difficult for me was the time we
spent in Montana, where he was constantly leaving. We'd just be
getting into a good routine, when things would change.

As our family grew and the children aged, I needed something
I could really hold onto. The demands the military placed on my
husband those first several years convinced me that he could not
be my rock. And really, I was looking further down the road than
my immediate circumstances anyway. I wanted the security of
knowing that God would be important to my children when they
grew up and moved away.

After lots of thinking, I determined that I wanted two funda-
mental things:

- Hope that my children could thrive within the military system in which God had called us to serve. Just
  getting them through eighteen years of life wasn't
  good enough for me. I wanted them to see blessing in
  it, to know that even in the difficult moments, God
  still saw them and loved them.

- Assurance that God would keep them close to Him, their feet solidly on the path He had planned for them. Although stories of returning prodigal children are inspiring, I didn't want any of my kids to deal with the heartache that accompanies those journeys.

Starting with Proverbs 22:6 (quoted at the top of this chapter) seemed logical to me. Yet while I trusted in its promise, I felt uneasy. I saw it as nothing more than what I call an "in the end" promise. If you start kids with God, they will end with God. Great. But I kept coming back to my second desire. What about all the time in between birth and death?

I searched Scripture and read books. I tried various recommendations, considered the teachings of all kinds of experts, and in the end I came to one conclusion. While Kathy and I can give you general precepts on raising children, tell you stories of where we succeeded and when we failed, the bottom line is that much about where our children end up is out of our control. Our children all have a gift from God that makes the results of parenting as much our children's responsibility as it is ours. God blessed them with free will.

Don't get me wrong. God will hold me accountable for how I parent. I must give it everything I've got, with His help, using the resources He's placed around me. But ultimately, my children must also choose wisely. Bad parents sometimes turn out sweet kids—think of Michael Oher, whose story was portrayed in the 2009 movie *The Blind Side*. And good parents sometimes live with rebellious children—perhaps you've read Franklin Graham's story, son of Billy and Ruth Graham, as he shared it in the book released in 1995, *Rebel With a Cause*.

Kathy will give you a lot more to think about, but I want to leave you with this. To have the best chance for success, whether your husband is home or deployed, you must study your children. Consider their personalities, work within their strengths, and guide them out of their weaknesses. Make sure to learn their love language and speak it regularly. And pray. A lot.

For many years, I took prayer for granted. I knew the great stories from the Bible of how someone would pray and God would change things. Yet I never really believed in its power when the words were coming from my mouth. I tended to either ask for little things that I knew could easily be accomplished, things I could point to when telling others that prayer worked. Or I would pray for impossible things, checking the box but never really expecting God to move the mountain before me.

Until the day He pointed out to me that He had already answered one of the desires of my heart, a prayer I had dared to whisper: that He would bring all my children to a saving knowledge of Him at a young age. God heard my heart and so, out of our three children, the child who waited the longest to ask Jesus into her life was just three weeks past her fifth birthday.

I've learned over the years that God loves to say yes to the prayers that echo His heart. Proverbs 15, verses 8 and 29 tell us that He loves to listen to the prayers of those who are striving to follow Him! So the most effective prayers are often those that ask something from God that He already desires to give.

God has provided many great books to help you pray for your children, some of which we list for you in the appendix at the end of this book. But if you've never learned to specifically pray for your children, here are a few of my heart's prayers to get you started.

- Pray that they would come to know Christ and desire a relationship with Him that lasts their entire lives.
- Pray that they would never be apathetic in their relationship with God, but always be drawn to love Him above all else. Pray that they would be bold in their faith, to the point that their example challenges you to draw closer to God.
- Pray that they would always get caught when they sin and that they would have a heart softened toward doing things God's way.
- Pray that they would be protected—physically, mentally, emotionally, and spiritually—from Satan and his plans for them. Ask that they would be able to identify when their enemy seeks to either distract or damage them, and that they would see the way out that God provides (1 Corinthians 10:13).
- Pray these same desires for their future spouse, asking God to unite them into a mighty force on the Kingdom battlefield.

FROM KATHY

> *He tends His flock like a shepherd: He gathers the lambs in His arms and carries them close to His heart; He gently leads those that have young.*
>
> —Isaiah 40:11

I grew up hearing that God wouldn't give me more than I can handle. I am here to debunk that theory. I have *many* times in my life been given more than I can bear. Quite frankly, the military life is more than I can take at times. Having nine children is more than I know what to do with. Having those children and raising them with their daddy gone for more than ten years of deployments so far during their lifetime, not including TDYs and training, is more than I can handle. But I praise God for Philippians 4:13 that says, "I *can* do all this through [Christ] who gives me strength" [emphasis mine].

We are going to be given so much more than we were ever meant to handle on our own. But thankfully, God knew that, and He promises that we don't have to face our trials alone. He says that through Him we can do all things. We can be attached to the military and learn to parent with our spouse on the other side of the planet. We can even learn to do it with great joy. It all must be done in and through Him, however, for us to find the strength to do it.

I wish that you could somehow see a snapshot of my family. But alongside the snapshot of them all smiling and looking at the camera . . . oh, wait! I don't own that picture! Have you ever tried to get nine children to look at the camera at the same time and *smile*? Getting stars to align on a whim is easier to accomplish, I assure you. But I wish you could somehow have a real glimpse of what we look like in the morning in our PJs. You would see our hair all mussed up, people arguing over who ate the last of the peanut butter cocoa puffs, someone spilling milk, and the two-year-old streaking through the house with no pants on chasing the cat!

People often have the misguided notion that God gave me so many children because I have a natural gifting toward patience and grace. The truth is that I believe God knew I lacked so much in this department, so He decided to give me the very thing that would force me to grow up into unselfishness. He knew I would either learn those things through Him, or kill my children or myself trying to mother them in my own weak strength. So I want to focus on a few biblical principles that have kept me sane and grounded through the many years of parenting in situations that were often more than I could bear on my own.

One of the main keys to parenting is to hold the heart of your child. At the close of the Old Testament, Malachi records God as saying, "See, I will send the prophet Elijah to you before that great and dreadful day of the Lord comes. He will turn the hearts of the parents to their children, and the hearts of the children to their parents; or else I will come and strike the land with total destruction" (Malachi 4:5–6). God closes the whole of the record of pre-messianic history in His Word with that statement. Why? Because it is the whole summation of what He has done for us, and how He will lead us in following Him.

God is the Father. We all become sons and daughters of Him when we hear that call on our life and know His heart for us. He sacrificed everything, including His own son, to show us how much He loves us. He longs above all things to have our hearts. When we can receive His great love for us, then we can submit our hearts and turn to love Him in return. God loves His kids. This is the model He has given us to teach us how to parent. We must begin to change our hearts toward our children before they can turn their hearts towards us. The way we do that is to turn our hearts to our loving Father first. We must look to the ultimate parent to learn how to parent.

One of the first things we see when we look to Him is the example of sacrifice. God is never selfish. He literally loved us to death. Now, I'm still alive to tell you about what I've learned, so I haven't succumbed to death by children in the natural yet. However, I assure you I have died. Every day I die a little more. I die to my selfish behaviors and personal gains. I crucify my flesh every time I lose a night's sleep to feed, nurse, or comfort one of my little ones. Each time I decide to forego my own desires in order to minister to the needs of those precious, often demanding, people, I am laying my life down again.

Sam and I have always wanted more for our kids than we had for ourselves. We have never claimed to be anything but sinners saved by grace, and we certainly don't know all there is to know about raising children. But we love our kids. We have made numerous mistakes and have failed our little ones more times than I care to recount, but we have always tried to give them the best that we had to offer at the time, even if our best was limited.

We sacrificed countless things for our children. In the beginning some of those sacrifices, such as losing sleep, seemed really hard. But over time you learn to stop complaining. Instead, you thank God that you actually had the physical strength to go day after day doing laundry and changing, bathing, and caring for those kids and still found time to cook a decent meal. You know you have overcome some of that selfishness when you can truly rejoice at a day where no one vomits and you were able to get a shower.

Sam and I knew when we started life together that we wanted children; we figured that two or three would be great. I began to tremble with fear, though, when we had three little ones under the age of five and I was clearly hearing from God that He wanted to send more. Sam's career was spinning at a crescendo level about the time I had baby number three, and although he hadn't been around much during those early years of marriage, the future promised that he would be around even less as time progressed.

I was so afraid that if the weight of parenting these kids was to fall on my frail shoulders, then I would fail and my precious children would not have the best that God could give them. I knew my weaknesses. I knew where Sam and I had messed up, and I did not feel qualified to do what God was asking of us.

I remember when God opened my eyes to some amazing truth a few years into our marriage and parenting journey. I was struggling to know how to be a good wife and love Sam, and how to be a good mom and love our kids. I felt like the more I tried to honor God in these areas of my life, the more hopeless I felt, because I truly did not know what I was doing. I wanted a biblical model of a home, but I couldn't quite figure out what that was supposed to look like or how I was supposed to get there. I often felt guilty, because I would struggle so much with being kind and patient with my family. The ugliness in me that I desperately wanted to change seemed to be the very battle I continued to fight within myself. I understood what Paul was saying when he said his flesh was contrary to his spirit and he would do the very thing he hated (Romans 7:14–25)!

Each time I was impatient or short-tempered with my little ones, I would feel like the worst mom ever. And so I would try harder. I would try to love my family more, but often I felt like I missed some invisible mark I couldn't even see, much less attain. I felt like I was in the dark, blindly groping to find the way that led to a home filled with the spiritual fruit outlined in Galatians 5.

I was reading Titus 2:3–5 (Contemporary English Version), when God illuminated a freeing truth to me. I'm going to write it for you to see if you catch the truth God shared with me.

> Tell the older women to behave as those who love the Lord should. They must not gossip about others or be slaves of wine. They must teach what is proper, so the younger women will be loving wives and mothers. Each of the younger women must be sensible and kind, as well as a good homemaker, who puts her own husband first. Then no one can say insulting things about God's message.

Did you catch that? The older women are to teach the younger women how to love their husbands and children! When I realized that truth, I was suddenly freed from the guilt of feeling as though I was failing at something I was supposed to innately know. As if becoming a bride should automatically mean that I knew everything about being a good wife. Or becoming a parent should somehow give me all the necessary knowledge to raise godly kids.

This realization showed me that I simply needed training. So I went hunting for godly women to lead me. And God was faithful to send them to me. It is for this purpose that Carrie and I have written this book. We don't claim to have all the answers, but we have lived long enough to now be the older women. It is our hearts desire, and our command from God, to go forth and share what we have learned with the women who have not yet learned these truths.

DISAGREEMENT IN PARENTING

Parenting is the most difficult thing I've ever done in my life, second only to marriage. More than anything else these are the two places that keep me on my knees asking God for help. And just as learning to love Sam is hard, learning to parent my children with Sam is hard. Loving the kids is easy for both of us most of the time, but coming together to share the same views and parenting ideals is not always easy for us.

There are so many areas in our parenting where Sam and I have disagreed through the years. It seemed right from the start that Sam would be gone frequently, so the daily tending and training of our first son was left largely to me. I was the one who figured out the sleeping, eating, pooping, and playing schedules. Because I breast fed our son, there was little Sam could do to help me when he was home. And although I welcomed his help when he was there, I found myself frustrated when he didn't adhere to my schedules.

So began our life of parenting together. And our life of parenting apart. Sam would do something that he meant to be helpful, and I would think he was actually trying to work against me and the needs of our children. He would give them chocolate milk at six weeks of age. He would bathe them and use the wrong shampoo. He would hold the children all the time. I was killing myself to try to feed, care, and train them up from infancy, and he unintentionally undermined half of what I was trying to do. Plus, I was struggling to even know what to do half the time, so when I would move forward with a plan only to have him randomly interrupt things, I got frustrated.

He was just trying to help, but because he didn't do things as I would do them, I got upset. When he would argue that he wasn't doing anything wrong and that I needed to loosen up, I would get defensive and feel as if he were disregarding all the thought, energy, and work I was pouring into the kids.

We didn't agree on toys, television programs, playmates, clothing choices, dietary and health needs, disciplinary actions, and the list goes on. Don't misunderstand me. We both loved our children. But the actual day-to-day parenting tasks were my responsibility, even when he was around. And so I established rules and boundaries that he undid every time he stepped through the door.

Parenting with Sam felt almost like parenting against Sam at times. I knew that wasn't what God wanted. As I learned how to be a better wife and mother, that pesky word *submission* kept rearing its ugly head. Especially when Sam and I wouldn't agree. God has reminded me on several occasions that our children are as much my husband's as mine, so he not only should have equal say in their training and development, but even more: because he is the head of our home. It doesn't matter if the task of raising and caring for their daily needs largely falls to me. The responsibility is still his, and he will stand accountable for that before God.

Just as in every other area of our marriage, we wives must learn to submit to the headship of our husbands when we parent our children. This is extremely hard when you have drastically different views on how to raise your kids. This can be even more difficult when you are saved but your husband is not. Although we've touched on the important role you have in your husband's life in helping to lead him to the Lord through your submission, we haven't discussed this in the arena of parenting.

Remember, we have learned that much of our calling as wives is to help our husbands succeed in their calling. In large part, that means that if he was called to be a father, then you were called to help him succeed at being a father, whether or not you get any thanks or appreciation for this great endeavor.

This might not resonate well with some of you, I know. You may be thinking that if he is head of the home and will stand accountable before God, why isn't he helping me parent more? Or, at least, why don't I get equal say, since I do more than half the work in the rearing of them?

But for the sake of our roles in the family, I have to realize that my life is surrendered. I am here to serve my God. I do this through serving my husband and serving my children by sacrificing my life for their training, discipline, and growth. I bend to the idea that my life is no longer my own and I will help my husband by raising his children, hoping that he will get great praise for the success of this lifelong project—even if in many ways he invests very little compared to the time and energy I will invest.

Our sacrifice in this area of parenting is the epitome of Christlikeness. Christ humbled himself before mankind and his Father. He gave up everything so that the children of God might be reunited with their Father. Christ kept the broken hearts of His fallen people always in the forefront, and it was for the joy of seeing us healed and united with our Father that He gave up everything. We must be so willing to see our children's hearts united to their daddy's hearts, and ultimately their Heavenly Father's heart, that we too are willing to lay our lives down. Daily.

1 Corinthians 7:14 says, "For the unbelieving husband has been sanctified through his wife, and the unbelieving wife has been sanctified through her believing husband. Otherwise your children would be unclean, but as it is, they are holy." This verse shows us that even if we are married to an unbelieving husband, our God will look upon our children as holy. This is critical to understand. God sees us as one with our husband, and our children are a product of our union. We want our children to be led into salvation.

How do you do this if your husband doesn't share your beliefs? You pray. Often. And you trust that God Almighty, who was big enough to raise you up from your own upbringing and your past sins to lead you into righteousness, is big enough to do that for your children. He perfectly placed those kids with you and your husband. He knew who they were going to be before the foundation of the world, and who their mom and dad would be. He knew all of that, yet He decided to trust you and your husband with the monumental task of parenting His precious creation. God knows what he is doing. He doesn't make mistakes.

We may make mistakes in our lives. But God doesn't. He uses even our errors and trials to grow us toward Him. Remember, He is literally moving heaven and earth to capture your heart (John 3:12–17). He will do the same for your children.

The differences in you and your husband might be very stark, but, with the grace of God directing you, you can learn to submit to a man who may not share your faith. Not only will that show him how much you love him, but it will show your children how much they should love their daddy.

This does not mean we have to love daddy's sin. It can be a delicate balancing act at times, trying to build a home in holiness and righteousness when your husband may continually open the door to the very things you are trying your best to shut out. I would encourage you to stay surrendered to Almighty God and present your needs and desires at His feet. He longs to give all good gifts to His children.

In Matthew 7:9–11, Jesus says, "Which of you, if your son asks for bread, will give him a stone? Or if he asks for a fish, will give him a snake? If you, then, though you are evil, know how to give good gifts to your children, how much more will your Father in heaven give good gifts to those who ask Him!"

Luke 11:13 says that our Father in heaven will freely give the Holy Spirit to those who ask. And it is through the power of the Spirit that you will find the strength and wisdom to know how to love and submit to your husband and lead and love your little ones. Stay at your Daddy's feet and let Him lead you in learning to follow your children's daddy.

LEARNING TO LET GO AND LET GOD

What if you are divorced and your children have a different father than the man you are married to now? Or what if you are trying to parent children to whom you didn't give birth? God knew that in advance too. His grace is sufficient. Remember Philippians 4:13, that we can do all things through Him . . . including raising our children in whatever situations we now find ourselves. God's truth doesn't alter, regardless of our changing circumstances.

Fostering a home of peace and encouraging a relationship between your husband and his children is vitally important. Remember, we want to turn the hearts of the fathers to the children. And then the hearts of the children will turn to the fathers.

Sometimes I think we let the hurts our husbands have caused in our hearts make us mistrust them with the hearts of our children. We have to learn to trust that our husbands won't mess up with our kids any more than we will. Learning to trust that God knew what He was doing when He gave those kids both their parents is part of learning to be a good parent. You have got to get in line and agree with God, even when you can't agree with your husband.

I'm not talking about getting in line with a man who is abusive. If you are married to a man who is abusing the authority God gave him over you or your children, you need to take the responsibility to get you and your kids out of that situation and to a safe place. God speaks directly to the abusive man in Malachi 2:13–16.

If you are in a situation where your husband is abusing you, you are obligated to protect your children and seek safety elsewhere. Do everything you can to ensure your and your children's physical and emotional protection. Then do everything you can to pray for your lost husband to come to a place of repentance and healing. Teach your children how to walk in forgiveness and to pray for their hurting daddy. If he can come to that place, it is God's greatest desire to extend redemption and restoration to your marriage. However, if he cannot, dear sister, you must seek your peace with the Lord for the direction of how best to move forward for the safety and well-being of you and your children, even if divorce is the ultimate price.

If this happens to you, please know that God will cover you where your husband did not. No one hates sin as much as God and no one went as far to offer a provision for it. He sent His son to die for all sin. And He paved a way for us to learn to walk in forgiveness for others because we know the fullness of the pardon undeservedly extended to us. Learn to walk in that grace and forgiveness. And teach it to your children.

Most of us, however, will not be in this situation. We may often feel sorry for ourselves, and with rumpled pride and a false sense of martyrdom we might think we are entitled to some rights that we justify in our own selfish minds. We think because we give so much to our kids, and our husbands don't, that we should have some extra praise, or thanks, or help.

That kind of selfish thinking will cause your children to also be selfish. If you want children who will lay their lives down before the cross, it starts with you laying your selfish expectations down there first. God will be your strength if you will allow Him to do what He wants with your life. Quit trying to get your husband to do what God is already willing to do for you.

I've learned to let go of many of the things I held onto so tightly when our children were younger. I've learned that if I'm the parent who has to exercise ninety percent of the discipline in our home, that's okay. I recognize the great influence I have in our children's lives by my leading them in prayer and devotions.

And although these are often led by me alone, which is not my first choice, that does not negate the power those things have in their lives.

Choosing to keep your children in church, whether your husband attends or not, is very important to your kid's spiritual walks. My father never attended church with my family when I was growing up. But my mother always left the invitation open for him. Encouraging invitation—without condemnation—in our walks before our husbands will draw them nearer to the cross. Respecting him and his opinions, rather than trying to guilt him into being a better father, will create that inviting atmosphere to help foster the change that only God can bring. My father, who finally surrendered his life to Christ after thirty-five years of marriage, can attest to that.

I have also learned to let go of my expectations of what I think parenting should look like in our home in more practical aspects. I have realized that sugary cereal, although not my favorite choice for our children's diet, will not kill them. I just limit the amount I purchase. I have also learned that video games, although not my first choice of suitable entertainment for my sons, will not lead them down a path of irresponsibility and foolishness when they play them occasionally with their father.

Sam, like most men, will encourage coarse joking with bodily noises among our children. And although I am trying to raise young ladies and gentlemen who have good manners, I've found they are not ruined by the time spent joking with their dad. In fact, quite the opposite. They all love to laugh but are also very well mannered, and they know how to relax and not take life too seriously. And they all love their daddy; he has captured their tender hearts.

I've come to realize that having dinner with daddy is more important than my idea of a timely dinner and bedtime. So we often wait to eat dinner until 7:00 p.m. so that we can all spend that time together. So I do baths and a snack at 5:00. I have to be flexible, and adjust to our life and my husband's schedule if we are going to share life as a family.

Maybe for some of you these things aren't hard choices. I am very controlling and so dying to my routine, my plans, and my schedules is hard for me. But whatever areas in your life you have to surrender in order to allow your husband to have authority over your children, you should learn to do.

GODLY ACCEPTANCE AND DISCIPLINE

One thing Sam and I do agree on is that our kids are not our own. They are God's. He didn't give them to us. He simply loaned them to us for a short season, to invest in them for His sake. With this idea firmly fixed in our minds, we have been able to make it over many of the hurdles that we don't agree on. I would encourage you to get this idea fixed in your head also.

As Carrie said, your children have a free will, just as you have. This truth is something that makes parenting a little less intimidating, because it removes the immense pressure of thinking we have to be perfect for them to be raised well. You won't ever have perfect kids, because they won't ever be raised by perfect parents. There is freedom in that truth. Your child's success and failures are influenced by you, but this truth of them standing alone be-fore Almighty God is one you must keep fixed in your mind.

Sam and I decided long ago that the greatest thing we could ever hope for our children was that at the end of their days they would hear, "Well done, good and faithful servant" (Matthew 25:14–30).

This is all my heart longs to hear for my own life, too. The more I walk with my God, the more I long for the sweetness of knowing that I have pleased Him. I am His child and I want my heavenly Daddy to be pleased with me. I want to run into His arms when I get home from this grueling school of life on Earth, and I want Him to hold me tightly and tell me how proud He is of me. Even though I fell down a lot and got in trouble often. Even though I forgot things, dropped things, and had to get paddled. I want grace, approval, and love in my life from my Father.

This is the desire that God put in the hearts of all His children. This is in the heart of your child. You and your husband have the awesome privilege and responsibility of being a model of God's love for your children.

Sacrifice and submission are two of the ways we can learn what God expects of us and how much He loves us. Understanding God's love through discipline is another important aspect to mod-eling godly parenting.

Hebrews 12:1–12 is a good place to start studying this principle. In this passage we are encouraged to run with perseverance and not grow weary or lose heart. One of the ways God says here that He will continually draw you closer to Him is through His dis-cipline. Verses 5–6 say, "My son, do not make light of the Lord's discipline, and do not lose heart when He rebukes you, because the Lord disciplines those He loves." It goes on to say, in verse 11, "No discipline seems pleasant at the time, but painful. Later on, however, it produces a harvest of righteousness and peace for those who have been trained by it."

I don't know about you, but I need to know that God loves me. I know that I want righteousness and peace in my life. So I must be willing to submit to the loving hand of my Father when, for my own good, He disciplines and trains me. Proverbs 15:32 says, "Those who disregard discipline despise themselves, but the one who heeds correction gains understanding."

We must look to this example of a loving parent when it comes to training our own children. There are many worldly concepts about disciplining, but godly discipline will bring understanding and godly change. Romans 2:4 says that "God's kindness is intended to lead you to repentance." This means that when He is bringing your sin to your attention and causing you to see it, He is doing it because He loves you. He is not trying to make you feel condemned. He wants you to see it and turn from it, finding freedom from the wages of sin and death.

When we see sin in our children, we must love them enough to show them truth and life by exposing their sin and correcting their behavior. It is an act of love to discipline them. Proverbs 13:24 teaches us, "Whoever spares the rod hates their children, but he who loves their children is careful to discipline them."

If you love your children, you will discipline them with a rod. To not use a rod is to show hatred for your child, the Word says. Many of you may have never heard of a "rod" before. At my house, it is a wooden spoon. Some people use a ruler. My grandmother used to use a switch cut from the hedge from the front of her house. No matter what the tool used to implement the action, a spanking has to occur using some type of device other than your hand.

Carrie and I told you in the foreword of the book that we are not very politically correct. I know that spanking is frowned on in our society. But if you examine our society, it is going to hell quickly. Personally, we are looking to God, not our culture, to help us raise our children. We don't want the same results that the world is getting. We want kids who are sold out for Christ and who walk in the blessings that come with that.

There is a very simple reason why God encourages us to use a rod rather than our hand to discipline our children. Our hand is used to embrace our children. When we use the rod, there is no confusion about the fact that we are disciplining. If we use our hand to both spank and hug our children, they won't know what to expect when we reach our hand toward them.

Some of you may have grown up without discipline or with a perverted use of it. Some of you may have been abused. The idea of using a rod on your one-year-old may make you feel like we are suggesting brutal methods to train a child. But if discipline in your life has been neglected or abused, then you must begin to allow God's truth to penetrate your heart and mind. God never intends for children to walk away from a disciplinary situation feeling harmed or humiliated. Correction should come with re-morse and repentance through conviction, but it should never hold shame and condemnation. Many of you have never been loved enough by your own parents to be disciplined correctly by them. God wants to show you, by His loving hand, how to correctly discipline and love your children.

You may shy away from using a rod on your kids. I would just encourage you to search the Word for your guidance. Throughout this book, Carrie and I have encouraged you to grow beyond what your upbringing or our society would tell you is correct behavior. Look to the one true God and ask Him what He thinks. His Word will always show you the best way as you journey with Him.

I will go a little further to say that in using a rod to discipline, you must never be heavy handed. We begin to train our children when they are quite young with this device. We certainly don't spank infants. But we do use a rod of correction and training from an early age. Children are usually much smarter than we give them credit for being. And although the pain will be slight when they are young, it will be enough to get their attention and teach them to want to avoid it again.

God does that with us. He hopes that the pain sin brings will cause us to want to avoid it a second time. God will allow us to sin. He won't keep us from sinning, but He will offer us every opportunity to get out of a tempting situation. And He will try repeatedly to show us a way of grace and peace by choosing obedience to Him. We must learn to do this with our children.

Disciplining our children in anger will only breed rebellion in them. Ephesians 6:4 says, "Fathers, do not exasperate your children; instead, bring them up in the training and instruction of the Lord." When we are disciplining our children as they get older, I always speak Proverbs 13:24 to them (that I quoted above). I begin by asking them if they think their daddy and I love or hate them. They always respond that they know we love them. I then ask them if we trust Jesus and believe His Word. They agree that we do. I then proceed to explain that if we believe His Word and if we love them, we must discipline them with the rod in order to be in obedience. We will not ever hate them, so we won't spare the rod. They understand and submit to the spanking. In twenty-one years of disciplining children, we have rarely had a child fight us on discipline.

When we are done with the spanking, we pray together. The child asks God for forgiveness of their sin and they apologize to me, or whomever the offended party is in our home. I then cover them in prayer and lift them before Jesus and thank Him that His payment was enough to cover this sin. Then we hug, and all is forgiven. It is a beautiful thing when children learn repentance.

Our children frequently see the rod between the ages of one and six. But honestly, after that time, we rarely ever have to spank a child. We spank them for disobedience or ongoing character training occasionally, but typically we can just speak to our children and they respond with tender hearts. Most of our children have accepted Christ by the time they are seven years old. We only have one five-year-old and one two-year-old who have not committed their hearts to Christ yet. (We pray for their salvation daily.)

This does not mean all of our children are angelic by the age of six. They are sinners who are saved by grace, just like their dad and me. We must continually work on their character and training, just as our God is continually growing us up in our faith and training us in righteousness. Obedience in our lives will directly affect obedience in our children's lives.

EFFECTS OF OBEDIENCE

There are spiritual ramifications in the lives of our children when we choose to be disobedient to God. Exodus 34:6–7 says: "The Lord, the Lord, the compassionate and gracious God, slow to anger, abounding in love and faithfulness, maintaining love to thousands, and forgiving wickedness, rebellion and sin. Yet He does not leave the guilty unpunished; He punishes the children and their children for the sin of the parents to the third and fourth generation."

I don't know about you, but that is a powerful motivator for me to stay in obedience to God. I don't want my sins to visit my children in the form of their punishment. I want to stand before God Almighty knowing my sins are forgiven and cast as far as the east is from the west. I want the cleansing of redemption because the blood of Jesus paid the price for me and my sins. And in that place I want to know I stand sanctified and justified, not fearful that there is some punishment yet to come, either to me or my children.

The amazing beauty of our God is that He sees us that way when we come into salvation! We don't have to fear that we look messy, even when we still mess up. And the other amazing blessing in this place is that because He sees us as sanctified, our spouse and children are freed from our past sins as well!

This doesn't mean that sins we commit won't affect them, past or present. It just means the debt has been paid and they won't have to walk in my guilt. I won't even have to walk in my guilt. Christ did that for me. He paid the price, so we are set free from needing to pay anything more.

There is however, the concept of sowing and reaping. If I have made poor financial choices in my past and my finances are a mess, my family may have to live in a more meager lifestyle until we can climb out of those problems my sin created. Or, if I chose to make mistakes in a previous marriage, we may all have to walk with a lifetime of dealing with some of the repercussions that could bring. When I choose to walk in my flesh and lose my temper, my children suffer for it. When I choose to be lazy and not walk in consistency with disciplining my children, their behavior shows this, and ultimately their personal spiritual walk is affected.

But I love the first part of that verse: "the compassionate and gracious God, slow to anger, abounding in love and faithfulness, maintaining love to thousands, and forgiving wickedness, rebellion and sin."

God is a gracious God. He is eager to extend His hand of mercy in our lives. He is always in pursuit of our hearts and wanting to grant us grace. I love knowing that my sin, no matter how great, can be forgiven by just bowing my knee before the cross and accepting the pardon given me there.

Choosing to walk the way Christ has called me to walk has direct implications on how my children will choose to behave. Just as you choose to model God, your children can model the behaviors and attitudes they see in you. I don't want my children to walk in selfishness, unkindness, or rebellion. So I have to model a selfless, kind, submissive life if they are to see it and learn from it.

Each one of us has been affected by our own parents, whether positively or negatively. As you journey on your walk with Christ and learn to parent as God does, you may begin to realize some lies, as well as some truths, that were spoken over your life and now greatly influence your own parenting choices. God's truth and grace are big enough to help you look at your own upbringing with forgiveness and thanksgiving knowing that all of it, the good and the bad, were all a part of bringing you to where you are today. You are in the hands of a loving heavenly Father who will teach you all things you need to know to parent your own children.

This principle of parental sin and redemption affecting our children is seen throughout Scripture. Achan's sin in Joshua chapter 7 is a good example of this. When Achan was disobedient, his whole family had to perish with him. When David sinned with Bathsheba, their first child died as a punishment. God did forgive David and ultimately sent him and Bathsheba another son, Solomon, who walked in the benefits of a son of redemption (2 Samuel 11–12).

The opposite is seen in Scripture as well. When a parent decides to follow after God in obedience, their children are given grace as a result of their parent's life. Noah's family being spared on the ark was due to Noah having found favor with God. Lot being led forth from Sodom before its destruction, along with his family, is another example. But this story shows us, too, that just because our family is extended grace by association with us does not mean they have to embrace it. Lot's wife turned back to the evil she longed for in Sodom and was destroyed.

In 2 Timothy 1:5, Paul writes to Timothy, who had an unbelieving Roman father, and Paul speaks of the incredible faith of Timothy's believing mother and grandmother who influenced him to come to Christ. Do not underestimate the power of influence you will carry over your children's decisions for Jesus. Just as 1 Peter 3:1–2 says that you can influence your husband, you can have the greatest impact on influencing your children to come into salvation through Christ.

Just like our walk with God, parenting is an ongoing journey. Just when you think you master something, you are in uncharted waters again. The heart of parents is to love their kids and give them their best. That doesn't change, no matter what season you happen to be parenting in. Just as the heart of God doesn't change for you no matter the season you are in. We must continue in faith to trust our God with all our hearts, as we earnestly seek to gain the hearts of our own children so as to direct their path toward Christ and adulthood.

In my own parenting journey, while pregnant, exhausted, trying to homeschool the children, and feeling overwhelmed with Sam deployed, there were days when I was sure I had blown it irreversibly with our children. But one day, while literally curled up in the fetal position on my bathroom floor after exploding at my kids, weeping and begging God to help me, He very gently spoke to me the verse from Isaiah 40 that I quoted at the opening of this chapter.

He reminded me that He was my Shepherd and my children's as well. He carried my precious lambs in His arms, close to his heart, while He gently led me and showed me how to follow Him. I was beating myself up, thinking that Sam and I would somehow neglect to give them all they would need to succeed in their lives. I was terrified that the wolves of this world would somehow sneak in and steal my children away. But God showed me that He was holding them. I wasn't holding my children: He was. He wouldn't let anything, not even my poor parenting, take them from Him and the plan He had for them. His protection was covering them.

What joy and peace that brought me. What freedom it allowed me to walk in. To know that my children wouldn't be ruined because they had a loud-mouthed, ill-tempered mother leading them and a father who was gone so often. My God held them in His sheltering arms. Sam and I could just keep following the Shepherd.

And that Shepherd very gently led me. He was more gracious with me than I ever seemed to be with my precious little lambs or with myself. This gave me the courage and the humility to keep loving my children.

Never underestimate the power of humility and forgiveness with your children. They are quite resilient. Just as we want our Lord's love and approval, our children want ours. They are so very quick to forgive us and love us when we admit our failings and ask them for forgiveness.

PARENTING IN DEPLOYMENTS

Our children's amazing ability to adapt in life is seen in the many deployments we have had to survive as well. Our children learn quickly how to live with daddy home or with daddy gone. Much of this is because I create a routine for those times when we face deployments. Their ability to transition into our life with their dad off to war is largely influenced by my actions and attitudes as I adjust to this season.

I have several things that I have learned to do that make deployments more bearable and help us all keep our spirits and attitudes positive. Keeping God in the center of our family, and certainly in the center of my own focus, is what will give me the strength to shoulder all the children's practical and spiritual needs as well as maintain our home and keep it running smoothly during dad's time away.

Usually, on the day daddy leaves I try to plan something fun for us to do to take our minds off the immediate pain and sorrow we feel at his departure. We usually either go to the movies, or rent a movie and plan on a fun dinner that I don't have to cook, along with a really fun dessert. Sundaes and milkshakes usually top my kids' list.

Over the next two weeks we will have many varied emotions throughout our home. Some children react more emotionally than others. I never tell them they shouldn't cry or feel sad. One of my friends told her girls that the very fact that they all feel so sad is really a wonderful sign of what a good daddy they have. If he weren't such a good daddy, they might not miss him so much. I love her take on it.

My children and I do regular devotions together in the Word, and we regularly pray together. We use the time while their daddy is gone to pray especially for him, but also to discuss how God has uniquely positioned our family for just this time. Just as we wives have had to learn that our husbands are called to be in the military, it is important to impress this truth on our children. They need to know that it is God who called their father to do his job. God has a plan and a job for your family, not just daddy. Even though our job of waiting for him is hard, it is very important, and God wants to help us with it. He wants us to trust Him in this place. We have the amazing opportunity, through deployments, of building a foundation of faith in our God into our children.

As I said earlier, kids are smarter than we often give them credit for being. They know the very real risks of their dad going away, especially if they are over the age of seven. Younger children may or may not fully grasp what daddy is doing or the danger he faces being at war. But even when they don't fully understand, I know that even my infant children have felt the effects on our family when he first leaves and we are all adjusting.

Moving into a routine schedule is very important. Meal and bedtime routines are especially critical for consistency and stability for children, especially during times of increased stress with deployments. Sometimes I choose to cook bigger lunches during these times and opt for easier dinner meals, like sandwiches. That way I'm not so wiped out by the evening, when I will need all my energy for baths and bedtime stories. Exhaustion is a real enemy during these seasons, as you won't have your husband to help in the evenings as he might normally do.

Learn to alter your life and to extend grace to yourself and your kids, so you can stay focused on the important things in life during this time, like loving on your children and spending extra time with them.

I have found that deployments are especially hard for children between the ages of seven and ten. Many of mine have nightmares during deployments at this age. I think younger ones don't really grasp the real threat of loss that war brings with it. And older children, at least ones who have gone through it several times before, have had enough time to mature in their walks with

Christ and learned to trust more in this area. But children that are just coming into the age of understanding, or those that may be older and facing for the first time a deployment season will struggle with the reality of having to face life and death with their dad.

This is when standing on the Word of God and helping them to understand early in life that we can trust God with our lives is so critical. Our lives are not our own, anyway: they are His. So we can trust, regardless of what He chooses, that it is good because He is good. We may not feel good about it, but that doesn't negate the truth. And our God loves us immensely and will always be our ever-present help in trouble.

One key to instilling this foundation of faith in our children is to train them to walk in joy in all circumstances. Not happiness, mind you, but joy. We can be sad but still have the joy of knowing that our God holds us even in our deepest sorrows. He will never leave us or forsake us. He has a plan for us, for our future, and for us to prosper.

The key to having this joy is having a spirit of thanksgiving. You must always remember to be thankful that God has called you to serve Him in such a mighty way. Always encourage your children to understand the magnitude of how much God trusts them to succeed in what He is asking of them in this military life. It will help them to trust Him more. Never allow resentment or complaining to come into their hearts, because that is the surest way to fear and distrust. This means you must guard your own heart carefully in order to emulate that joy to your children, so they can follow your lead.

Remember, children will follow what they see being lived out in front of them. That knowledge, probably as much as my personal desire for growth in Christ, has kept me on my knees and seeking to follow Him when I might have otherwise quit. I don't ever want my children to quit. I want them to have faith greater than mine. I want to see them succeed in places their dad and I struggled. I want so much more for them than I ever wanted for myself. My love for them is greater than they could ever comprehend, and I know from that truth that my God loves me more than I could ever grasp. I hold onto Galatians 6:9, "Let us not become weary in doing good, for at the proper time we will reap a harvest if we do not give up."

Creating boundaries for your life and allowing yourself some margin will help you tremendously in shouldering the multiple responsibilities and stresses that will accompany deployments. Remember to do enough to keep busy and make time pass quicker, but don't do so much that you can't get the rest you need and your kids will need you to have to minister to them.

I usually plan a big weekend at least once a month, or even every three weeks, during deployments. We will plan a trip to see family and friends, if they are close enough. Or we will plan to go to an amusement park, zoo, or even the beach for a day. The point isn't really the activity so much as having something exciting and out of the ordinary on the calendar to look forward to. Learning to anticipate a fun time coming up in three weeks is a whole lot easier than learning to wait patiently for nine months for daddy to come home.

Time is a difficult concept for children to understand. Biting off chunks of time with fun activities helps pass that time more easily. The cost of the event or even the activity itself isn't what matters. It is the buildup of the anticipation and the marking off days. By the time you do four big weekends, you could be nearing the end of a deployment!

Depending on how much communication you have with your husband during deployments, the children may be able to talk to or even see Dad via Skype. My kids saw their dad only three times during all our years of deployments. We got to Skype with him two times during his final deployment, and during another deployment we had one VTC (video teleconference) at his unit the week of Christmas.

We wrote letters and pictures and sent packages, and we emailed when he had that available. We loved phone calls, but they were very sporadic and, due to their inconsistency and limited opportunities, often the kids didn't get to talk to him much, what with time differences and time limits. It is hard to let nine children plus mom talk to dad when we have only five minutes a week on the phone. I learned to let two kids each get one minute at the start of a call, and then I got whatever was left. I tried to make sure that each one of our children got at least one chance to talk to their dad each deployment.

Again, learning to build a foundation in the Lord is key to building trust in God during deployments. Sam and I stand together in encouraging our kids that we know without a doubt that God called us to this life, whatever that may hold for us. Sometimes that means having daddy home, and sometimes that means having daddy gone for a long time. But we also instill in our children that this earth is not our true home either. We both eagerly await the time when our God will take us to our real home in heaven where we will always be together, without any more separation.

Helping children embrace Christ, the cross, and a Kingdom mindset is truly the only thing that matters in raising them, whether you are in the military lifestyle or not.

I realized when we got to the teenage years for the first time that our kids were going to have to make and learn from their own mistakes—sometimes without our input. I had hoped to protect my children from all of life's pain, but there were some lessons they just had to learn the hard way. But even as their father and I had made countless mistakes in our lives, we always fell forward toward the cross when we fell. Our children, having witnessed so many of our failings, were quick to embrace the cross when they realized their own shortcomings. Creating a safe place for them to fail and learn from their mistakes was necessary.

Learning how to balance grace and mercy with accountability and responsibility as we lead them is difficult. I've found that I have to sustain the energy to be their greatest cheerleader in encouragement, but also to hold them accountable as they learn to take ownership for their own daily lives, responsibilities, and faith. Character development is still continuing during these years—for them and you. As parents, our faith and trust in God is stretched to new lengths as we seek to determine which circumstances we should let them figure out alone, and which we should still intervene to assist them.

But God is faithful to show you what your teenagers need in order to succeed. And continuing to hold their hearts and let them know your best intentions are for their best interests will go a long way in establishing a close relationship into their adulthood. I love our teenagers. And I love our adult children and the relationships we now have with them; they are the fruit of a lifetime of effort and love.

3 John 4 says, "I have no greater joy than to hear that my children are walking in the truth." Sam and I hold to that closely. We don't expect perfect children. We just pray that our children will learn to embrace the Truth. If they stay in the light, they will attain the greatest thing they could ever have: life and life abundant in our Savior. Not a life without pain and problems, but a life filled with hope and redemption through repentance.

We thank God that He is the ultimate Father and that He has taught us how to parent our children, as He has led us. We thank God that His grace is extended to us, and that His love for our children is even greater than ours is for them. No matter whether Sam and I are together or oceans apart, our God is always covering and holding our lambs. And He continues to gently show us how to love those young ones, even as He calls all of our hearts to His.

CHAPTER 9

FACING COMMON MILITARY LIFE STRESSES

When I heard these things, I sat down and wept.
—Nehemiah 1:4

FROM CARRIE

If we all came together and compiled a list of our top stressors in military life, I imagine most of us would name many of the following:

- deployment—dealing with everything at home without your spouse;
- deployment—what might happen to him while he's gone;
- moving—leaving loved ones and familiar places;
- moving—the actual process, particularly if he's gone;

- dealing with TRICARE (military healthcare system) and/or DEERS (Defense Enrollment Eligibility Reporting System);
- finances.

I can identify with all of these. I was pregnant with our second child when my husband joined the Air Force, so I was not only dealing with putting our house up for sale while he went to Basic Training, but also learning to be a parent without his presence. I'm not sure which concerned me more—the deployments that separated us or the night shifts he worked providing security with a cute, single brunette.

Moving wasn't a new process to me, but I'd never done it alone. Family of some sort had always been there. But more than once now in our years together I've prepped or unpacked by myself. And it always costs more to move than you think it will.

And don't even get me started on DEERS! I think our youngest child was eleven before they got his social security number entered into their system. I got so tired of going in to renew an ID card or change something in Tricare and being told I needed to give that piece of information to them. Again.

Probably my biggest stressor, though, is one I caused myself. It's one I see in my closest military friends. No, that's not true. It's one I see in all my closest friends, even the civilian ones. And although I'm very guilty of it, it's one I'm learning to combat with greater frequency. You could call it the Wonder Woman Syndrome.

You may recognize the symptoms I exhibited. I could handle anything life threw at me, or at least with my children's help I could handle it. If I just did enough research, I could fix or assemble anything all by myself. Or move any piece of furniture. Or face any deployment. Or . . . You get the idea.

I still remember the night I returned home to Alaska after a visit in southern Texas. My husband was deployed, so my two children and I had spent a month with my parents at their winter home. We'd been flying all day, and our pastor was supposed to pick us up at the airport. Supposed to. He forgot.

So there I was, standing in the middle of Ted Stevens Anchorage International Airport at midnight, after flying over 3,500 miles across three time zones, with my two-and-a-half-year-old and eleven-month-old. Yes, I had friends living on base who would have come to get me. I even had a sister who lived in town. But what did I do? Determine that I was not calling anyone at midnight to come rescue me. Instead, I found an ATM, withdrew every bit of cash we had left in our checking account and—hoping that I had enough cash—hired a taxi to take us home. That sweet cabbie not only fastened the baby's car seat securely in his back seat, but when we pulled up to the house, he quickly sent me inside with my tired children while he carried all our luggage inside for me.

Did I need to struggle that night? No. Absolutely not. Our pastor even called early the next morning to apologize, after realizing that he'd forgotten us. He told me I should have called. And I should have.

So let's call this fierce determination to do it all by ourselves what it is: sin. It's pride, ladies. It's a stubborn unwillingness to show weakness. A tenacity to look like we have it all together. And it's not God's plan for us.

Now, we absolutely must not swing to the other extreme, acting with such frailty that we convince ourselves or others that we are incapable of doing anything. We need to stand on our own two feet, putting to good use the gifts and talents that God put into us (2 Thessalonians 3:6–13). We must find balance.

One of my favorite biblical examples of this is the rebuilding of the wall around Jerusalem. God told the Jews for years through various prophets that He would bring discipline if they continued to disobey Him, but they largely ignored Him. Finally, God allowed their enemies to come in, destroy their temple, and take them into captivity. It was decades before groups of Jews began returning to restore their city.

Zerubbabel led the first group of Jews back to Jerusalem in 538 B.C., followed by Ezra with a second group in 458 B.C. Although these groups worked to restore the temple, they were still defenseless with no wall to protect them.

This concerned Nehemiah, the cupbearer to King Artaxerxes of Persia. So he prayed that God would grant him favor with the king, and when God provided an opening, he humbly asked for vacation time to go rebuild Jerusalem. Since the king was agreeable to this, Nehemiah pushed further, asking for letters for safe passage and for timber from the royal forest. Nehemiah 2:8 says, "And because the gracious hand of my God was on me, the king granted my requests." Not only that, but Artaxerxes also sent army officers and horses for the journey.

When Nehemiah arrived in Jerusalem, he took three days to investigate the wall before he told anyone what was on his heart. When he finally spoke out and said, "Let us rebuild the wall," the people agreed (Nehemiah 2:17–18). When their enemies began to plot against them, Nehemiah posted a guard (4:7–9). When the threat became bigger, he got the people involved in protecting the wall, unifying families to work and fight together (4:13–20). And what happened? Something beautiful:

> So the wall was completed on the twenty-fifth of Elul, in fifty-two days. When all our enemies heard about this, all the surrounding nations were afraid and lost their self-confidence, because they realized that this work had been done with the help of our God.
>
> —Nehemiah 6:15–16

Do you see how all this displays God's plan for interdependence? In our stubborn pride, we power through life like we need no one. Yet imagine if Nehemiah had tried to rebuild the city wall with that foolish notion. Did he need help rebuilding the wall? Yes! And when did he first ask for help? Before he even left to see what the project looked like. Remember—he asked the king for letters of safe passage and wood to rebuild key structures before he even left Persia. In fact, he went further than that. He asked for wood to build his own house for the short time he'd be living in Jerusalem!

Perhaps you are thinking that you don't have such a grand project as rebuilding a wall. You are merely trying to raise a child or two and keep your house clean. Or get to work each day and survive this current deployment.

Sweet one, you are short-sighted. God has placed you exactly where you are for a purpose. He wants to use you and love on you right where you are. He also wants to prepare you for the next phase of your life. After all, Nehemiah was merely cupbearer to the king, but it was Nehemiah's placement within Artaxerxes's palace that started his remarkable journey.

What legacy do you want to leave? That you merely survived what life threw at you? That's what a servant tried to tell his master, in a parable Jesus told in Matthew 25:14–30. In this story, Jesus tells what the Kingdom of Heaven will be like. "It will be like a man going on a journey, who called his servants and entrusted his wealth to them. To one he gave five bags of gold, to another two bags, and to another one bag, each according to his ability. Then he went on his journey" (verses 14–15).

The servants with five and two talents each went out, worked hard, and doubled their master's money. However, the servant with one talent tried another approach. When his master returned, this servant said, "I knew that you are a hard man, harvesting where you have not sown and gathering where you have not scattered seed. So I was afraid and went out and hid your gold in the ground. See, here is what belongs to you" (verses 24–25).

The master was not pleased with him. He said, "You wicked, lazy servant! So you knew that I harvest where I have not sown and gather where I have not scattered seed? Well then, you should have put my money on deposit with the bankers, so that when I returned I would have received it back with interest" (verses 26–27).

God grants us opportunities. Sometimes they look fun and inviting. Sometimes they look like obstacles, and sometimes they look like storms. But when we dig in and invest in God's Kingdom by loving on other people, by determining to trust God more, and by learning to live this life together with Him and others, then God is glorified and our talents are multiplied.

This lesson might be hardest to apply after a move. As I write this chapter, I am just four months removed from an out-of-state relocation myself. I left behind dear friends I trust with my whole heart, a job I loved, and stability within a loving community for my kids. Yet I knew that God wanted us to trust Him and transfer to another base.

It was a hard move, perhaps the toughest one we've experienced to date. To add to the stress of the change, God moved me from a time of frenzied activity to a time of rest. At first, I welcomed the reprieve. Now I am struggling with loneliness.

It is difficult, particularly for introverts, to break into the bonds of friendship at new places. It can be wearisome to invest yourself into new groups and activities so you can find out where you fit in. It is scary to think about pouring yourself into new people, not knowing if they will like you or accept you.

I get it.

But my empathy does not give you or me permission to be lazy. God wants us to live, work, and play together with other people. For one reason, because other people will encourage us, challenge us, and propel us to greater Christ-likeness (Proverbs 27:17, 1 Corinthians 12:24–26, Colossians 3:16, 2 Timothy 2:1–2, 1 Thessalonians 5:11, Hebrew 10:24–25).

Furthermore, who better to ask about good doctors, the best shopping areas, and reliable mechanics than someone who has lived in the area for several years? Think of all the stressors listed at the beginning of this chapter. Now think about how many of them would dramatically decrease in the presence of a couple of good friends.

We were made to worship our God. And we were made to live in community. I encourage you to take a step. Lay down a small piece of independence and embrace a piece of interdependence. If you don't make friends easily, ask God to show you someone who desperately needs a friend. You might just find someone you don't want to live without.

FROM KATHY

For our light and momentary troubles are achieving for us an eternal glory that far outweighs them all. So we fix our eyes not on what is seen, but on what is unseen. For what is seen is temporary, but what is unseen is eternal.

—2 Corinthians 4:17–18

Can you think of the worst day of your life since you've been married? I can think of five knee-buckling days that were so horrific that I honestly did not think I would survive them.

But I did.

The crisis on each one of those days was unique, and each brought its own unique type of pain. One of these crises was when I thought I had lost my husband because of infidelity. Another was when I was informed that I was being reported to social services for being a negligent mother. (The allegations were untrue.) Then there was the morning I got a call informing me that my cousin, who was like a sister to me, had been killed in a car crash. And I will never forget the day we waited for our two-year-old to come out of exploratory surgery—to determine if he had cancer or not.

Each one of those days sent my mind reeling and my heart racing. I felt sick to my stomach, and I literally fell to my knees out of fear and desperation. Those events challenged my faith—to near the breaking point. I was blindsided with the intensity of those circumstances and powerless to do anything about them. But the Holy Spirit graciously carried me and held me each of those times.

The fifth crisis might seem to you (in comparison to the first four) like just any ordinary day. But it stands out in my memory as, literally, a day from hell, and one that I never want to relive. Unlike the others, I was given the opportunity to prevent it, but I didn't. So it was largely my fault.

Sam had deployed two weeks earlier. We hadn't yet had any contact with him, and I was beginning to feel the stress of not knowing if he had made it safely in country. We had five children at the time, ages nine, six, four, two, and six months. I had decided to not homeschool that day, but instead load up the kids for the thirty-minute drive into town, where we would run a ton of errands and then return home for a late lunch. I had a plan, so I set out to tackle my full morning. I warned the kids that we weren't eating out, as funds were tight and mommy wanted to hurry so we could get back home, so I wouldn't have to nurse the baby while we were out.

Everything went wrong. I forgot my ID and realized it ten minutes into my drive, so we had to drive all the way home and start over. A kid vomited in the backseat due to car sickness, so I had to pull over and clean that up. Traffic was terrible. I had to get all five kids in and out of car seats half a dozen times, for half a dozen stops, that on my own would have taken me only five minutes each, but due to the kids and car seats they took twenty minutes each. I had to wait in a DMV line for close to an hour with all those now tired and hungry kids—only to hear that DMV couldn't help me.

As I finally pulled into the commissary parking lot, with the kids starving and exhausted, I hesitated. I looked back at my children's weary little faces and I heard the Lord whisper, *"Not today. It can wait."*

But the cat didn't have food. And we were out of milk. And I was down to two diapers. I had to go. I was already there, for heaven's sake. I did not want to be forced to load all those kids up again the next day for yet another trip into town. We could pull ourselves together and push through just another thirty minutes, decided Super Mom.

So I dragged my children into the store and I started shopping. We went ahead and got two carts, because I figured if we were there, we were doing the shopping—full-on once-a-month shopping. I put my hand to the plow, and I wouldn't look back. Or so I thought.

About twenty-five minutes into this ordeal, and with one cart over half-full, my infant son was screaming his head off because he was so tired and hungry. I could not keep going until I had at least offered him something to eat. But I hadn't brought in the diaper bag, so I had no blanket to nurse him under.

I decided to sit on a bench that happened to be near the dairy products. I put both carts beside each other, with the two-year-old in one, and I sat behind them, trying to discreetly offer my son a breast. He was crying so hard that he couldn't even eat. My milk came down, however, and I started spewing milk all over my blouse. I was literally soaked in a matter of moments.

In the meantime, my four-year-old and six-year-old were arguing, and the four-year-old started crying uncontrollably. That's when the two-year-old decided to stand up and put one foot in her cart and one in the other cart. This produced the same effect as someone putting one foot on a rowboat and one on a dock. The carts began to separate, and her little legs just split farther and farther apart. All this while I'm trying to juggle a baby and a milk faucet.

My nine-year-old was desperately trying to get my attention and alert me to the impending disaster, and just in time, I looked up. I frantically reached out to grab the toddler, hold onto the infant, cover my exposed breast, and not fall down myself in all the commotion. And just at that moment, an elderly gentleman walked past me, glanced my way, and said coldly, "I bet you wish you didn't have so many kids."

At that moment, I wanted to die. I literally wanted the ground to swallow me whole. I wanted to sit right there on that bench and just scream and cry and quit.

But my children were all there and they just looked at me, with their big round eyes pleading with me to get them out of there and care for them. So we put the screaming baby in the seat and we headed straight to the checkout. I still needed diapers, milk, and cat food.

When we got to the car, I just sobbed. I mean I literally sobbed uncontrollably. My children all just sat there, with quiet tears streaming down their sweet faces, not even knowing what to do or say to their messed up mom. By God's grace, the baby had finally fallen asleep out of sheer exhaustion.

By the time we got home, it was nearly 4:00 p.m. No one had eaten since breakfast and I still had to unload the groceries and fix a meal. We ate cereal for dinner. Then I checked our phone and realized I had missed the only call I was going to get for the next two weeks from my husband. I had missed the call by about twenty minutes.

That was one of the five worst days I have ever had to survive. And it was my fault.

God had cautioned me against trying to push any further. But I was so sure I could do it that I ignored His urgings to head home. From the time I left home, I should have known that the day was not going to go smoothly. By 10:00 a.m., I should have stopped doing whatever it was I had thought was so important. Instead, I should have focused on my kids and their needs rather than insisting on completing my agenda and my schedule. I missed giving my children what they needed, and in turn I missed the gift my Father was trying to give me: the phone call from my husband, as well as a lot more peace and joy in my day.

My older children still remember that day. Although all my kids have repeatedly told me through the years that I'm a great mom, there are moments even now when I can still see their sweet little faces that day, with tears silently streaming down their cheeks. And my heart aches, because I know that I had my priorities all wrong, and I failed my children miserably.

As Carrie has said, part of being able to shoulder all the burden of stress, work, and parental responsibilities during deployments is knowing when to ask for help. Some of you may not like asking for help. Well, you need to drop your pride and quit being selfish.

You might think that not asking for help is the epitome of *un*selfishness, but I disagree. When you are being prideful and refusing to ask for or receive help, there are multiple selfish actions happening. One, you are robbing someone else of a blessing in heaven, because they could have served our Lord through serving you and your family. Two, you are robbing your children of seeing the beauty of "every joint supplying" in the body of Christ (Ephesians 4:16). And three, you are robbing God of the opportunity of showing you something more of Himself. You are selfishly depriving all of those people of great blessing just so that you can hold onto your pride and gain nothing but exhaustion and weariness.

Is it really worth holding onto your pride, when you could exchange it for peace?

But along with getting help, we also have to know how and when to create boundaries. We need to know our limits, especially when help is very limited. We have to learn how much we can handle and leave enough margin in our lives for the unexpected. More important, we have to learn to listen to the Holy Spirit, because He will warn us of our limitations or temptations. Learning to hear the voice of God and being obedient to it are critical for you to have peace in your life.

God cares about you and will be with you on the worst days of your life. He will carry you through the critical, unexpected, uncontrollable days, including life and death situations. But He also cares deeply about your practical needs and the everyday stresses of living life without your spouse there to help, and He cares about those days when you have errands to run and groceries to buy while having to manage a bunch of small children.

Ask God for help. He will send it to you! He never asks us to do something without equipping us for the task, or else He sends the help to ensure that we can accomplish all He is asking. But we must learn to ask. And we must learn to be obedient to what He says to us.

And remember to be thankful for the help He sends. Don't complain if it isn't what you thought it would look like or doesn't offer the relief you had hoped it would bring. Sometimes He may tell you to buck up and take care of something by yourself. Sometimes He will tell you to stop doing something you either think you need to do in your strength or that you enjoy, because He wants you to change your priorities so He can lead you through a particular season of trials.

Sometimes we get overly weary because we wallow in self-pity and end up spiraling into a negative mindset. Because our life doesn't look like we want it to look, we think we have the right to complain. Complaining will deplete our energy and result in depression and exhaustion. But the joy of the Lord shall be our strength! Psalm 28:7 says, "The Lord is my strength and my shield; my heart trusts in Him, and He helps me. My heart leaps for joy and with my song I praise Him."

When we allow our hearts to trust in Him, we are helped! And joy should be the natural byproduct of knowing that God is in our lives and standing with us in our trials. We should be overflowing with gratitude! We have absolutely no excuse to not be thankful, in whatever circumstances we may find ourselves in, because we know that our God holds us, both in the temporal and the eternal.

Now I'm not saying that when your car breaks down and strands you and the kids that you should do backflips. I am saying that when that happens, you ask for help and you rejoice in the provision God will send. And you remember to find joy in the fact that the car merely broke down instead of having a wreck. Or that the sun is shining and you aren't having to change a tire in the rain. You practice being thankful to your Father in heaven, who has never and will never leave or forsake you on this rough day or any other, and you see the glory in that truth.

PRE-DEPLOYMENT STRESSORS

One way you can practice being thankful is by taking steps to ensure there is less stress, by doing some pre-deployment planning. God is an organizer, and we can learn to follow His leading. 1 Corinthians 14:33 says, "For God is not a God of disorder but of peace."

Pre-deployment planning will go a long way in helping you find some of the help and peace you will need to prevent a crisis. It will allow you and your husband some reassurance that at least some things will be easier on you while he is away. This can allow you both to be thankful and more at peace as you face the many months of separation.

Planning a checklist of practical things to get done before he leaves, and a list of things to help you run your home while he is away, can create order in your home and bring immeasurable peace to you both. The following is a list of suggested things to think about before he leaves.

- Stock up on light bulbs, batteries, and house air filters.
- Make sure you service your heating/air system before he leaves—and have a repairman's number ready to call in case of emergency repairs.
- Make sure you know how to turn off the main water line and where the fuse box is at—and know how to check fuses.
- Get the car's oil changed, and change it again every three months—mark your calendar.
- Make sure the wipers and lights are all working on the car—if possible, get the car serviced before he leaves.
- Check the car tire pressure—and if possible, change a tire once together before he leaves, so you know how.
- Make sure you know how to jump start your car and have jumper cables.
- Get a tool box of your own and equip it (hammer, flat head and Phillips screwdrivers, pliers, duct tape, super glue, nails, flashlight, extension cord, extra batteries).
- Decide who will do the yard work—you or someone you hire.
- Get a power of attorney.
- Make sure your name is on all accounts that you will need access to in order to pay or stop payment on something.

- Locate at least one person who will be willing to babysit for you when you need a sitter, and budget for that at least twice a month. Once for errands/appointments, and once for you to go to a ladies' function or to a movie with a friend!
- Have the name and number of at least one car mechanic and one plumber written down.

This is certainly not an exhaustive list, but it is one that I like to look at before Sam deploys. You may have other issues, like who will care for your pets on holidays while you travel, and babysitting needs beyond the occasional appointment or much-needed break. But whatever your personal needs, make sure you address as many as you can before your husband deploys. Seek the Lord and pray about what issues you may need to address with your husband. God will actually prepare you ahead of time for some crises before they occur.

I remember when Sam was about to deploy, just three weeks after we had our sixth baby. I was emotionally and physically exhausted, and the impending deployment was throwing me over the emotional edge. Sam asked me what he could do to help me. After crying and begging him to get out of the deployment somehow, which was not going to happen, we started to go through a list of things that were stressing me the most at that time.

I realized that the housework was overwhelming me. I could keep up with the children, the schoolwork, the cooking, the laundry, and straightening the house, but it seemed as if I never had the time or energy to tackle the deep cleaning that needed doing at least weekly, such as scrubbing toilets and mopping floors. My house looked straight, but I knew it wasn't as clean as it should be, and that worry was constantly hanging over my head and causing me frustration.

So we hired a housekeeper to come help me do a thorough cleaning twice a month. At first I resisted. I thought I shouldn't be paying someone to do something I was capable of doing. But when I took the time to do those chores, I was dropping the ball somewhere else in our life. Focusing more on our kid's needs and schooling was more important than toilets, but I could only go with dirty toilets for so long. Rather than have to sacrifice clean toilets to have time with my kids, hiring help became a way for me to have peace of mind with my housework while not sacrificing the people and things that were of greater priority to my life.

I was worried about the expense for that help. But when our men are deployed there is the blessing of family separation pay, and hostile fire pay, and hazardous duty pay that we can be thankful for. So, we decided to budget for help with my housekeeping. It was a huge blessing to me. After the deployment, I actually kept the help on for a once a month cleaning day. Then after we had another baby, we upped it back to twice a month. For our family, this is a priority.

For some of you, budgeting to eat out more may bless you. Some of you may want to get help with yard work. I don't mind cooking or mowing, so I'd rather have the help cleaning. But each of us could use some help. And each of us can and should consider ways to help alleviate some of the stress we will face, especially through deployments. I encourage you to spend some time praying about some practical things you and your husband could do to help you while he is gone.

EXTENDED FAMILY AND FRIENDS

Some of you may have family nearby and so you have an abundance of help. You should praise God for that blessing! My parents moved near us several years ago, and it has meant so much to me to have their love and support.

But for some of you, your extended family and in-laws, or ex-laws, may actually be one of your major stress points in your life. This is not uncommon. I encourage you to stay before the Lord for wisdom in knowing how and when to communicate with family members who may cause you stress, especially when you have to handle that alone without the support of your husband nearby.

Family and friends who do not understand the lifestyle you have been called to live can often cause you more grief through their careless comments and ignorance. Sometimes this can be intentional, but frequently this is not maliciously or intentionally done. They really don't understand that they make things worse by complaining to you about their son's deployment, or their son-in-law's absence from the holiday gathering.

There was a time when I felt I had to run interference between my husband and his family, just so they would know what was happening in his life. Sam and his mother and siblings were not very close when we first married, and if I didn't call his mother, she was never called. When she was dying of cancer, I was blessed to help care for her. It allowed me to invest in her and in Sam's family in a much greater way than I ever had before. Her illness and passing was very hard on his family, but it brought them much closer together. Death has a way of either tearing a family apart or uniting them. Thankfully, we were blessed with a new closeness.

Sam and I are also blessed with family that is extremely supportive of our military career. Both of my grandfathers and my father served in the military. Sam's family also has a rich military history. This is helpful because they understand that we have little to no control over our vacation time or our ability to join in larger family functions around holidays.

I have had friends, though, who can't seem to understand that I can't plan a vacation to go see them with my husband. I can plan things without my husband, but rarely with him. And often I don't want to plan things without him. I'd rather share as much of our life with him as possible. Often I miss the ladies' retreat or even an evening out with friends, because I opt for precious time with my man and my family.

The kids and I don't put our life on hold while Sam is deployed, but we would rather plan our vacation time and finances around something we can share with him when he returns. So we tend to miss out on things that people would like us to attend. But we have to prioritize our life as God leads us and not worry about what other people expect from us. This includes our parents and siblings, who may not understand that our marriage and family will take priority over time with them.

We understand that others love Sam and are also glad when he returns from a deployment, but we have always made it extremely clear to everyone that our family time will take precedence over time with them. Especially when our time with him will still be very limited. We are as loving as possible in expressing this, but sometimes people get offended. All we can do is express our desire to love them, but also express the importance of placing our family above other relationships and obligations.

Hebrews 12:14–15 says, "Make every effort to live in peace with everyone and to be holy; without holiness no one will see the Lord. See to it that no one falls short of the grace of God and that no bitter root grows up to cause trouble and defile many." We are commanded in Scripture to try to live at peace with everyone. That includes our coworkers, neighbors, the rude person at Walmart, and our extended family. Sometimes it is easier to be nice to the lady at Walmart, who you can largely ignore, than your mother-in-law who you have to face at Thanksgiving.

The term *holy* literally means "to be set apart." God is holy. He is set apart from sin and is the completion of love and righteousness, something we can't even begin to approach in our fallen sinful state. But we can approach the throne of grace through the amazing redemptive blood of Jesus Christ. When we come into salvation, we are set apart through Christ, and we gain the right to walk in holiness and righteousness. As the verse above says, we are to walk in that holiness and be a reflection of Christ in us to all who see us. We must be careful to guard against bitter roots in our hearts or unintentionally encouraging that growth in other's hearts.

This is a path that must be carefully and prayerfully tread out with our extended family and friends. Many of you have come into salvation and your unsaved family may think you have jumped onto the crazy train, because of your drastic life changes. Although figuring out how to love your extended family while drawing lines in the sand for your own family's choices may cause some stress, God will be shining out for them to see. Even when you create boundaries that they won't understand, that path of holiness may be the catalyst to ultimately draw them into Christ.

Do all that you can to keep the lines of communication open with your and your husband's family, and pray for those relationships. Above all, seek God for wisdom about how to deal with them, how to honor God yet still reflect love, even to those who might refuse it. You can never control someone else, but only your own choices. Always choose to love. Love includes placing boundaries in our lives. But love also extends grace. I encourage you to stay on your knees while learning to love your extended family and friends, since they might honestly struggle to understand and encourage your military lifestyle.

MILITARY ORGANIZATIONAL STRESSORS

Another arena where you may need to pray frequently about how to set up boundaries and extend grace is within the military organization itself. You would think that within that community you would find a sense of understanding and support. And you do, to some degree. But often the expectations from within your husband's team or command can be overwhelming and frustrating.

I don't ever remember me signing enlistment papers or swearing an oath to the United States military in any fashion. I do not wear a rank on my sleeve. But there are many unwritten codes within the military. In many respects, whatever my husband's rank, I wear it too. Dealing with command responsibilities or obligations due to your husband's position can be hard. Officer's wives have even more expectations laid upon them than enlisted wives. We must learn to work as unto the Lord when we are thrust into our husband's workplace.

I must regularly encourage both Sam and myself with the words of Colossians 3:23–24: "Whatever you do, work at it with all your heart, as working for the Lord, not for human masters, since you know that you will receive an inheritance from the Lord as a reward. It is the Lord Christ you are serving." Sam and I both have to remember that we are working for our God, but in doing that we are also ambassadors for the Kingdom.

I am astonished how often I've felt that the same soldiers we stand beside to defeat foreign enemies are the same ones we fight in our hearts here at home. Jesus calls us in Luke 6:27–42 to learn to love our enemies and not judge others. Sam has had to deal with people around him throughout his career who have been quite foolish and often abusive with their authority. It is during these times that we must remember each day Who we really serve and work for. We must remember to humble ourselves and trust that God will deliver us through these tough seasons. Hopefully He will reveal more of Himself to us, and we will be able to reflect that image of Him to those who see us.

When Sam was with 3rd Special Forces Group, I was heavily involved with the FRG (Family Readiness Group) for about a year. It was my first glimpse into the inner workings of the military. During my time with the organization, our men deployed to Haiti, and staying connected with them and trying to gain information about our husbands' whereabouts and safety became top priority to me and the women in the group, so we could keep our ladies updated.

I remember being completely shocked at the lack of organization and communication we were extended. I knew they couldn't tell us information that would put our men in jeopardy, but they would often give us false information, either because they didn't know the status of our men or didn't care enough about us to find out and communicate the truth.

When one woman heard from her husband, she would quickly grapevine the information to the rest of the group. This became dangerous, however, because often the information was incorrect or misleading for other teams. Then you would have women in a panic about something that didn't concern their own husbands. So we would try to discern the truth from the Rear Detachment, only to be even more frustrated because of their lack of concern.

I understood that they didn't want to deal with a bunch of gossipy, overly emotional women, and quite honestly that is what a large majority of those women were. But there was also a huge amount of disrespect for legitimate concerns within these women's lives. I remember several ladies about to have babies, who just wanted to know if they would need to ask extended family to come help them with the newborn, or if they could count on their men to make it home in time. I also recall several serious family health issues and extended family deaths that were not acknowledged by command as important enough to notify the husbands. You must remember, this was twenty years ago when we didn't have the Internet or even phone lines where our men were. Cell phones did not exist. We would go weeks without communication from our men. So we became dependent on the Rear Command to inform us of their status and to let them know about our needs.

Another thing that was hard was dealing with the women themselves within that group. As I said, there was a lot of gossip and emotion. Many of those ladies complained and were extremely negative about everything. That is very hard to deal with when you are trying your best to get information to them and support them. The FRG planned many activities to bring ladies out to fellowship and gain encouragement from one another, but often they left more depleted because all they did during their time together was find reasons to complain. It was a feeding frenzy of unwholesome, destructive, idle gossip about everything from the military command, housing conditions, commissary prices, and even their husbands.

Philippians 2:14–15 says, "Do everything without grumbling or arguing, so that you may become blameless and pure, 'children of God without fault in a warped and crooked generation.' Then you will shine among them like stars in the sky." We have to go through life without complaining, or else we will look just like the rest of the fallen world. If we want to shine for Jesus, we need to polish up our hearts with a good rubbing of thanksgiving.

Ladies, we must remember to be thankful in all situations. Grumbling and complaining about our life and our situations will not make us feel better. I'm not saying you can't occasionally vent your frustrations to a good friend, but you must be very cautious about whom you share your struggles with, and be sure to safeguard your thoughts and tongue. God knows you have unique challenges in your military home, but He has also given us so very much for which we should be grateful.

Some of the benefits of our chosen profession include housing accommodations or an allowance for your own choice of housing. Also, we are given great privileges with the commissary and the gas prices on post. And although the system is not perfect, we are given healthcare for our needs. Dealing with Tricare can be troublesome to say the least, but in this day and age any insurance company can be trying. I have civilian friends who don't have insurance and so have to decide if they can afford to take a sick baby to the doctor, or if they must instead buy groceries. Ladies, we are blessed, and we must remember to be thankful when we are dealing with frustrations within the system. The key to having joy in this life is to remain thankful.

God allowed us to be in the particular unit or organization we currently find ourselves in. He knows who your husband will have to work with. He knows who you will have the opportunity to work with during your time at a duty station. We must try to remember that our service within the military organization and with other military spouses is a way to further the kingdom of God. This realization should give us a good incentive to press on even when it is difficult and should allow us to find joy even in trying circumstances.

MILITARY SOCIAL STRESSORS

One other great area of stress that I have experienced within the military is the team expectations of my husband on a personal and social level. Many of these expectations are extended to myself, or at least I am expected to comply with whatever they are dictating to him.

For example, when my husband's team would go TDY or on a short training trip, the team would spend their off-duty hours going out together after work. This wouldn't have been bad if they just wanted to grab dinner together. But often it resulted in the guys wanting to end up in a strip club or bar. Sam didn't want to join them there, of course, and was often ostracized for not participating.

Sometimes he would go and sit alone in the car until the wee hours of the morning so that he could be the other men's designated driver. And although I was glad he wasn't getting drunk, I was so frustrated that he was forced to go along in the first place.

Now you can say he wasn't forced, but he really wasn't given much choice. These are men he must develop a relationship of trust with; these are the men he must lay his life on the line with, so he must maintain a cordial working relationship with them. But in order to do that, he has to spend time with them on a personal level. He is going to live with these guys in close quarters for months on end and they will get to know things about each other they probably don't even want to know, so being transparent with them early on is crucial. This can be extremely difficult if your husband tries to adhere to a spiritual or moral code that the other men don't. For Sam, being with the guys, even if he was only the designated driver, was a way to show that he was one of them.

Sam always made it clear that he would not support their choice to engage in infidelity. He let them know he loved his wife, and infidelity or going to strip clubs was not his idea of building a healthy marriage.

But not drinking was an issue for us early in our marriage, and Sam is not a drinker, so it became an issue, as we were expected to regularly attend team functions and parties as a couple. And although I'm the most sanguine person I know, this was very hard for me. Fellowshipping and enjoying people is easy . . . unless they are drunk. Which is exactly what we had to contend with many times when we went to someone's house for a cookout or gathering. And we usually had our children with us to witness these people getting drunk.

I began to dread every single outing with those people. We learned to show up early, eat quickly, and hope our kids would get fussy so we would have the excuse to leave sooner rather than later. I usually kept them from naps so they would be really tired and prone to fussiness before going to those events. I set up my own sabotage so we could escape sooner!

Sam and I had many discussions about alcohol due to these trials. We were both raised Baptist, and drinking was totally unacceptable in our churches and families. Plus, I had an extended family history of alcoholism. So neither of us had much interest in drinking or, before being adults, were thrust into these situations of feeling peer pressure to drink.

Before we were walking with the Lord, in the very early days of our marriage, Sam had been stationed in Germany for two years. He did drink some then, and I would get very angry at him for it. It wasn't so much the drinking that bothered me. It was the getting drunk and losing his capacity to maintain control. I knew he was setting himself up for a fall if he opened those doors, because drinking always occurred in bars where women were just waiting to be picked up. But by the time he was on a team, we were walking with Christ and we had new issues to wrestle with. What was the biblical truth about drinking? Did we have a responsibility to the people on his team to try to connect to them on their level by sharing a drink? Did we need to separate ourselves in order to show holiness? What freedoms did we have regarding drinking and within what restraints did we have to walk?

These were the questions that Sam and I began wrestling with. And they are important questions. After all, drinking is totally acceptable in the military, as well as in many other professions and areas of our society. Business dealings often take place over drinks. Football games are watched while sharing beers. Champagne is served at weddings, and a glass of wine is often served at dinner tables.

So how are we as Christians to view all this? What does the Bible say about drinking?

Jesus was very familiar with alcohol within His own culture. His very first miracle was turning water into wine at a wedding (John 2:1–11). Growing up in a conservative church, I heard some people argue that this wine was not fermented, but just grape juice. But clearly in the passage in John, the master of the banquet talks of the effects of inebriation from wine, so obviously guests sometimes drank too much wine and became somewhat drunk. The master said that the best wine, the wine that Jesus served them, was saved until the last. This means it was a quality wine, not merely a weakened imitation fruit juice.

It's a mystery to me why Jesus's first miracle involved alcohol. I do know that I don't want a weak, imitation Savior. I want the full-on power of drinking the Spirit of God. I want to know that after tasting the cheap imitations the world offers me, my Jesus saves the best for last! He has shown me He is the real thing. He is

100% proof! I want to drink deeply of the fruit of the vine of life and experience the full effects that will have on me.

Ephesians 5:15–18 says, "Be very careful, then, how you live— not as unwise but as wise, making the most of every opportunity, because the days are evil. Therefore do not be foolish, but under- stand what the Lord's will is. Do not get drunk on wine, which leads to debauchery. Instead, be filled with the Spirit." Learning to fill ourselves with the Spirit of God is far more important than filling our stomachs and satisfying the appetites of the flesh.

Alcohol in and of itself is no more sinful than anything else we consume. 1 Corinthians 10:23–24 says, "'I have the right to do anything,' you say—but not everything is beneficial. 'I have the right to do anything,' but not everything is constructive. No one should seek their own good, but the good of others." Anything that we partake in to the point of overindulgence is sinful. It is greedy and selfish. I know that I have freedom to enjoy a piece of cake for dessert on occasion, but it would be gluttonous for me to devour an entire cake. This is true for any food or drink.

Colossians chapters 2 and 3 discuss at length the freedoms we have through Christ: freedom from human traditions, religious holidays, and even food. The law of Moses put many restrictions on the Jews' diet, but nowhere did it prohibit drinking alcohol (unless someone was under a vow before the Lord). But Scripture does say that we aren't to drink to the point of drunkenness. Christians have complete freedom to eat foods that the Jewish people were strictly forbidden to eat. Based on Scripture, our free- dom is extended to alcohol as well.

Paul writes to Timothy to "stop drinking only water, and use a little wine because of your stomach and your frequent illnesses" (1 Timothy 5:23). Clearly, Paul would not encourage Timothy to partake in something sinful. In 1 Corinthians 8:9–13, though, Paul instructs us to be careful about exercising our freedoms with food and drink when dealing with others. He cautions against letting our freedom become a stumbling block to those who are spiritually weaker.

If you are at liberty to consume alcohol, then you should prayerfully consider how this liberty may or may not affect others who might observe you. For example, if you know you are free to have a glass of wine, but you do so in the presence of a friend who is not saved and for whom alcohol is an idol, you are being a stumbling block to them. You may be giving them reason to justify their continued use of something that they abuse to their own detriment. Romans 14:19–23 summarizes this idea beautifully:

> Let us therefore make every effort to do what leads to peace and to mutual edification. Do not destroy the work of God for the sake of food. All food is clean, but it is wrong for a person to eat anything that causes someone else to stumble. It is better not to eat meat or drink wine or to do anything else that will cause your brother to fall.
>
> So whatever you believe about these things keep between yourself and God. Blessed is the one who does not condemn himself by what he approves. But whoever has doubts is condemned if they eat, because their eating is not from faith; and everything that does not come from faith is sin.

I encourage you to pray about where you and your spouse should stand on this issue. It is one that you will have to face in your military career. The choices you make must line up with where your conscience has freedom to walk. I caution you against making these decisions based on what others around you will be doing. This is one of those places you should work at honoring your husband and honoring your God while not causing anyone else around you to stumble. As it says in the verses above, whatever you believe about these things, keep between yourself and God and walk with a clean conscience before your Maker.

Alcohol, like anything else in our lives, can display either our freedom in Christ or our bondage in sin. Alcoholism, though, is very destructive to a marriage and a family. If you or your spouse have a drinking problem, then God wants to deliver you from this unhealthy addiction and bring you freedom. As in all things, Christ is the healing answer, and my prayer is that you, your spouse, and your family will all find the redemption and freedom God has for you. I encourage you to pray about this problem and seek godly counsel. Seek your Father's help if you find yourself in this painful place.

FINANCIAL STRESSES

Financial stress can and does affect everyone at some point, whatever their career choice or station in life.

God has made many references to money throughout his Word in order to help us gain understanding about how to handle this resource. He makes it clear that He is to be first in our lives, and anything that vies for His position of Lordship in our lives is an idol. Money is to be used with great restraint and wisdom. It is, after all, a tool that God uses to accomplish things i. the lives of others in His kingdom.

How we choose to use this resource and how we view it is of extreme importance in our walks with Christ. Jesus said, "Where your treasure is, there your heart will be also" (Matthew 6:21). He goes on to say in verse 24 of the same chapter, "No one can serve two masters. Either you will hate the one and love the other, or you will be devoted to the one and despise the other. You cannot serve both God and money."

One of the foundational beliefs in the Christian faith is that you should tithe a tenth of your income to God. Hear me when I say you tithe to God. Not to men. God laid down a standard of what He would ask of us from our finances in order to keep our hearts turned to Him and our hearts unselfish and uncorrupted by the wiles of money and wealth in this world.

The tithe is used by God to move His church forward. The resources brought into the local churches and ministries are used by God to advance His kingdom. It says in Galatians 6:6, "Anyone who receives instruction in the word should share all good things with their instructor." In other words, make sure you help pay your pastor a salary so He can continue to preach! Make sure the church light bill gets paid so you have a place to meet and others can come and find Christ. Bring the tithe to the local body you are serving and being served in.

The first instance of seeing an offering freely given is by Abel in Genesis. He freely brought from the firstborn of his flock. Cain simply brought some of his fruits, not the first fruits (Genesis 4:1–16). God is not interested in our leftovers. He wants to know that we bring the first of what we have to honor Him and to acknowledge His blessing and provision in our lives.

After all, does God need money? He certainly doesn't need our money. But He is always after our heart. And if we hold too closely to our funds or somehow believe they are ours to spend as we wish because we earned them, we are grievously mistaken. Is He not the giver of all good gifts, as spoken in James 1? He graciously gives us our jobs and livelihoods. In reality, one way to look at His request of a tithe is like realizing that He is only keeping 10% of what is rightly His as He gives you the other 90%! Isn't everything His when you surrender your life and all that is in it to Him?

I mention the tithe to you because some of you do not walk in obedience to this command. It says in Malachi 3:8–10,

> But you ask, "How are we robbing you?"
>
> In tithes and offerings. You are under a curse—your whole nation—because you are robbing me. Bring the whole tithe into the storehouse, that there may be food in my house. Test me in this, says the Lord Almighty, and see if I will not throw open the floodgates of heaven and pour out so much blessing that there will not be room enough to store it.

Some of you may not be tithing and so your finances are suffering as a result. I encourage you to begin to trust God with this area of your life. You will need to prayerfully take this before your husband and seek his leading as well. God will always bless a heart that is surrendered to Him. Stepping out in faith in this area will always bring blessing. It is the only place in Scripture God tells us to test Him! He will not disappoint you when you trust Him in this area of your life.

Besides the tithe, there are many other principles in Scripture that teach about how to handle money and how we are to view it. It talks of debt, and how we should seek to avoid it if we can. It also talks of planning for our future and saving up for an inheritance to pass to our children, both spiritually and financially (Proverbs 22:7, 21:20, 13:22). Matthew 25:14–30 discuss at length the importance of being a good steward not only with finances, but with all gifts God entrusts to us.

If you are not on a budget or don't know how to budget, Carrie and I strongly encourage you to check out some of the resources in the back of this book. We want to see you find freedom in your finances. God doesn't promise great wealth, but He does promise to meet all our needs. We must seek the Giver and not the gift as we reach out to God. How much money you have is not what is important in your life. What you do with those resources and how you choose to honor your God is vitally important. He knows your needs and He greatly desires to liberally pour out His wisdom in your life and show you how to use the financial gifts He provides you.

Some of you may have never considered allowing God to direct how you order your finances. He is faithful to direct each of us in how to spend our funds in a way that will honor Him and provide for our families. As with everything else in this book, we encourage you to surrender this over to your Lord and allow Him to direct your path. Pray for wisdom for both yourself and your husband as he leads your family's financial decisions. God will be faithful to help you when you seek Him.

EXCHANGING STRESS FOR REST

It is critical that you hold onto 2 Corinthians 4:17–18 when you face the stresses of this military life: "For our light and momentary troubles are achieving for us an eternal glory." Jesus said in John 16:33, "I have told you these things, so that in Me you may have peace. In this world you will have trouble. But take heart! I have overcome the world."

Our troubles and stresses are light and momentary when we look at them through the eyes of eternity with our Lord Jesus Christ. Our God has every desire to give us peace and joy in this life, whatever our current circumstances may be. Dear sister, we pray you are encouraged to stay the course this day. 2 Corinthians 4:16 says, "Therefore we do not lose heart. Though outwardly we are wasting away, yet inwardly we are being renewed day by day."

Seeking the heart of your Father and learning to listen to His voice and obediently follow His leading will always bring you rest. Jesus is calling you. He is offering you the help you desperately need to make it through this day. Will you listen and obey?

Come to Me, all you who are weary and burdened, and I will give you rest. Take My yoke upon you and learn from Me, for I am gentle and humble in heart, and you will find rest for your souls. For My yoke is easy and My burden is light.

—Matthew 11:28–30

CHAPTER 10

LIVING WITH THE FEAR OF DIVORCE AND DEATH

I lift up my eyes to the mountains—where does my help come from? My help comes from the Lord, the Maker of heaven and earth . . . The Lord will keep you from all harm—He will watch over your life; the Lord will watch over your coming and going both now and forevermore.

—Psalm 121:1–2, 7–8

FROM CARRIE

Starry-eyed, I walked down the aisle to my groom, the man who agreed with me that the word *divorce* would never enter our vocabulary. No argument would be so bad or differing opinions so great that we couldn't find a compromise. Only death would part us. It wasn't long, though, before marriage got "real" and those well-intentioned thoughts were tested.

So far, we've kept our vows made on that day in 1996. Not that it was always easy. Not that we still don't have days when I wonder what I was thinking when I said yes to his marriage proposal. Thankfully, though, as the years progress, those questioning moments get farther apart.

Statistics on marriage and divorce are disheartening no matter how you look at them. It's commonly said that fifty percent of all American marriages will end in divorce, although that statistic is very misleading. That number most likely comes from the assumption that since we have roughly 2.4 million marriages a year and 1.2 million divorces a year, then we can just take those two numbers, divide them out, and get the number of marriages that will end in divorce. It's really not that simple.

Several articles on the World Wide Web and in psychological journals discuss this in far more detail, but let's just determine for our purposes that divorce happens a lot, and the United States is very high on the list of countries in the world with the most divorces.

In addition to the many stressors we've already discussed, military families are dealing with a modern American culture where deployments complicate relationships, divorce is quickly recommended, and happiness is promoted over commitment. Add in the inherent danger that is included in many MOSs and the assumed risk when working in several overseas locations, and fears of divorce or death can overwhelm the best-intentioned wife.

So let's ground ourselves in truth and define clear boundaries for the battlefield ahead of us.

THE MARRIAGE COVENANT

We live in a day of contracts. You have to sign a contract for cell phones, utilities, and even medical appointments. While it's very common to sign our name on the dotted line, do we really understand what that symbolizes? Or recognize that a contract is very different from the marriage covenant?

Legally, a contract is an agreement between two or more people in which the first person will (or will not) do something for the second. In return, the second person will provide some sort of benefit to the first. In other words, when you sign on the dotted line at the doctor's office, the doctor provides his medical training and advice in return for you paying (or authorizing your insurance to pay) his bill. Both people involved get something.

A covenant works differently. It is simply an agreement between two or more people to do (or not do) something. Neither party gets an expressed benefit or preauthorized consideration. Which means that neither side gets an easy out if they feel slighted, neglected, or underappreciated.

It's why we call the promises we give during the wedding *marriage vows*. Those words are more than simply a promise to love, honor, and cherish. They are a solemn pledge before God Almighty and everyone in attendance at the ceremony to do exactly what we're saying. Period. Even if the other person falls short on their commitment. And Scripture is very clear on what God thinks about breaking a vow:

> If you make a vow to the Lord your God, do not be slow to pay it, for the Lord your God will certainly demand it of you and you will be guilty of sin. But if you refrain from

making a vow, you will not be guilty. Whatever your lips utter you must be sure to do, because you made your vow freely to the Lord your God with your own mouth.

—Deuteronomy 23:21–23

Now I want to be sure that everyone understands that this is the ideal, God's best plan for all of us. I know some of you reading this have been touched by divorce through your parents or siblings. Some of you will already be on your second or perhaps even third marriage, and some of you are contemplating divorcing your spouse right now.

WHEN DIVORCE IS PERMISSIBLE

The Bible recognizes that we do not live in an ideal world, and so it gives guidelines on when divorce is permissible. The exception clauses are few, but significant. It should be noted that just because one of these situations occurs in your marriage, this does not mean that divorce is mandated. Divorce should be your course of action only after you've spent much time in prayer and sought wise, biblical counsel.

First, God allows an unbelieving spouse to walk away from a believing spouse. Please note that this principle does not apply in reverse! Paul states this clearly in 1 Corinthians 7:

If any brother has a wife who is not a believer and she is willing to live with him, he must not divorce her. And if a woman has a husband who is not a believer and he is willing to live with her, she must not divorce him . . . But if the unbeliever leaves, let it be so. The brother or the sister is not bound in such circumstances.

—1 Corinthians 7:12–13, 15

In these verses, Paul is not advocating divorce, but peace. He follows this up by saying, "God has called us to live in peace. How do you know, wife, whether you will save your husband? Or, how do you know, husband, whether you will save your wife?" (verses 15–16). Paul allows for the possibility that the unbelieving spouse may be so curious as to why the believing spouse humbly accepts a separation or divorce, that they will turn to investigate Christ and thereby become a believer.

Is this possible? Sure. Easy to live through? Of course not. If this is your situation, cling to godly friends who will both remind you of the ultimate goal of salvation for your spouse, and cry with you when the weight of your reality seems unbearable.

Secondly, God allows divorce in the case of sexual immorality. Now this is a broad category so let's define a couple of terms.

Legally, adultery is voluntary sexual relations between a married person and a person who is not the spouse. Non-sexual intimacy with someone other than your spouse is not technically adultery, according to our judicial system. This means that someone might have a purely emotional affair without committing actual adultery. (Understand, I am not condoning an emotional affair. I'm merely spelling things out.)

However, we need to keep in mind that God holds Christians to a higher standard. Jesus repeatedly says in the Gospels that sin includes the heart's desires as well as the physical act. On this issue, Jesus attacked it bluntly in the Sermon on the Mount recorded in Matthew 5–7: "You have heard that it was said, 'You shall not commit adultery.' But I tell you that anyone who looks at a woman lustfully has already committed adultery with her in his heart" (Matthew 5:27–28).

Fornication is sex between unmarried people. Both it and adultery fit into the broader term *sexual immorality*, which would also include every other sexual activity involving two or more people that is outside of what God allows. To put the rules in their most basic form: sex is for a husband and wife, alone, after the wedding ceremony (Genesis 2:22–25, 1 Corinthians, 7:1–5, Hebrews 13:4, Romans 1:21–32). Everything else falls into the sexual immorality category. Among many other acts, this includes rape, incest, prostitution, homosexuality, bisexuality, and bestiality (Galatians 5:19–21).

Kathy will talk more about this in the next chapter, so I merely want to say that in the case of sexual immorality, God permits divorce. Jesus says in Matthew 19:8–9, "Moses permitted you to divorce your wives because your hearts were hard. But it was not this way from the beginning. I tell you that anyone who divorces his wife, except for sexual immorality, and marries another woman commits adultery."

Finally, we must consider the case of treachery. In Malachi 2, God is speaking to the Israelite priests. If you've never read this book, just know that they were really messing up and God had some very strong warnings for them. I like how the Amplified Bible writes verses 13–16:

> And this you do with double guilt; you cover the altar
> of the Lord with tears [shed by your unoffending wives,

divorced by you that you might take heathen wives], and with [your own] weeping and crying out because the Lord does not regard your offering any more or accept it with favor at your hand.

Yet you ask, Why does He reject it? Because the Lord was witness [to the covenant made at your marriage] between you and the wife of your youth, against whom you have dealt treacherously and to whom you were faithless. Yet she is your companion and the wife of your covenant [made by your marriage vows].

And did not God make [you and your wife] one [flesh]? Did not One make you and preserve your spirit alive? And why [did God make you two] one? Because He sought a godly offspring [from your union]. Therefore take heed to yourselves, and let no one deal treacherously and be faithless to the wife of his youth.

For the Lord, the God of Israel, says: I hate divorce and marital separation and him who covers his garment [his wife] with violence. Therefore keep a watch upon your spirit [that it may be controlled by My Spirit], that you deal not treacherously and faithlessly [with your marriage mate].

Those verses hold a lot of good stuff, but I want you to make sure you get the main point of the passage: do not deal treacherously or faithlessly with your spouse. Those who find themselves in this situation may have biblical grounds for divorce. Cases of spousal abuse would be treachery. Or an unrepentant spouse who repeatedly commits the same offense. Or a spouse who abandons their family. (See also 1 Timothy 5:8.)

I want to pause here and reiterate—divorce is not *mandated* in any of these situations. If your husband has a gambling addiction that is putting you or your children at risk, a separation may both be wise and serve to get his attention focused on seeking help. Before you end your marriage, though, I strongly encourage you to talk with a Christian counselor who adheres to biblical standards and holds marriage as highly as God does. And if you or your children are in physical danger, find a safe place.

To the rest of us, the ones not facing abandonment, fornication, or treachery, but are unhappy and struggling? Here is your guideline from the Apostle Paul: "To the married I give this command (not I, but the Lord): A wife must not separate from her husband. But if she does, she must remain unmarried or else be reconciled to her husband. And a husband must not divorce his wife" (1 Corinthians 7:10–11).

Some situations are clearly more difficult than others. A quote from Ruth Graham comes to mind: she said she'd never considered divorcing the Reverend Billy Graham—but murder had crossed her mind! All of us have had times when we were being particularly pigheaded or difficult to live with. If your husband has an injury or disease that causes irritability, depression, or other such emotional instabilities or physical weariness, this verse can seem cruel or daunting. We'll talk more about that in a couple of chapters.

More than anything, what I want you to understand is that the legal option of divorce, except in the cases listed above and under wise, biblical counsel, needs to be off the table and out of your mind. You being unhappy is not a reason to divorce. Him being grumpy more often than not is not a reason to divorce. Neither are bad financial decisions, new orders to a place you do not want to go, constant arguing, unmet expectations, or any other excuse you want to put out there.

If anything in that last paragraph sounds like you, then I have advice for you. You won't like it. I wouldn't have wanted to hear it a time or two in my marriage. But it's sound truth: it is time for you to grow up, accept responsibility for your marriage, and seek counsel from a mature Christian woman or couple.

WORKING ON YOUR MARRIAGE

Healing a marriage that is in distress takes time and effort, but it is possible. Kathy and I have both walked through times that have destroyed other marriages. Each situation is unique, so the solutions I offer are broad. But here are three keys that changed me and my marriage.

You may know me well enough by now to know that the first key I'm going to offer you is prayer. You must get past the desperate prayers for God to simply save your marriage. What do you really want? What do you fear? Those are perfect places to start conversations with God.

One day when I was praying for God to change a particular aspect of my husband that really irritated me, God asked me a question. He said, "What if I see things differently?" I tried a couple of rebuttals, but ultimately, I got very quiet as I considered this. My mind circled in two directions. First, what if I were the problem in that irritation, not my husband. And second, what if God saw something more important in my husband that needed changing first?

So now I pray for God to have the freedom in my husband's heart to change what He deems most important. I ask for God to keep him moldable and pliable in God's hand, for his ears to be attuned to God's voice, for his eyes to see where God is working, and his desire to be to work with Him. Sometimes I ask God to help my husband understand me better, and I often ask for God to give him great wisdom in leading our family.

I also learned to ask one thing for myself as I pray for my husband: that I would see where God is working within him—because those irritations that bug me aren't really too bad when you see evidence of a changed heart in other areas.

A second key I discovered is taking the time to seek God. You may have heard people say that you can't change other people, so work on yourself. That's the general idea, but let God be the focus of the process. Reading your Bible, getting involved in Bible studies either on your own or with a group, and finding an accountability partner who will regularly ask you if you've opened your Bible recently are more than good ideas: they are keys to growth. And as you change, as your relationship with God improves, you will begin to see a positive effect in the relationships around you.

Which leads to the third key: seek godly relationships. You need to look critically at your friendships and make sure they are ones that encourage you to remain steadfast in your marriage vows. Does that person you confide in tell you to pray, or to run away? Do they encourage you to step out in faith, or to seek what makes you happy? Do they challenge you to trust God, or to follow your heart? It's much easier to stick with God's plan and have hope for His restorative power if those surrounding you believe with you that God can heal your marriage.

WHAT IF HE LEAVES YOU?

Over the last several years, Kathy and I have talked with a lot of women in difficult situations. Occasionally, I could clearly see things within the hearts of these wives that needed changing, particularly if they wanted to save their marriage for the long-term. Frequently, both husband and wife were causing problems and both needed their hearts changed.

A couple of times, though, a woman we know was truly doing things well—not perfectly, but being godly—and she still ended up with divorce papers in her hands. While all divorce is sad on many different levels, these cases, where one spouse is striving to follow God while the other is running from God, are truly heartbreaking.

If this is you, know that as I wrote this I stopped writing to pray for you. You likely already know all I am about to say, but let me remind you of three basic truths.

First, you are loved. Isaiah 41:10 says that God will strengthen you, help you, and uphold you. Romans 8:35–39 tells you that nothing can separate you from the love of God.

Scripture also says, "Greater love has no one than this: to lay down one's life for one's friends" (John 15:13). The moment you said your marriage vows, you agreed to lay your life down for your husband. Perhaps this act of laying down your life is more real to you now than it has ever been before. In this difficult place that you now walk, remember that God still loves you. Psalm 147:3 says that the Lord "heals the brokenhearted and binds up their wounds."

Secondly, you are wanted. Deuteronomy 7:6 says that you are chosen to be one of God's treasured possessions, and Jeremiah 29:11 says that God knows His plan for you. Only something that is wanted is chosen and planned for. But God doesn't stop there. Jeremiah 29 continues by assuring us that His plans are to give us hope! I pray with the Apostle Paul that, even in this very difficult place where you find yourself, the "God of hope [would] fill you with all joy and peace as you trust in Him, so that you may overflow with hope by the power of the Holy Spirit" (Romans 15:13).

Finally, you are not forgotten. More than once, Bible heroes such as King David cried out for God to remember them. Yet David also knew God was present in his life. In Psalm 9:18 David writes, "God will never forget the needy." And Psalm 23, a favorite for many people, assures us of God's provision and protection.

A FINAL THOUGHT

As you consider your marriage, and before you read Kathy's thoughts on facing the fear of your husband dying on the battlefield, take these words from Psalm 23 to heart. See the care and concern that your loving Heavenly Father has for you.

> The Lord is my shepherd, I lack nothing. He makes me lie down in green pastures, He leads me beside quiet waters, He refreshes my soul. He guides me along the right paths for His name's sake. Even though I walk through the darkest valley, I will fear no evil, for You are with

me; Your rod and Your staff, they comfort me. You prepare a table before me in the presence of my enemies.
You anoint my head with oil; my cup overflows. Surely
Your goodness and love will follow me all the days of
my life, and I will dwell in the house of the Lord forever.

FROM KATHY

Brothers, we do not want you to be ignorant about those who
fall asleep, or to grieve like the rest of men, who have no hope.
—1 Thessalonians 4:13

It was late in the evening, and I was playing a game of solitaire
on the computer after having put the last of my children to bed.
Sam had deployed just three weeks prior. The phone rang, and I
jumped in my skin as I instinctively began to pray while reaching
for the phone, hoping it would be Sam. We had spoken only a
couple of times since his departure.

As my hand touched the phone I saw the caller ID and my
heart stopped. It wasn't the normal string of numbers that indicated my husband was calling from halfway around the world. It
was a local number from the base. My eyes darted to the clock as
I picked up the phone and my mind raced.

Nine forty five? They wouldn't call you if he . . . Please God no. They
show up at your door not phone you . . . Please God no.

"Hello?" I waited to see who would speak from the other end
of that dreadful phone.

"Mrs. Barnett, this is Sgt. Smith calling to inform you that there has been an incident regarding men within your husband's unit. We want to assure you that your husband is fine. On April 25, we regret to say that Richard Herima was killed in action while serving his country, and . . ."

My husband is fine. Sam is fine. I didn't recognize the other name. Wait? What did he say? Who did he say?

The man was still talking, but I hadn't heard anything else he said, due to my heart pounding in my ears and my thoughts racing so frantically.

"Wait. Who did you say was killed?" I blurted out, interrupting the man's rehearsed speech.

Silence for a moment. "Uh . . . Richard Herima," he says, and you can tell he has to go back up to the top of the page to find the name.

"Do you mean Rick *Herrema*?" My heart was in my throat once again as the realization began to dawn on who he was talking about.

"Uh . . . yes, I mean, Herrema. Sorry, I didn't know how it was pronounced."

"But he's on Sam's team! He's new. He is young! He is DEAD?! Are you telling me Rick Herrema is DEAD?! Where is my husband? When did you say this happened? Was Sam with him when he died? Are you sure Samuel Barnett wasn't injured in this incident? Are there other casualties of any kind?"

My questions tumbled out of my mouth as fast as they entered into my head and my heart was flying even more quickly. I was up on my feet pacing the floor nearly screaming into the phone.

The poor man at the other end of the phone was at a loss to know what to say for a moment.

"Mrs. Barnett, I can't answer these questions. I simply don't know. We will update you as soon as we have new information. But I can assure you that your husband is fine."

I knew in my heart that my husband wasn't fine. And I wasn't fine.

In my mind, I could see Rick Herrema standing before me just four weeks earlier, on the last Sunday the guys were home. He was a handsome young man, just twenty-seven years old; he had not yet married. He told Sam he was waiting for God to bring him a wife. I invited him home to have dinner with us after church that Sunday. He said thanks, but he had a roast cooking in his crock-pot at his house. He grinningly told me that he would take me up on the offer of dinner when he got home next time.

As I hung up the phone, I collapsed onto the floor and wept. I wept with relief that Sam was okay. I wept with immense grief, realizing that Rick's family had been notified that he would never return to them. I wept over my own wave of guilt for feeling relief that it was not my husband. And then I was back to crying out why this had to happen to someone so young? To one who clearly loved the Lord and had waited for God to bring him a bride: a bride who now would never appear. Then I was thankful she hadn't, so she wouldn't now be dying inside with him.

My heart broke. And somewhere on the other side of the world, my husband's heart broke as well.

When Sam was finally able to call me the next day, he was so far away. His heart and voice were further than Iraq. He wasn't able to communicate any details to me until he returned home four months later, but Sam had been just eighteen inches from Rick when he had been shot and killed instantly. Sam had to complete the mission leading his team, and then he was determined to get Rick's body out with them on the chopper. He carried the 160-pound body of his friend for over a mile, while both were in full kit.

Rick never came home. And Sam came home forever changed.

War changes men. It changes us. Death is so real. It is so over-whelmingly real sometimes that it chokes you. Three of my dear-est friends have received those calls in the late-night hours, voices informing them that their husbands had been shot. I talked late into the night on the phone with them or left my house and flew to their side to comfort them, as they waited to hear if their man would make it back to the States alive.

Trying to comfort someone who has lost or is facing the poten-tial loss of their loved one is extremely difficult. It causes a range of emotions within all of us: grief, helplessness, anger. Death at any time is difficult, but death in the military comes with a sense of pride and purpose, yet also with a sense of undeniable pain: pain that can bring with it guilt to everyone involved.

It may seem strange to feel guilt over the death of a fallen sol-dier, but it is a feeling Sam and I both have shared in these tragedies. Sam knows he is called to do the work he does, and so he serves in confidence. But when he loses a friend in battle, he is quickly reminded of his own mortality and the reality of how fragile life is. He questions whether he could have done more to help save his friend, and he wrestles with anger at the war in general.

The solid understanding of God's purposes in fighting a war become somewhat hazy when the overwhelming loss of a friend permeates his life and thinking. He feels grief that he lives and an-other man doesn't. He feels guilt that he momentarily questions

God's purposes. Ultimately, he finds his peace by laying all of his feelings before the cross and continuing to walk in obedience to the Lord for the call he feels so strongly on his life.

The magnitude and complexity of emotions that our soldiers face through seeing the atrocities of war and the death of comrades is vast. Ultimately, the only place they will be able to find their peace is at the cross. Jesus alone is big enough to take all that we are and all that we face and make it wholly different.

For me, I feel guilty that I am relieved that it wasn't my husband who died. I am deeply grieved for the loss of the fallen soldier and his family. So once my fear for Sam is assuaged by my relief over his safety, I will then be flooded with guilt at my seemingly inconsiderate selfishness during someone else's most desperate hour of loss. Again, taking these feelings before the cross and laying them there is how I am able to overcome them.

I have attended more funerals than I care to recount. I have taken meals to grieving widows whom I love dearly; some I don't know personally, but someone I know does. I have cried over the loss of men I knew and many I was never privileged to meet, but who died for me none the less. Their death paid for my freedoms in this country.

I know Rick's parents probably struggled with the sacrifice of their son for a nation that would in many ways never acknowledge or appreciate the gravity of the price paid for its freedom. No one would identify with that more than God Almighty, who laid His Son down for all nations, only to be rejected.

It is in these moments that I realize afresh that our soldier's sacrifice is the epitome of Christlikeness. These men truly loved; as Scripture says in John 15:13, "Greater love has no one than this:

to lay down one's life for one's friends." They loved as Christ loved. They laid down their lives to pay for the freedoms of others, regardless of whether those people would ever appreciate it or not. When Christ came He gave all He had to pay for the freedom of all mankind. Freedom from slavery and sin.

CHRIST FACED DEATH

Facing death means facing grief. It means facing suffering, pain, and loss. Most important, facing death means facing fear. I believe that when Jesus was faced with death He felt all of these things. He had known the death of loved ones before He had to face His own crucifixion. We saw Him weep with the loss of Lazarus, even though He knew that God was going to bring Him back to life (John 11). I think Jesus wept not only for His own loss but because He felt great compassion for His friends who were grieving.

I feel like I know that grief. I have never lost my husband to death, yet I have watched others lose theirs. I weep for them and with them. Even when I know the man will be in glory with our Lord, so we have cause to celebrate, I weep. Jesus wept. He knew the pain of watching the suffering of His friends. Death rips a great void of emptiness where once there was fullness of life, and the loss is so gaping and raw when it first occurs that it tears at the hearts of all who witness it.

We know too, that Jesus must have personally experienced the suffering of losing a loved one. Because He gave instructions for John to care for His mother after His death, we know that his earthly father, Joseph, had to have already passed away (John 19:26–27). And He didn't bring him back to life. Jesus knew the pain of losing a man He loved intimately and followed closely. So as he watched His friends suffer the loss of their brother, Lazarus, He understood their grief and in His compassion grieved with them.

We also know that Jesus faced fear when He faced His own death. It is recorded in Matthew chapter 26 that He asked the Father if there was another way for Him to fulfill all that needed to be done for mankind. He asked if the cup of death couldn't be taken from Him three separate times. But in each of those requests, He was willing to surrender His fear and lay it in faith to receive God's will for His life over His own. Are we willing to do that?

Isaiah 53:11–12 says,

> After he has suffered, he will see the light of life and be satisfied; by his knowledge my righteous servant will justify many, and he will bear their iniquities. Therefore I will give him a portion among the great, and he will divide the spoils with the strong, because he poured out his life unto death, and was numbered with the transgressors. For he bore the sin of many, and made intercession for the transgressors.

It is because Jesus had faced death and understood the power it held over us that He was resolved to set us free. He knew the pain. He knew the grief. He knew the fear. But He knew a greater fear . . . the fear of the Lord. He knew the power of almighty God and He knew His purpose was to come and do for us what we were powerless to do for ourselves. His love for you and me was so great that He did not shy away from sin and death's destruction. Instead, He took them on Himself so that we might be set free. And He overcame them! And now we too can overcome!

Christ faced death so that we might join Him in the light of life. He took on all my sin and shame so that I might know the freedom of righteousness and hope. It says in Isaiah 61:1–3 that "He has sent me to bind up the brokenhearted, to proclaim freedom for the captives and release from darkness for the prisoners . . . to comfort all who mourn, and provide for those who grieve in Zion—to bestow on them a crown of beauty instead of ashes, the oil of joy instead of mourning, and a garment of praise instead of a spirit of despair."

Christ knew better than anyone what suffering was. He knew what grief and pain felt like better than anyone who has ever lived on this planet. He faced the fear of death and overcame it. He took on all of our sin and in exchange gave us eternal life, if we but accept His gracious gift (Romans 6:23). He knew we would have to face fear. All men face the fear of death, unless they find their life and courage in the truth. Christ said, "I am the way and the truth and the life. No one comes to the Father except through Me" (John 14:6).

Jesus knew that all mankind was doomed to eternal death and separation from God if He didn't pay the price for our sins and pave a way for our life. He gave up all for you and for me. The price He paid was sufficient for all eternity. For every sin. For every fear. We can rest in knowing that we are carried by our Creator. Each of us was created by our God for a purpose in His kingdom. We can and must learn to rest in the sovereignty of our God and in His infinite wisdom for our lives.

FACING OUR FEAR OF DEATH

Psalm 139 speaks of the Creator handcrafting each of us, and knowing and valuing everything within us. Verse 16 says, "All the days ordained for me were written in Your book before one of them came to be." Job 14:5 says, "A person's days are determined; You have decreed the number of his months and have set limits he cannot exceed."

God knew when He made you how many days you were to serve on this earth. He knows everything before it happens. This knowledge is what the Psalmist says is "too wonderful for me, too lofty for me to attain" (139:6). Psalm 37:23 says, "The Lord makes firm the steps of the one who delights in Him." Philippians 1:6 says that "He who began a good work in you will carry it on to completion until the day of Christ Jesus."

God knows what He is doing with your life. He knows what He is doing with your husband's life. There is nothing that you or your husband will ever face that God didn't know it first and allow it to happen. He has a purpose in all things in our life. Especially the things that cause us to face death. Sin is death. Jesus not only faced sin, He took it on Himself. He stared death in the face and arose victorious. He did that so you and I might be able to overcome the death of sin every day of our lives. He didn't just do it so we can have eternal life in Him after our earthly bodies pass away. He did it so that while we are yet in this flesh on planet Earth, we might know the joy and freedom of life eternal right now!

We can face our own sin of worry and fret and learn to overcome it. We can learn to trust in our God and find peace instead of fear. There was great purpose in Christ's life and in His death. There will be also in the life and death of each of His precious children.

So often we worry about our husband's lives while they are deployed. And I'm not saying I don't know that place of worry. I do. But Matthew 6:27 says, "Can any one of you by worrying add a single hour to your life?" Worrying about our men won't help them. And it most assuredly won't help us. We must learn to trust in our God. We must learn to look beyond the temporal into the eternal.

Romans 8:28 tells us "that in all things God works for the good of those who love Him, who have been called according to His purpose." He doesn't say that all things are good. He doesn't say all things will feel good. He says *in all* things He works for the good of those who love Him and are called by Him for *His* purposes. God has a purpose in our military. He has a purpose in your husband's service there. He has a purpose in you learning to honor and respect the call on your man's life as you learn to love the man as He calls you to do. And if God were to call your husband home and you to walk this life in widowhood, there is good in that purpose too.

But of course there would be pain. And no one knows pain better than Jesus. No one is better acquainted with grief than him. My prayer is that none of you reading this will ever have to face the death of your husband in military service. But I know that each of you will face that fear. And there is pain even in the facing of the fear.

I remember asking God one time out of fear, "What would I do if You took Sam from me?"

And I clearly heard His response, "What *would* you do if I took Sam from you?"

It wasn't what I wanted to hear. But it forced me to face death. To look at the reality that I had no guarantees that Sam would live with me until we were old and gray. No guarantees that he would see our children into adulthood. No promise that either of us would live even one more day. And in facing that truth, I was able to face my fear and realize that no amount of worry would change anything. God has a plan. He will see it carried out. I can either fret, or I can rest in that knowledge.

God spoke to Joshua as he faced the fear of battle. In Joshua 1:6–9 He says,

> Be strong and courageous, because you will lead these people to inherit the land I swore to their ancestors to give them. Be strong and very courageous. Be careful to obey all the law my servant Moses gave you; do not turn from it to the right or to the left, that you may be successful wherever you go. Keep this Book of the Law always on your lips; meditate on it day and night, so that you may be careful to do everything written in it. Then you will be prosperous and successful. Have I not commanded you? Be strong and courageous. Do not be afraid; do not be discouraged, for the Lord your God will be with you wherever you go.

God wouldn't have told Joshua so many times to be strong and courageous unless he was feeling weak and scared. Joshua needed God's encouragement to stay strong in the battles God was calling him to fight. So do we. We must do as Joshua was commanded: meditate on God's Word day and night. It is in His Word that we find truth, and we find our courage and strength when we walk in that truth.

Our God will always be with us no matter what battles we face in the natural or in the spiritual. Learning to trust God with our men on the natural battlefield is a spiritual battle we must fight and win. We must hold fast to the truth of the gospel of Jesus, the finished work of our Lord and Savior on the cross.

Paul urges Timothy to be faithful to the life God has called him to live and to walk not in timidity, but in a spirit of power, of love, and of self-discipline (2 Timothy 1:7). He goes on to say,

> Join with me in suffering for the gospel, by the power of God. He has saved us and called us to a holy life—not because of anything we have done but because of His own purpose and grace. This grace was given us in Christ Jesus before the beginning of time, but it has now been revealed through the appearing of our Savior, Christ Jesus, who has destroyed death and has brought life and immortality to light through the gospel.
>
> —2 Timothy 1:8–10

Death has lost its power and its sting. We no longer have to fear death. And when we face it, we can live with hope and assurance that God holds us and is working out His perfect purposes for our lives. That doesn't mean we have to enjoy it, but it does mean we are free from the fear of it.

God has more for us than just what this flesh can see or do. And He has placed a high value on the lives of His children. He values the lives of you and your husband. Nothing you or your husband will ever walk through is without great worth within the kingdom of God. Nothing your children will have to face is without purpose, either. In Jeremiah 29:11 God says, "For I know the plans I have for you," declares the Lord, "plans to prosper you and not to harm you, plans to give you hope and a future."

God knows each of our lives and ordains each of our days. Trust that He loves you, and even when facing death, He brings light and life to both you and those around you. I pray that you never know the pain of the sacrifice of your husband's life. But for all those who have, and for those who will yet lay their lives down for me and my freedoms in this great nation, I thank them. I thank God for them. I thank God that they were willing to give all they had to follow after the call of God on their lives and to defend their friends. This amazing blessing is one I never want to be complacent in honoring.

I pray that I also rise each new day with the fresh revelation of what my Jesus did for me. And I pray that you too, dear sister, will know the way, the truth, and the life that Jesus has for you as you live out your personal calling in and through Him, no matter where that journey takes you in life or death. And I thank you. Thank you for sharing in the sacrifice of time spent with your men, even if not in death. Thank you for your amazing service to our country. But more importantly, thank you for seeking to honor your God through uplifting your precious husband and valuing his sacrifice for me and my family. I am eternally grateful. And your God is eternally blessed.

CHAPTER 11

THE PAIN OF PORNOGRAPHY AND INFIDELITY

Not that I have already obtained all this, or have already
arrived at my goal, but I press on to take hold of that for which
Christ Jesus took hold of me. Brothers and sisters, I do not
consider myself yet to have taken hold of it. But one thing I do:
Forgetting what is behind and straining toward what is ahead,
I press on toward the goal to win the prize for which God has
called me heavenward in Christ Jesus.

—Philippians 3:12–14

FROM KATHY

Pain is subjective. There is a pain chart at the doctor's office
that ranges from one to ten, with one being no pain and ten being
unbearable pain. When I gave birth to my first few kids, I would
have said childbirth was some of the most intense pain I had

experienced in my life, and I gave the nurse a nine and sometimes a ten on my pain scale rating during labor.

Then one day after I had four children, I was sitting in the ER for several hours agonizingly waiting with a broken arm that was nearly a compound fracture. I decided that was my ten on the pain scale. Childbirth was suddenly downgraded to a seven based on this new level of pain in my life. But I have to tell you that when I gave birth again, I really wondered how I could have downgraded it that much: was there an eleven?

I had a similar experience with pornography and infidelity in my marriage. I once thought that I couldn't know any greater pain than the realization of my husband's addiction to porn. But then I felt the agonizing revelation of infidelity, and suddenly my pain scale shifted.

Dear reader, I don't know the state of your marriage right now. I don't assume to know your level of pain. All I can tell you is that I have known great pain in my own heart and I know Carrie has as well, and I want you to know that I am praying for you as I write these words.

Pain, even seemingly unbearable pain, is almost always survivable. We may not want it to be. We may wish, as I did with that broken arm, that someone would just shoot us and take us out of our misery. I know that when I experienced the sin of infidelity in my marriage, I spiraled into an abyss of darkness. I didn't know where or how I would find the strength to rise up again, and there were moments I just wanted it to take me down to the grave and leave me there.

But that didn't happen. God sent a new dawn. He sent His light into my darkness and with it He sent hope. He sent strength to endure the pain I wanted to escape. He didn't remove the pain. He taught me how to live through it. He helped me to slowly creep forward and crawl toward that light of life. He held me closely as I struggled with the will to press onward. He sent me encouragement through His Word and through His children who had already passed that way and were eager to aid me in my journey back from the abyss. He began to minister to the broken places in my heart, and to reveal to me my own faults and the places where that crushing and destructive sin was not just my husband's, but my own as well.

In many ways, the climbing back up from that pit meant climbing past the layers of the sin in our marriage that had become a grave to us. The further I climbed to the fresh air of truth and freedom in Christ, the further I got from that earthen chasm filled with the suffocating stench of lies and sins that had held us captive. But it was an arduous journey. It was messy. Sometimes as I reached out to take hold of the next handhold, I found myself slipping backward. I had to grasp and fight desperately to hold my ground, to hold onto the progress Sam and I had made in climbing out of the darkness.

There are few things in my life that have caused me such intense pain as sexual sin. I was introduced to pornography at a very early age, so my introduction to sex was one of immense curiosity, but also the sense that this was something hidden; something that must be kept secret. I was enticed by it, yet I also felt guilty, knowing I was interested in something that was clearly not intended for my eyes.

Satan has a way of creeping into our senses and enticing us with the forbidden. The world surrounding us tells us that sex is exciting, mutually physically satisfying every time it is performed, and something to be exposed and exploited (as on a magazine cover). The enemy of our souls tries to keep our focus on the flesh and the things that are appealing and satisfying to the sensual nature within us. 1 John 2:16 says, "For all that is in the world, the lust of the flesh, and the lust of the eyes, and the pride of life, is not of the Father, but is of the world" (KJV).

We are surrounded by the world and all of its offers of satisfaction and happiness. Yet Jesus said that we must be in the world but not of the world (John 17:14–16). He prayed that, while we are seeking to follow Him here, we might be protected from the evil one, Satan, who has always been out to deceive and mislead us, to steal, kill, and destroy. To keep from being ensnared by Satan, we must seek to follow the Word of God and stay close to the commands we find there. Only there will we find the life and protection God has provided for us (John 10:10).

Here's a question for you. When was the last time you went to a lawyer's or doctor's office and saw hard-core porn openly hanging on the wall? Would you find that acceptable? Then why is there such an open acceptance of pornography in the military? After all, being a soldier is as honorable a profession as being a doctor or lawyer or other public servant. Soldiering is often spoken of in Scripture as being honorable, legitimate, and respectable, along with judges, physicians, pastors, farmers, and craftsmen. But of all these honorable professions, only in the military is there a widespread acceptance of pornography. Pornography permeates the military culture. Not only is it openly condoned, it's often even encouraged. Why is pornography considered acceptable for military professionals but not for other professions? Because when our men are overseas for months on end, they can't have sex with their wives, and their flesh longs for satisfaction. And the enemy is always ready and willing to grant his solution to our longing and need for intimacy. But Satan's solutions are deceptive answers for the genuine needs within our flesh and our souls.

Sometimes our enemy's suggested solution to the longing for satisfaction comes in the form of a relationship with someone other than our spouse. Suddenly, the covenant that we once held closely is as distant from our minds as our spouse is across the ocean, and we sink into the deception that someone else will meet our unfulfilled needs. And like all lies of the enemy, once we are caught in his trap, we struggle to find a way to be free again. We struggle to hear truth. We find ourselves being pulled further from the light of love, and soon we find ourselves in a darken place of despair, not even sure how we got there.

We told you early in this book that this calling to be a military wife is a high calling. I know of no other wives who have to endure all that we do to be married to our valiant men. Very few professions call husbands and wives to face the separations we face in deployments and so open us up to the temptations of Satan through our fleshly desires.

We must learn to look past the dark temptations and lies of this world and look to our Almighty God who longs to show you truth in all things. He wants desperately to reveal to you a way to love Him, and through that experience new truths on how to love your husband. God wants to teach you about real intimacy. He wants to uncover His beautiful heart for you and encourage you to trust Him with the unveiling of your own heart to Him. He wants to draw you into an intimacy that is more satisfying than any relationship you have ever known. And in that, He longs to show you a beautiful intimacy with your husband that will reflect His love and life.

I want to encourage you, wherever you may be: God is with you. He is there beside you, sometimes holding you, sometimes prompting you to gain your strength to move forward in spite of the pain. He loves you, and He has so much more waiting for you than you can now see in the dim light of your surroundings. Press forward to take hold of the life and light He is extending to you.

SEXUAL SINS AND THE LAW

To learn the truth about pornography and infidelity and their effects, we must look to the Word of God, our foundation for all truth. It is here we discover God's purposes for sex and the repercussions of misusing this gift of His.

Sex is a gift from God. It was a precious gift given first to Adam and Eve to share in their marriage. God intended marriage to be a beautiful representation of Christ's amazing love for His bride, the Church. Ultimately, marriage, along with sex and the other gifts of intimacy that come with marriage, were designed to parallel His love for the church.

Carrie has already briefly outlined the scriptural boundaries of sex. The list of items that fall under sexual immorality is broad, but the obvious parameters include: adultery, incest, prostitution, homosexuality, and bestiality. The Bible indicates that sex was designed for one man and one woman to be shared within the bounds of marriage. I would like to expound on this somewhat to illuminate not only our boundaries, but also our freedoms.

Most married couples would agree that adultery is not healthy for a marriage, whether they are seeking to follow God's Word or not. Most people don't get married with the idea that someone else will be welcome in their marriage bed. We all desire to be loved and cherished for who we are. This is why we vow to forsake all others and to remain faithful to our spouse.

No woman I know would welcome the knowledge that her husband had taken another woman to his bed. That is adultery. But what does the Bible say about indulging in pornography? Is that adultery? What about emotional relationships between your husband and another woman? Or between you and another man? What if no one climbed out of their marriage bed into someone else's?

As believers, we have to be careful about technicalities, because sometimes they lead us down a slippery slope of justification of sin. Galatians chapter 5 talks about not abusing grace to justify sin. The Pharisees said they were eager to cling to the whole Mosaic law, but their hearts were far from honoring God. Jesus discusses this observance of the spirit of the law versus the letter of the law in Matthew chapter 5, which I discuss below.

Titus 3:3–11 talks about the freedoms we find in the knowledge and salvation of Jesus Christ. The first part speaks of how we once were foolish, and enslaved by the deceptions of passions and pleasures. Once we experience the grace of rebirth and renewal in Christ, though, we are justified and can walk in a new hope, which profits not only ourselves but those around us. But verses 9–11 go on to say that we should, "avoid foolish controversies and genealogies and arguments and quarrels about the law, because these are unprofitable and useless. Warn a divisive person once, and then warn them a second time. After that, have nothing to do with them. You may be sure that such people are warped and sinful; they are self-condemned."

I share these verses with you because I have spoken to people about what the Bible says regarding sex, and occasionally someone will want to debate what the Word says. But if they are merely trying to justify their own sin, then debate is unprofitable and useless; I will not engage in foolish controversies.

Many people say that the Old Testament no longer applies to our lives, because Jesus fulfilled the law and so we are free from it. I understand that Christ came to fulfill the law. The first eight chapters of Romans outline this fully, but consider the opening of chapter 8:

> Therefore, there is now no condemnation for those who are in Christ Jesus, because through Christ Jesus the law of the Spirit who gives life has set you free from the law of sin and death. For what the law was powerless to do because it was weakened by the flesh, God did by sending His own Son in the likeness of sinful flesh to be a sin offering. And so He condemned sin in the flesh, in order that the righteous requirement of the law might be fully met in us, who do not live according to the flesh but according to the Spirit.
>
> —Romans 8:1–4

The law is there to outline sin for us so that we might be made aware of our desperate need of a Savior. The rules within the law are useful to guide and to show us the heart of God's perfection which, without Christ, would be unattainable for us. The law seeks to protect the people of God from themselves and from their own sinfulness. But in so doing, it also shows us the beauty of God's heart for us. He longs to protect our hearts, minds, and bodies from sin.

When God gave the Ten Commandments to Moses, He was summing up the rules He intended for all men to live by, not just the Jews. God wants everyone to know the rules for holy living, rules that will keep us from sin. The over 600 Mosaic or Levitical laws recorded in the first five books of the Old Testament then expound on these commandments. God gave these other rules because He knew that the Israelites would need clarification in some areas. For example, He gave some rules to protect their physical health, such as the rules concerning mildew, outlined in Leviticus 13:47–59. I don't believe these rules were directly related to any type of sin in the Israelites lives. God simply wanted to protect His people from struggling with sickness and unhealthy living. They probably didn't understand the scientific and medical effects of things like mildew and skin infections and how to keep themselves clean and healthy, so God gave them specific rules to protect them. He still does that today.

To debate the validity of the Old Testament rules regarding our modern-day marriages is futile. Are we free from the law? Yes! We are free from the condemnation and uncleanness that filled our lives before Christ! But through the law, we can still see the boundaries that God set up to protect us from sin. For this purpose, knowing the law and the rules is critical to see some of our boundaries more clearly.

To argue over the validity for our lives of any portion of Scripture is foolish. If it weren't important, God would not have put it there for us! So even though we are able to walk in freedom through Christ, we should never throw out the value of knowing and understanding the law and its purposes. For this reason, we will be looking to both the Old and New Testaments for God's thoughts about sex.

People are all sinners, and we are all prone to want our own way instead of God's way. We will even cling to the letter of the law if we can use it to justify our sin. For example, I told my children the other day that they weren't allowed to have any cookies while I left them at home and I ran some errands. I was bringing dinner home, so I didn't want them to spoil their appetites. They were amazingly obedient. They didn't eat any cookies. They ate ice cream!

It is in all of our hearts to find a way to get our own way.

God knew this, so He had Moses record an entire chapter in Leviticus (chapter 18) about unlawful sexual relations. He didn't just rest with Exodus 20:14 in the Ten Commandments, "You shall not commit adultery." Why not? Because He knew that men and women would find a way to justify sin in their lives, if they weren't given specific rules. It wasn't enough for Him to say, "Do not have sexual relations with your father's sister" (verse 12), and "Do not have sexual relations with your mother's sister" (verse 13). Just as with cookies and ice cream, He had to specify in verse 14,

"Do not dishonor your father's brother by approaching his wife to have sexual relations; she is your aunt."

Really? To my mind, the whole aunt thing was already covered in verses 12 and 13. But God knew that someone would say, "Well, He never actually said my uncle's wife was forbidden." Our natures are so like the serpent's! It makes me think of that ancient garden where he questioned Eve, *You must not eat from any tree in the garden?* (Genesis 3:1). He knew full well that only one tree was mentioned. But we often begin to want what we can't have. We begin to wonder about the forbidden fruit within our grasp and think that maybe it's okay to just touch it.

And like Eve with the forbidden fruit, we begin to see that it is pleasing to the eye, and we desire it and what we think it will bring us. But also like Eve, we will be disappointed. We will find only sin and death if we don't adhere to the commands of our God. We must be careful not to try to wiggle out of what we know is not righteous in order to justify something that seems desirable.

Jesus addresses this fact in Matthew chapter 5, with regard to adultery: "You have heard that it was said, 'You shall not commit adultery.' But I tell you that anyone who looks at a woman lustfully has already committed adultery with her in his heart" (verses 27–28).

Jesus brought the revelation of the spirit of the law so that in walking by the Spirit, we could fulfill the letter of the law. He meant that if you are already longing for someone other than your spouse, then your heart has already sinned. You might not have done the deed of actually jumping in the bed with someone else, but you have desired to do so. Therefore, you are an adulterer.

This is much harder than the original law. Jesus doesn't leave any room for us to justify our sin. Jesus summed up the whole law into two statements: Love the Lord your God with all your heart, soul, mind, and strength, and love your neighbor as yourself (Matthew 22:36-40). In all that He did, He purposed to show us that God is after our hearts, above all things. When He has our heart, our actions will naturally follow His ways and laws. In the same way, when we are looking for satisfaction in our sexual desires only from our spouse and we treasure our spouse in our heart, then we are going to naturally want to be faithful to them, both physically and emotionally.

Galatians 5:16–26 expresses this beautifully:

> So I say, walk by the Spirit, and you will not gratify the desires of the flesh. For the flesh desires what is contrary to the Spirit, and the Spirit what is contrary to the flesh. They are in conflict with each other, so that you are not to do whatever you want. But if you are led by the Spirit, you are not under the law.

> The acts of the flesh are obvious: sexual immorality, impurity and debauchery; idolatry and witchcraft; hatred, discord, jealousy, fits of rage, selfish ambition, dissensions, factions and envy; drunkenness, orgies, and the like. I warn you, as I did before, that those who live like this will not inherit the kingdom of God.

> But the fruit of the Spirit is love, joy, peace, forbearance, kindness, goodness, faithfulness, gentleness and self-control. Against such things there is no law. Those who

belong to Christ Jesus have crucified the flesh with its passions and desires. Since we live by the Spirit, let us keep in step with the Spirit. Let us not become conceited, provoking and envying each other.

SEARCHING DEEPER FOR DIRECTION

I love looking at Scripture to discover what God has to tell us. Studying it and digging to see the original meanings in the languages it was written in, Hebrew and Greek, are fascinating to me. I know many of you may not share my fascination, and that's okay. I would like to look at a couple of passages of Scripture and break them down a bit, though, to help us discover some nuggets of truth we might otherwise miss.

The King James Version (KJV) of Galatians 5 verse 19 reads, "Now the works of the flesh are manifest, which are these: adultery, fornication, uncleanness, lasciviousness." The Greek for the word fornication in this passage is *porneia*. The Greek *pornos* is the form used to describe a fornicator, which is defined in *Strong's Exhaustive Concordance* to include adulterer, committer of incest, harlot, whore, male prostitute, indulging in unlawful lust, or practicing idolatry.[5]

Instead of *lasciviousness*, the New International Version there uses the word *debauchery. Debauchery* is defined in the dictionary

---

5 *Strong's Exhaustive Concordance of the Bible* (Nashville, TN: Thomas Nelson, 1990) s.v. "fornicator."

as "1. excessive indulgence in sensual pleasures; intemperance. 2. (Archaic) seduction from duty, allegiance, or virtue."[6]

There are a couple of things I find interesting in looking up all these meanings and definitions. One is that the root for the word *fornication* is the same root from which we get our word for *pornography*. That tells me that if fornication was a sin, then so is the use of pornography, which is in keeping with what Jesus said in Matthew 5.

Some other things that jump out at me from the definitions are that unlawful lust is considered idolatry, and that one definition for *debauchery* is "to be seduced from virtue or duty." We hold to our virtue when we hold to the duty we committed to our spouse in our marriage covenant. We must be very careful not to be seduced from this place of virtue.

As I struggled with sexual sin in our marriage, I needed to know what God said was acceptable and what wasn't. I wanted to believe that Sam's and my love was pure and lovely, because we did love each other so much. But I couldn't trust anything that Sam and I might decide was acceptable. I knew we had clearly violated the statutes of God in our marriage covenant, but I was no longer sure what to believe was pure. We had listened to the world and to the deceptive lies of the enemy for so many years that when we were in that broken, fragile place of rebuilding, I wanted to know without a doubt that we were building fresh on the solid-rock foundation of God's Word and nothing else.

---

6 *Random House Dictionary Online*, 2014, s.v. "debauchery," accessed 21 February 2014, dictionary.reference.com/browse/debauchery?s=t.

The transgressions mentioned in Galatians chapter 5 that people are prone to commit are numerous and all are not sexually related. However, I found when I was processing through the sexual sins in my marriage, I could identify nearly all of them within myself. I wasn't one to drink or engage in orgies, but I recognized that I had made Sam an idol in my life, which I discovered was one of the definitions of fornication. I also found myself jealous, and prone to fits of rage. God graciously and gently pointed out my selfish ambition and hatred that were residing in the depths of my broken, mangled heart.

And He loved me there. He forgave me there. He began to show me that not only did my husband have sin in his life with his addiction to pornography, but that my heart was equally guilty of sin. We both needed forgiveness. First from our God in heaven, and then from and for each other.

If you have identified with any of the sins in this chapter, then I want to encourage you: there is hope. The first step is to admit your own sin and seek forgiveness from your God and from your husband. Perhaps your husband is the one in sin and you aren't sure how he will react to your newfound knowledge. I encourage you to pray for him and seek God in how to proceed in addressing these issues with him.

But whether the sin is your own or your husband's, you will be affected, and your response should be the same either way. Seek forgiveness. Both as it is received from your Lord and from your spouse, and then as it is to be given by you to your spouse. Repentance is the first step toward redemption. After that, you must seek to stay in God's Word and seek godly counsel for the health and healing of your heart and marriage. When we seek our Lord, we will find Him. His love and grace is big enough to help you through this place.

When I was struggling in this place and trying to work through forgiveness of our many sexual sins, I found that staying in God's Word was imperative. Several Bible studies and books helped me overcome my hurts and to seek not only my own forgiveness from God, but to have the grace to extend forgiveness to my husband. Beth Moore's *Breaking Free*[7] was invaluable in helping me find my liberty and forgiveness during my season of searching. I also sought godly counsel from some amazing women during those years of rebuilding. Counsel founded on the Word of God is the only counsel that will bring godly change.

EFFECTS OF PORNOGRAPHY

Pornography has far-reaching ramifications in the hearts and minds of all those whose lives are touched by it, because it affects the intimacy of our relationships. Sex is a gift from God to be shared within the bounds of marriage. Unlike mandatory physical needs such as food, water, and sleep, sex is not an essential part of life; we don't have to have it to survive. Sex is a gift, however, that helps us to meet another essential need within the human soul. The need for intimacy is hardwired into the very hearts of all men and women, and this need must be met in order for us to not only survive uncrippled emotionally, but also to thrive. Ultimately, the deepest intimacy that anyone can ever experience

---

7 Beth Moore, *Breaking Free* (Nashville: LifeWay, 2009).

isn't of a fleshly nature at all. It is the intimacy we share with our God Himself. No other relationship can come close to the intimacy and fulfillment we find with Him alone. And God will not share His place within our lives with anything or anyone else. He must be solely first.

But God orchestrated marriage to be a reflection of His love and relationship with us. So He wanted to give us an intimacy that would not compare to any other and that was to be kept solely for the pleasure and passion between husband and wife. And so He gave us the gift of sex.

Whenever we choose to place anything above our relationship with God, we have created an idol. We have chosen to engage in loving something else: something that is far inferior to the one true God. Nothing could ever compare to His glory and grace in our lives, and no one could ever compare in their ability to pour out a lasting, genuine love, as He does. Yet we can be deceived into thinking we can find satisfaction and fulfillment with something less than Him—but that idol will always leave us feeling empty and used.

Pornography is like this. It is a far inferior imitation of the genuine gratification and fulfillment we can find through sex within the healthy bonds of marriage. Sex was designed to bring about a physical, mental, and spiritual connection between a man and woman, a connection that would bind them closer to each other than to anyone else on this earth. It was never meant to be used selfishly just for the physical gratification it would bring. And although sex involves the flesh, it also has major mental and physiological effects.

Neurons in the brain are stimulated by thoughts of sexual activity and intimacy, and when a person reaches orgasm during intercourse, chemicals are released in the brain that give the person a natural high, similar to a drug-induced high. Because it brings us pleasure, we want to repeat this feeling. So you should definitely desire to engage in sex within your marriage. Just as a person who has experienced a pleasurable and addictive drug will long for their next hit, a person who has experienced sex will long for their next encounter. This is one reason the Bible says in Song of Songs not to awaken love too soon, meaning don't awaken your sexual longings too early in life or you will be prone to want to satisfy them prematurely. You would put yourself in danger of falling from righteousness prior to marriage, due to the desire to satisfy your flesh. This is why we should withhold sex from our lives until we are married. Then we are free to fulfill our longings without any fear of sin.

Also, the brain was designed by God to remember things. When we are learning anything in life, our brain creates pathways within itself to help us remember. This is why it becomes easier and easier to do things when rehearsed over time, such as tying your shoe without thinking about it, or being able to recognize the word *the* without having to actually read it anymore. This is also why it is hard to unlearn something if you have learned it wrong.

Our brains can be trained to achieve sexual stimulation and satisfaction through the use of pornography and masturbation. The longer it is done that way, though, the more difficult it is to correct our brains and retrain them to find stimulation and satisfaction through the means God intended, our spouse. Our minds and bodies will long to re-encounter the pleasurable chemical and physical release within our brains and flesh in the same way we originally learned and practiced it.

Within the bounds of marriage, there is no problem. A husband and wife mutually long to be together and enjoy one another, and there is nothing wrong, and everything right, with that. God designed us to want that! He wants you to want to have sex with your husband. He wants you to long for him. Just as He designed us to want to long for Him.

But what about when the sexual gratification comes through the use of pornography? Then the person who chooses to find their high alone will distance themselves from the one they should be sharing it with. They have lusted after someone other than their spouse, and are guilty of sharing this special gift with another, which is why Jesus said it is in fact adultery. They have taken the intimacy of sex outside their marriage bed and used it for themselves alone, leaving their spouse out of their experience and choosing to engage in selfish gratification rather than mutual edification.

Some people argue that pornography isn't wrong if the husband and wife choose to both use it in their bed as a couple. That is not true. Jesus said that to look on anyone other than your spouse with lust is adultery. Inviting anyone into your bed, whether they are in person or in a picture, is still committing adultery. You have elevated your personal satisfaction above the desire to press into intimacy with the person you are with. It is sin.

Remember when I said we are in a dangerous place when we try to justify our behaviors with the letter of the law? We have to be very careful with sexual activities, to make sure we are choosing to honor both our marriage covenant and our God, who so blessed us with it. God meant for sex to be a great blessing in our lives, but when we engage in our sexual gratification outside our marriage bed, we are left feeling hollow and used.

BENEFITS OF SEXUAL INTIMACY

What is intimacy within marriage and Christ's intimacy with the Church intended to accomplish? How does sexual intimacy with our husbands parallel the relationship we as the Bride Church have to our Bridegroom, Christ? I found myself asking these questions as I was seeking the Lord for His direction in my marriage and trying to find healing from the wounds of our sins. As I was praying and searching the Scriptures, I found several benefits to sexual intimacy that mirrored our relationship as the Bride Church to our Bridegroom Christ.

The first of the benefits of sexual intimacy is procreation. When God first gave sex to Adam and Eve in Genesis 2:24–25, He said they would become one flesh and would feel no shame in that place. God commanded them to be fruitful and multiply (Genesis 1:28). God also spoke this to Noah in Genesis 9:1 and again in verse 7.

When we become intimate in marriage, one of the results can be children. This means we have people born out of that relationship whom we are to love, train, nurture, and point to God. Similarly, when we grow more intimate with Christ, the natural byproduct is to grow the Kingdom family of God. When the Church presses into Christ, others are drawn into that life and we are to love, train, nurture, and point them to God.

The second thing I discovered was that God created and blessed us with sex for recreation. This was a freeing discovery, because I was struggling with feeling as though any pleasure found in sex was somehow sinful, because of the many sexual sins we had fallen into. These doubts created an almost prudish reaction within me, which was just another snare from the enemy to keep me from intimacy with my husband. The enemy also tells us that sex is for recreation, but when done his way it will never satisfy our needs for intimacy. It was very healing and freeing to me to see the beauty and joy that God designed for a healthy sex life to bring to a marriage. In Proverbs 5:15–19 the Lord says,

> Drink waters out of thine own cistern, and running waters out of thine own well. Let thy fountains be dispersed abroad, and rivers of waters in the streets. Let them be only thine own, and not strangers' with thee. Let thy fountain be blessed: and rejoice with the wife of thy youth. Let her be as the loving hind and pleasant roe; let her breasts satisfy thee at all times; and be thou ravished always with her love. (KJV)

In Genesis 26, we see the story of Isaac and Rebekah in the palace of Abimelech, king of the Philistines. The king looks out his window and sees Isaac caressing his wife. I love the KJV, which says he looked out and saw them *sporting* on the lawn below. This to me sounds like they were playfully enjoying one another as one would enjoy playing a game!

Do we enjoy our marriage bed? God intends us to enjoy it. When we begin to look past the world and the imitations it offers, we can begin to find freedom from shame and guilt. Our

Christian liberty allows our marriage to be passionate, exciting, fun, and fulfilling.

God gave us an entire book in the Bible devoted to showing the beauty of marital intimacy and the joys found through sexual intercourse. Song of Songs is filled with gorgeous passages showing us the freedoms we are meant to enjoy in our marriage beds.

When it speaks of milk, honey, honeycomb, and wine, it is referring to deep kisses. Do you kiss your spouse passionately anymore? Do you remember when your husband's kiss was the thing you longed for most? And what of our Lord? Have you ever longed for the deep things in Him? When I am in worship, I feel the kisses of my Lord, and I long to go deeper. Have you longed for more in His presence? Kisses are an intimate picture of our Lord drawing us face to face and meeting us there with nothing else between us.

When you see the passages in Song of Songs referring to myrrh, spices, a garden, and a well, you are looking at the beauty of how God made a woman able to open herself up to receive her husband. Practically speaking, it is her opening her legs. But do we fully open ourselves to our husbands? Do we open our hearts as well as our physical bodies during sex? God wants you to find forgiveness, trust, and freedom to enable full access of your heart as well as your body to your husband.

Are we open to our Lord? Do we lay ourselves out before Him, totally naked and unashamed, and allow Him into the most intimate places of our lives that we have for so long hidden in darkness with shame and guilt? He loves you very much and wants so desperately to love you there. To hold you there. To touch not your body, but your heart and your soul. He longs to be drawn into you. But you must open yourself to Him. Just as you must open your physical self to receive your husband, you must open your spirit to receive your God. There is love in that intimacy that cannot be matched by anyone else. And there is joy and fulfillment unlike anything you will ever experience elsewhere.

In reality, until we learn to open ourselves up to our God, we can't truly open ourselves up to our husbands. God's relationship with you must be the most important in your life. When you place Him first in your intimacy, He gives you the grace you need to extend and receive the intimacy you long for with your husband. This is true especially when there is the pain of betrayal in a marriage. God's eternal faithfulness is the place where we find our fulfillment and our value as a woman. It is only when we trust ourselves to be loved by Him that we can begin to trust our hearts to others.

Song of Songs 7:10–13 shows a couple making love in a vineyard. The woman actually dances before her husband. This is not a prudish relationship! This is a couple that can be naked and not ashamed before one another. This is a couple that is not afraid of being exposed to the light of day and to one another. They are clearly enjoying bringing pleasure to one another. God made our bodies so that we could be captivated and blessed by the sharing of them with our spouse. He means for us to be unashamed both before our husbands and before Him.

There is great freedom within scriptural guidelines for us to enjoy our spouse in our marriage bed. In fact, if you can't find a clear command forbidding something, then it is okay for you and your spouse to prayerfully consider the benefits of some act within your bed that would be mutually acceptable and pleasurable. I say this because when you start searching for answers about things like oral sex, anal sex, sexual toys (such as vibrators), and cybersex during times of separation (with your own spouse only or it would be adultery), you won't find a whole lot of Scriptures referencing these issues directly. But remember, we are free from the Mosaic law through Christ. How much liberty you personally have is between you, your God, and your husband. In all that you do, you should purpose to walk with a clean conscience before your God.

Paul references this concept in Romans 14. He talks about how all food is clean to eat because we are all free in Christ. The Jewish Mosaic law had strictly limited the foods that were considered clean for the Israelites. This is exactly what Christ came to set us free from. But Paul said that just because you may have found freedom in this area, you should be very careful not to cause someone else to stumble because of your freedoms, if they personally haven't found that freedom in their own life yet. He says in verses 14–15, "But if anyone regards something as unclean, then for that person it is unclean. If your brother or sister is distressed because of what you eat, you are no longer acting in love."

If one of you feels that something is fine with their conscience but the other does not, then it is better to put love ahead of personal satisfaction. Your marriage bed should be a place where you both mutually agree to the things your consciences are clear with before the Lord. I encourage you to seek the Lord's thoughts to find your freedoms, and prayerfully lay your decisions before your husband. I pray that you are both mutually benefited and blessed by the joy and peace you find.

If there has been sexual abuse of any sort in your life, then your heart and your willingness to participate in certain things may be inhibited. For this I would encourage you to stay near to the heart of your God. He longs to bring you freedom not just sexually so that you will know greater freedom in intimacy with your husband, but also within your mind and heart—which are no doubt damaged and in need of healing—so that you can be drawn into greater intimacy with your loving Heavenly Father.

How willing are we to bring not only our sins before our God, but the most intimate parts of our hearts, the things we have kept hidden in the darkness of night, beneath covers of shame? How willing are we to expose ourselves to this God who longs to meet us there? Are you willing to begin to trust that there is a God who will never leave you nor forsake you and who is big enough to heal your pain? When we are washed by the blood of Christ, we are clean. Christ calls us to walk in the light of life. We are called to life, and life abundant! When you can begin to believe this, you are well on your way to finding joy in life, and hopefully joy in your marriage bed.

This brings me to the next benefit of sexual intimacy in our marriages. In addition to procreation and recreation, sex also was meant to bring comfort to married couples, as well as a way to relieve stress. Remember, when sexual orgasm is reached, there are chemicals released in the brain that not only bring pleasure, but also can bring an immediate release of stress, which can cause a more restful sleep immediately following.

In Genesis 24:67, we are told that Isaac married Rebekah and took her to his bed and was comforted over the death of his mother. In 2 Samuel 12:24–25, David is recorded as having gone to comfort Bathsheeba through joining her in their marriage bed after the death of their child. It was through this encounter that God sent Solomon, whom He named Jedidiah, which means sent and loved by God.

Not only was sex designed to bring comfort through a physical chemical release in the body, but also through the emotional connection of intimacy that brings comfort to the mind and heart. When we are intimate with the Lord, there is evidence of the fruits of the Spirit, as seen in Galatians chapter 5: love, joy, peace, etc. And the Holy Spirit is referred to as the *Comforter* (John 14:16, 26, 15:26, 16:7 KJV). God intended for you to find comfort in your marriage through the intimacy of sex with your husband just as He intends to bring you comfort through intimacy with His Spirit.

This can be hard to accept if you are feeling betrayed due to pornography or infidelity in your marriage. The one thing you may *not* want to do to seek comfort is to have sex with your husband. But I encourage you to press into the heart of God and to remember that this dark place will get lighter, and that with forgiveness and time, you can find great comfort in your bed again. And often, this is the place your husband may most need to know he is forgiven. To withhold intimacy here may do more damage to him and do little to help you recover. Remember that during a season of rebuilding, you must both remember to deal gently with one another's hearts and try to act unselfishly, with God's help and guidance.

The final blessing that sexual intimacy brings into our lives is that it is a means of avoiding temptation from the enemy and maintaining righteousness. 1 Corinthians 7:2–5 says,

> But since sexual immorality is occurring, each man should have sexual relations with his own wife, and each woman with her own husband. The husband should fulfill his marital duty to his wife, and likewise the wife to her husband. The wife does not have authority over her own body but yields it to her husband. In the same way, the husband does not have authority over his own body but yields it to his wife. Do not deprive each other except perhaps by mutual consent and for a time, so that you may devote yourselves to prayer. Then come together again so that Satan will not tempt you because of your lack of self-control.

When we don't have sex frequently, we are prone to temptation by the enemy. This is why I would argue that being a spouse in the military with frequent deployments makes our marriage trials harder than the trials of most other marriages. It is a whole lot easier to fight temptations from the enemy when we are finding sexual satisfaction within our marriage beds. But that is hard to do if you are separated by an ocean for months on end.

Just because we are called to face these difficulties does not allow us to justify breaking the commands of God and our marriage covenant. This is why our understanding and embracing of such a high call means that we must embrace Christ in order to find success. We lack the self-control, as Paul said above. But he also said later, in Galatians 5, that when we choose to walk by the

Spirit and not by the flesh, we will bear fruit and be able to accomplish that which we could not do on our own. Self-control is the final fruit in that list of the fruits of the Spirit. It begins with love. If we are to finally bear the fruit of self-control, we must first begin the cultivation of love, joy, and peace in our spirits.

Song of Songs 2:14–15 says: "My dove in the clefts of the rock, in the hiding places on the mountainside, show me your face, let me hear your voice; for your voice is sweet, and your face is lovely. Catch for us the foxes, the little foxes that ruin the vineyards, our vineyards that are in bloom."

There are foxes that will slip in and destroy your vineyard if you don't go there regularly to tend to and protect the good fruit there. Your marriage bed is a place where you plant seeds of truth and cultivate godly fruit. The enemy is out to steal, kill, and destroy all that you work to produce. By going to your bed regularly, you are able to keep the enemy out. That place of intimacy offers protection "in the cleft of the rock," and there is a shield of protection in the hiding places of the mountain where you go to meet your husband intimately, face to face.

Exodus 33:22 describes God hiding Moses in the cleft of the rock when they were in their most intimate place. God revealed Himself to Moses and yet protected him at the same time. We must do this in our marriages. We must begin to reveal ourselves and protect one another. Guard your marriage and all that it holds, both inside and outside the bedroom.

BECOMING AN OVERCOMER

While you are struggling with overcoming places of pain and hardship in your marriage, you must remember the value of spiritually covering one another. I'm not talking about covering up sin. Sin must be brought into the light if we are to be set free from it. I am talking about covering the heart of your man.

Proverbs 17:9 says, "Whoever would foster love covers over an offense, but whoever repeats the matter separates close friends." This means that you should be extremely careful whom you choose to share your marital struggles with. You will cause further separation between you and your husband if you are not wise in where you seek counsel and encouragement. Also, 1 Peter 4:8 says that "love covers a multitude of sins."

We must maintain righteousness when we are struggling in our marriages. We must remember to keep no record of wrongs (1 Corinthians 13:5). I know that is difficult if you are trying to overcome the pain of pornography or you are trying to recover from the knowledge of infidelity. We have to stop playing the broken record in our brains that tells us we aren't worthy, or replaying some painful image or hurtful conversation with our husbands. We have to learn to lay down our pain and hurt before the cross.

As we said earlier, the renewing of your mind comes through the watering of God's Word. God alone can heal you. He graciously heals through His truth and through the gift of time. Time will heal wounds in our hearts just as it heals flesh wounds. But just as a wound must be cleaned, so must God cleanse our wounds with truth to remove the infection of lies that would seek to kill us. And just as a wound needs the covering of a bandage, so do our hearts need the covering of love. We must have grace in the tender, raw places of our hearts when we are wounded. We must learn to forgive.

When pornography or adultery has entered into a marriage, it can cause one to feel violated and betrayed. Both spouses can feel a range of emotions, including: anger, fear, shame, guilt, worthlessness, and hopelessness. I know both Sam and I felt unclean. The world and the deception of the enemy told us that sex was for recreation and for personal pleasure.

One thing you must know is that Satan can't think of anything original in his own mind. He can only copy from the things of God. Then he twists them and tries to take credit for them. And because he steals from God, there is always an element of truth and beauty in everything he presents. It will be appealing and attractive. He simply perverts the pure things of God into a twisted, inferior imitation. Satan makes everything selfish because that is all he knows. Everything he offers will cause you to satisfy the longings within you by selfish means. But God designed us to be satisfied only when we can learn to be selfless. And He designed us to be truly satisfied sexually when we can enjoy sex selflessly within the bounds of marriage.

God meant for sex to be satisfying. He meant for it to be pleasurable. He meant for it to be a way to connect with your spouse, to become so close that you are no longer two separate people but one flesh. Ultimately, God wants us to be able to become so unselfish within the church that we can share one heart and one mind, as it says in Acts 4:32. My husband and I were so separated in our hearts due to the painful destruction of our marriage that was caused by our sexual sins, that during the rebuilding we struggled to feel even a tiny bit of unity in our hearts and minds. Our flesh was one, but sometimes even the physical gratification we would find in our bed felt selfish to me, because that was sometimes all the fulfillment I took from it.

As a woman, I wanted desperately to connect and feel secure satisfaction with Sam on an emotional level. Sam's needs were somewhat different. He and I both had to rebuild trust with one another, but for Sam, the moment he was able to confess his sin to me and to God he felt clean. There is freedom in the cleansing blood of the Lamb. Praise God! But Sam had no idea how to heal my heart and reassure me that his repentance was real, nor did he know how to trust me with his heart.

I knew we were forgiven for our sin, but I still felt dirty. I felt like sex was dirty. I felt like every time my husband desired me physically he was just trying to satisfy his flesh, and that seemed so unspiritual to me that I almost didn't want it. I wanted more than physical gratification. I longed for my heart to feel satisfied. I didn't understand much of what I've just shared with you. It was only as I learned what God's truth was about sex, instead of what I had been taught by a dying world, that I was able to transform much of my thinking.

I also struggled with my worth and my beauty. I believed that if I were prettier or thinner Sam wouldn't have gone elsewhere. If I were smarter or more exciting in bed perhaps I could have kept him entertained enough to not want to stray. So I struggled with trying to perform for Sam in bed. But that wasn't real. I was motivated out of my fear, not my desire to meet Sam's needs and have my own met. It was still selfish on my part because I was trying to hold onto Sam, keeping him in a place of idolatry in my heart. God had to show me my sinful motivation and again help me to renew my mind with truth.

1 John 1:9 says, "If we confess our sins, He is faithful and just and will forgive us our sins and purify us from all unrighteousness." That means that when you are washed by the blood, you are made clean. I had to continually stay in the Word to fight off the lies that the enemy would whisper that I wasn't enough for my husband. The lies that I was still dirty, that my sin would always be with me. I would cling to Romans 8:1–2, which says, "Therefore, there is now *no condemnation* for those who are in Christ Jesus, because through Christ Jesus the law of the Spirit who gives life has set you free from the law of sin and death" [emphasis my own].

Psalm 103 is probably one of my favorite Psalms. I encourage you to read it through completely. Verses 10–12 read, "He does not treat us as our sins deserve or repay us according to our iniquities. For as high as the heavens are above the earth, so great is His love for those who fear Him; as far as the east is from the west, so far has He removed our transgressions from us."

I love that. I love knowing that He has forgiven me. And from that place of forgiveness, I can find the strength to forgive my husband when he has hurt me. I will choose not to repay him according to his iniquities, because God did no less for me. And in that place of forgiveness, I find freedom.

As I purposed in my heart to seek God for help in my marriage, I found that not only the sins committed within my marriage needed healing. I found there were places in my heart from my past that also needed healing. Some of you reading this will have to face deep places of hurt concerning sexual sin in your lives. Some may have suffered sexual abuse, rape, or an abortion. All of these will cause gaping wounds that need much healing and counsel. Until you begin to find healing in these places, they will affect your marriage, even if the sin wasn't directly related to your spouse.

The same is true for the hurts within your husband. Carrie will address how to deal with their hurting souls in the next chapter. We strongly encourage you to seek solid godly counsel. Look for those Christian sisters who can hold your hand and help lead you out of the dark pit you may need to climb out of. I thank God for the faithfulness of His Word, and the love of His children He has sent to me in my life to help guide me into His truth and freedom. He longs to lead you there as well.

I also offer a caution. We must be very careful about establishing relationships with other men, Christian or not. If you are seeking counsel with a male counselor or pastor, you should always have a woman there when you are talking to them. Even if you are just going to speak briefly in the church foyer. Always choose to err on the side of being overprotective with your marriage and safeguarding your intimate relationship with your husband. Most acts of infidelity do not occur because someone is looking to have an affair. They happen because they begin to share a part of their heart with someone other than their spouse. When we share the intimate places of our heart with someone else, especially when that person is giving us comfort, we risk becoming too emotionally involved with them.

There are signs when infidelity occurs. I don't believe a woman who says she had no idea it was coming. There are always warnings if we look for them. I don't say that to frighten anyone reading this, or to say that if you see weaknesses in the following safeguards in your marriage that you should automatically assume your husband is having an affair. But I would suggest that if you do see some of the following signs, you are possibly disregarding the value of your marriage and you aren't investing enough energy to protect it. Don't ever grow complacent in the precious relationship you share with your husband.

1. Is your normal sex life as frequent or fulfilling as it has been in the past?

Now let me add conditions to that. In the first few weeks after having a baby, during deployments, or seasons of extreme duress or health issues, your sex life is going to be affected. But examine how much time and energy is being invested in your bedroom. Being busy with raising kids and living life is not an excuse to place sex on the back burner. I have nine children and my life is always full and exhausting. But, clearly, from the sheer number of children I have, you can see that I did not stop having sex because I was tired!

I have purposed in my life to put my God first and my husband second. That means my children, friends, and ministries will sometimes have to wait while I meet needs within my marriage. Making time to ensure I have the energy to give to my husband at the end of the day is important to the health of our marriage. I often say no to other things so I can have the strength and longing to enjoy my husband in our marriage bed at the end of the day. When I realized the value of that and the blessing it was to my husband, I began to reap bountiful blessings within my marriage. My husband was eager to give me his energy in other areas of our life outside the bedroom when his longings within the bedroom were met.

I'm not saying you should have more frequent sex out of fear that you will lose your husband. I do recommend that you focus your energy with purpose. The enemy is looking to gain a foothold in your marriage anywhere he can. Don't give him any room in your bedroom. Keep your man wanting to come home. Don't ever give him a reason to want or need any of his physical or emotional needs to be met somewhere else.

2. Do you spend your leisure time together or largely apart?

This is a particularly difficult one for me. Sam likes to do things I don't like to do. For instance, he loves to ride road bikes. He wanted to include me in his passion and he bought me a $700 bike with all the accoutrements to go with it. I hated it. I tried, but riding twenty-five miles at 20+ miles an hour is not enjoyable to me. I like jogging, but he doesn't like that. We've recently started taking a walk together a couple of times a week. We just walk for a couple of miles, but it is wonderful. We get to talk and communicate without the children with us.

If you don't enjoy the same things as your husband, don't use that as an excuse to not spend any of your leisure time together. There had to have been something you liked doing together when you were dating, or you wouldn't have wanted to marry. Find those things again. Begin to date one another again. Keep looking until you find something you both like. It could be doing yard work, playing Scrabble, or riding motorcycles! But keep searching until you find something! Sharing your time outside the bedroom is healthy, and it promotes better communication and more satisfaction in your relationship.

3. How many of your emotional needs are being fulfilled by your spouse?

This one is perhaps a little harder to immediately answer. When I was struggling with Sam, I wasn't drawn into infidelity because I wanted an affair. I just found a person who spoke into my life in the ways I best receive love. You may recall that I love words of affirmation. When Sam wasn't meeting my needs in this way and someone else stepped up to affirm me, I was drawn to share my heart with that other person.

God showed me other unhealthy ways I was filling my emotional needs. One was watching romantic movies. I would get my "feel good" from a chick flick. Another was from reading a lot of Christian romance novels. Now there is nothing wrong with watching a discreet PG-rated movie or reading Christian romance novels. I happen to love reading, and I think my coauthor has written some of the best on the market. But during the time I was trying to love my husband with all of our weakness and failings, I was doing him a serious disservice by continually comparing him to a fictional character—one who always seemed to say the right thing and stroke the heart of his heroine perfectly. Most fiction romance novels are written by women, so they know what women want to hear. But my poor man usually didn't know what to say. By watching those movies and reading the books, I was always setting him up for failure, because he wasn't saying what I had scripted in my head that he should say to me! So I would encourage you: if you are finding your intimacy fulfilled between the pages of a book other than the Bible, put it down and seek the fulfillment between the sheets of your bed!

We also must be extremely careful with social networking. Many people share their lives online and seem eager to share in your life, but it's often superficial and can even tend toward gossip. I always discourage much social networking for people who are working on their marriage. If you are struggling with your primary relationship, why would you invest time and energy in countless other people? You don't have it to spare. Their opinions shouldn't come anywhere close to mattering as much as your husband's, and they don't need to know the intimate details of your marriage, anyway.

4. Do you or your husband have a friend or co-worker of the opposite sex who you talk to frequently? How often without others around?

I can't stress enough the importance of guarding your conversations with other men, especially when you are sharing anything emotional. And joking around with witty comments is emotional. It creates a sense of joy and laughter that perhaps you haven't experienced within your marriage for some time. You must guard your emotions on every level and guard your conversations with everyone other than your husband. For those of you who work with men, you must be diligent to protect your marriage by keeping yourself and your heart only for your husband.

If your husband works with women and this is a particular sticking point for you, then you need to work extra hard at creating those boundaries. Perhaps your husband sees no need for that and so doesn't share your eagerness to create those boundaries. I would encourage you to pray frequently a hedge of protection over your husband's eyes, ears, and heart. I would also encourage you to work hard at meeting his needs at home, so he has no need or excuse to go looking elsewhere to have them met.

5. Do you have complete access to each other's passwords and accounts for all things financial, as well as communication outlets (email, phones, social networking)?

If your husband has a phone or computer that you don't have access to, then you need to gain access to them. If he tells you that he can't let you have access because it has to do with his job, you need to exercise caution to determine if he is trying to hide something from you. But if the equipment from his job is unsecure enough to be carried from his military office into his car or home, then it isn't high security, and his job isn't that secret. Why would he need to keep that secret from you, his wife?

I can tell you that my husband has an extremely high security clearance. Very few ever work where my husband works. He has held positions that required him to know government secrets and military dealings that most people do not know. I'm not trying to make him out to be James Bond, but the things he did were not what the typical soldier engages in. I say all of this to say that there were many things my husband had to have access to that I could never see. But as much as he was able, that man shared everything with me. He trusted me to keep the information safe, and I trusted him to keep my heart safe. There is very little or nothing that your husband should have to keep secret from you.

After we dealt with secrets in our marriage that had caused us pain, I struggled knowing that Sam worked in a place that would be off limits to me on many levels. But Sam worked very hard to keep every area of his life open for me to see. He has had an email and phone that I didn't have access to, but they couldn't be reached except behind the walls of the compound in which he worked. The places where I couldn't go and the experiences he would have that I couldn't share, I had to learn to trust God with. That usually looked like me learning to trust my husband. Remember, God uses our marriages to mirror our relationship with him.

You also need to look at your own choices. Are there things you are keeping from your husband? I submit to you that if your husband doesn't have full access to all your accounts and passwords, you are withholding places of intimacy from him. You should purpose to stay open with your husband in all areas, even if they seem insignificant.

6. Can you account for each other's whereabouts on most days?

Obviously, during deployments this will be nearly impossible for you to know. I often only had a vague idea of my husband's whereabouts. I usually knew the country, and sometimes a city, but I never knew where he was staying or how he spent his days.

But when he is home, do you know that if you showed up at his work he would be there? Or more importantly, does he know where you are spending your time? I knew a woman who would spend hours shopping and never told her husband. She had an addiction to spending money. She didn't want him to know, so she didn't tell him. She even went so far as to secretly take out credit cards in his name so that he wouldn't know how much money she had spent. She ended up spending them into bankruptcy, and the man claimed he never saw it coming. My question to him would have been, was he watching for the signs I've just given you? There were many secrets, but few safeguards in that marriage.

Some of you reading this are on the brink of divorce. Many of you just read Carrie's chapter and you understand your biblical grounds for divorce, but you aren't sure if you should stay or leave. Some may be wondering if you have grounds for divorce because of your husband's repeated use of porn and his unwillingness to stop. Yes, you do have grounds. The Word makes it clear that the use of pornography is the same as adultery, and adultery is grounds for divorce.

But that doesn't mean you should get a divorce. Only you can stand before God Almighty and know what you are supposed to do. But I can tell you this: you can live with far less on your own than you can live with Christ by your side. If you have never surrendered your heart to Christ before now, or there are areas in your marriage that you have withheld from the touch of Christ, I implore you to hand them to your Lord today. I encourage you to try trusting God in places where you can't trust your husband. Begin to try to love your husband despite his sin. Remember, this is where Christ loves you.

Fighting *for* your husband can look like *fighting* your husband. But it shouldn't look like that. Fighting for your husband means dying to your wants and desires. It means facing pain and death, and through forgiveness in Christ, being able to see hope and life.

If your husband struggles with porn, but he loves you very much and wants to be in your marriage, then dear sister, I encourage you to try. If there has been infidelity but there is repentance, then I implore you to try. I encourage you to press into your man and find intimacy there. I encourage you to press into your Jesus for all the places in your heart that your husband can't fill—and perhaps isn't even supposed to fill.

I'm not saying you should condone his sin, but if he loves you and is willing to try, then I ask you—Jesus asks you—to seek peace and forgiveness before you seek divorce. Your willingness to love him as God loves you will show him Christ and could be the very thing that draws him into salvation and freedom from his sin.

Proverbs 30:21–23 says, "Under three things the earth quakes, and under four, it cannot bear up: under a slave when he becomes king, and a fool when he is satisfied with food, under an unloved woman when she gets a husband, and a maidservant when she supplants her mistress" (NASV). Each of these four people is someone who is in a position of submission and is suddenly uncovered by their authority, or displaces that authority without having the ability or anointing to properly fulfill the required duties of the position. A married woman who is unloved causes the earth to tremble. God never intended for you to be unloved by your husband. He knew that without the love of your husband, the needs of your heart would not be met and your world would not only tremble, but no longer bear up.

Isaiah 54:4–8 often spoke to me when I felt unloved and not covered by my husband.

> Do not be afraid; you will not be put to shame. Do not fear disgrace; you will not be humiliated. You will forget

the shame of your youth and remember no more the reproach of your widowhood.

For your Maker is your husband—the Lord Almighty is his name—the Holy One of Israel is your Redeemer; He is called the God of all the earth. The Lord will call you back as if you were a wife deserted and distressed in spirit—a wife who married young, only to be rejected," says your God.

"For a brief moment I abandoned you, but with deep compassion I will bring you back. In a surge of anger I hid my face from you for a moment, but with everlasting kindness I will have compassion on you," says the Lord your Redeemer.

I pray that you are not an unloved wife. I pray that your husband loves you. Even if you are both broken and unsure of how to climb out of the darkness you now find yourself in, I pray that you are loved by your man. Whether you are or not, there is a Man who will never leave you or forsake you. There is a Man who wants to speak to the places of hurt in your heart and breathe life into both you and your husband. I pray that you both meet this Man, Jesus, and that you can come to find the peace and redemption that only His love and kindness can bring you. No other place of intimacy will ever fulfill you like knowing Him. Seek Him today, dear sister. Let Him begin to lead you out of your painful pit of darkness and into the everlasting light of truth and forgiveness.

CHAPTER 12

LIVING WITH A WOUNDED SOUL

To have and to hold, from this day forward, for better or for worse, for richer or for poorer, in sickness and in health, to love and to cherish, till death do us part.
—Traditional Wedding Vows

Therefore we do not lose heart. Though outwardly we are wasting away, yet inwardly we are being renewed day by day. For our light and momentary troubles are achieving for us an eternal glory that far outweighs them all. So we fix our eyes not on what is seen, but on what is unseen, since what is seen is temporary, but what is unseen is eternal.
—2 Corinthians 4:16–18

FROM CARRIE

I'm not sure I would use the words Paul used above—light and momentary troubles—to describe my life. I know the Bible teaches that to the Lord a thousand years is like a single day, so to Him my life on this earth is only momentary (Psalm 90:4, 2 Peter 3:8). But to me, sometimes my single day feels like a thousand years.

Although my husband came home slightly changed after his first deployment to Saudi Arabia in early 2000, it was after his second deployment in 2001 that I noticed bigger changes. But I excused these warning signs because we were preparing to move, and he'd been to a different country, experienced stresses I could only imagine, all within the confines of *just doing his job*. War changes people, and it should. I've learned that standing guard during so-called peaceful times also changes people.

I certainly do not want to negate the very real sacrifices of our brave men and women who have gone to war. I cannot adequately describe my feelings as I walked the Vietnam Veterans Memorial, watching veterans from World War II, Korea, and Vietnam take in the 58,195 names listed there. I was a jumble of pride and anguish, wanting to honor the men who came home, yet so heavy-hearted for the families of those who didn't.

Some will make a distinction between military members who serve in a time of peace and those who serve in a time of war. While I agree that wartime definitely changes many aspects of the military community, in some cases a better distinction might be with the MOS one works. Some of our bravest people literally put their lives on the line even when we are not at war, while others never deploy outside of their home state even in the midst of raging battles.

Thanks to the War on Terror, the terms PTSD (Post-Traumatic Stress Disorder) and TBI (Traumatic Brain Injury) have hit the mainstream media. Before the 21st century, few outside of medical professionals could easily roll those acronyms off their tongues. Yet neither is limited to wartime activities.

Both are simply the effects of trauma. A car accident or playing tackle football can just as easily cause a TBI as a bomb blast. A newspaper article I read just before writing this talked about the rate of PTSD in children who live in gang-controlled inner cities as rivaling that of soldiers and marines returning from Afghanistan.

Sometimes PTSD can sneak up on people. Because grief is cumulative, a person in the midst of multiple tragedies can occasionally find themselves unable to get past what would otherwise be a small disappointment.

My husband had what I would label a relatively safe job overseas. He worked security details: ACPs (Access Control Points), perimeter checks, and the like. I wasn't a fan of the nights he worked alone in deserted locations along foreign perimeters, and I liked his gate detail checking for bombs on incoming vehicles even less. But to him? He was just doing his job.

That's a common phrase for our veterans. Ask the heroes of Operation Market-Garden, who parachuted in with either the 82nd or 101st Airborne Division behind enemy lines in 1944 Netherlands. Or the Air Force helicopter crew who rescued an F4U Corsair pilot in 1950 in North Korea. Or the Navy corpsmen who offered medical aid to their Marine regiments while taking fire in 1966 Vietnam. Or the many soldiers, sailors, airmen, marines, and guardsmen who stood on the battleground with evil over the last several years.

The question becomes this: What do we do when the job comes home? I'm not talking about the many stressors already discussed within the pages of this book. I'm talking about the soldier who comes home missing a leg. The marine who comes home badly burned. The sailor who comes home angry and distant. The mental and physical wounds of war can sometimes be seen and sometimes only felt, but they are all very real.

For my airman, the first sign I noticed was irritability. Then decreased sleep. Then a pulling away from the family. And although I know that his multiple diagnoses over the years have helped his mental battle with everything going on medically within him, I'm not sure they've helped me. Sure, I now have medical or biological reasons for his temperament and behavior. But it's still a battle for me at times to simply not label him as lazy, or unconcerned, or uncaring.

I know those labels are not the truth. But sometimes, especially in my darkest moments, they feel like truth. I fight apathy, giving up, and taking the easy way out. Taking any way out. I struggle to maintain faith in God's goodness, a positive outlook, and knowledge that today is blessed.

Do I still hang onto hopes of celebrating fifty wonderful years with my husband? Yes. I do.

BACK TO THE BASICS

This discussion really takes us back full circle to where we started: Who is your Savior and Lord? Where is your trust? If Jesus is truly your Lord and the Bible is more than just a storybook, then what the Word says matters. And as much as I don't like it some days, the truth is very simple.

I vowed before God, family, and friends to love my husband for better or for worse, in sickness and in health until death parted us.

The Bible does not give me a path to divorce if I don't like the wounds of war.

There it is. Double-checking Scripture only cements the truth. Old Testament law says, "If you make a vow to the Lord your God, do not be slow to pay it, for the Lord your God will certainly demand it of you and you will be guilty of sin . . . Whatever your lips utter you must be sure to do, because you made your vow freely to the Lord your God with your own mouth" (Deuteronomy 23:21, 23).

Jesus tells us to follow through on our word even when we wouldn't consider it a vow or promise.

> Again, you have heard that it was said to the people long ago, 'Do not break your oath, but fulfill to the Lord the vows you have made.' But I tell you, do not swear an oath at all: either by heaven, for it is God's throne; or by the earth, for it is his footstool; or by Jerusalem, for it is the city of the Great King. And do not swear by your head, for you cannot make even one hair white or black. All you need to say is simply 'Yes' or 'No'; anything beyond this comes from the evil one.
>
> —Matthew 5:33–37

And we can't forget a verse commonly quoted in marriage ceremonies. In Genesis 2, Adam says Eve would "be called 'woman' for she was taken out of man." The next verse says, "That is why a man leaves his father and mother and is united to his wife, and they become one flesh" (verses 23–24). After quoting these verses out of Genesis, two of the Gospels record Jesus saying, "What God has joined together, let no one separate" (Matthew 19:6, Mark 10:9).

Let me pause for a moment to be absolutely clear. I know the realities of life after war. I've heard personal stories, and I've read the statistics. Your home may be a war zone. If you are experiencing any type of abuse, seek advice from a pastor, counselor, First Sergeant, or someone who will help you see clearly what is going on in your home and aid in keeping you safe. If you or your children are experiencing physical abuse or are afraid for your safety—get out. I'm not advocating divorce, but sometimes a temporary separation is best. Pray a lot, seek wise counsel, and keep yourself safe.

But that was not my problem. I did not fear my husband; I was frustrated and confused. As I began to seek God over what to do with the chaos in my marriage, a verse in Psalm 50 greatly encouraged me. The writer of this Psalm, Asaph, compares those who truly follow God with those who merely appear to follow God. Verses 14–15 say, "Sacrifice thank offerings to God, fulfill your vows to the Most High, and call on Me in the day of trouble; I will deliver you, and you will honor Me."

I love that! It's like a personal message straight to my heart. God knew that sometimes as we fulfilled our vows we would be standing in the day of trouble. And here He promises that when we call, He will do more than hear us. More than answer us. He will deliver us.

Soak in that encouragement for a moment because you will need it for this next part.

While God absolutely promises to deliver you, He does not promise to change your circumstances. As my husband's health deteriorated and pain overtook his body, we had to give up some dreams and change some ideas of what we thought we'd do. That's been hard on him, on me, on us, and on our kids, but along the way I learned three lessons.

LESSON 1: LOVE

The first lesson that God drove home in my heart was the fact that He loved me. I knew this in my head and I believed I knew it in my heart, but nothing quite drives that fact deep into your being like walking through the valley of the shadow of death (Psalm 23). I remember times of utter despair, not knowing what was wrong with my husband, fearing it would always be as bad as it felt, worrying that he wouldn't fight with me to salvage our marriage from the devastation that I saw all around us.

One time in particular is crystal clear in my memory. He hadn't slept in two days and was highly irritable. We fought, and he raced off on his motorcycle. I ran to our room, sat on the edge of the bed, and sobbed. Contemplating divorce, yet knowing that wasn't the answer. Not wanting to stay, but at the same time not wanting to leave. I felt trapped. Alone.

I unleashed my despair on God, admitting that I couldn't continue this way. As I prayed, calmness slowly invaded my being. For perhaps the first time in my life, I imagined I was curled up in my Heavenly Father's lap, His protective arms around me. I knew life could be different if I chose it, and at that moment, I determined to choose it.

I began to pick up studies like *Lord, Teach Me to Pray in 28 Days* by Kay Arthur, and I devoured them. I forced myself to find the silver lining in every cloud, no matter how big the cloud seemed. And I resolved to find some relationships that I could take deeper, forcing myself to open my heart and let people see more of me than I'd ever before allowed.

No, this did not change my husband or my circumstances. But my outlook gradually morphed, and I now can say without any doubt that God is in control and God is good. Always. Even when it doesn't look like it.

LESSON 2: REALITY

Second, God taught me to acknowledge reality. That may sound strange, particularly when I tell you that I tend to see things concretely. But I also tend to minimize things, both good and bad, and not fully recognize their impact on my mental or emotional health.

Major General (Retired) Robert Dees, in his book *Resilient Warriors*, says, "The warrior who does not intellectually or emotionally recognize the existence of evil and the reality of pain and suffering is far more subject to being blindsided, swept totally off of their feet."[8] That was me! Intellectually I understood evil and suffering, but emotionally—I minimized both.

This is why the flood of emotions overwhelmed me. My melancholy phlegmatic personality didn't know what to do with this imperfect chaotic life I found myself living. (See chapter 7 if you missed the discussion on personalities.) And the fears

---

8 Robert F. Dees, *Resilient Warriors* (San Diego, CA: Creative Team Publishing, 2011), 35.

confronting me about my marriage and my husband forced other issues to the surface as well. Years of pain that I had underestimated and downplayed would no longer be contained. With the help of my pastor, a licensed family therapist, I opened the door to these emotions, and I found God standing there.

Together, He and I looked at the mess. The process was difficult, but God helped me be honest. Over several months, He walked me through dark places, shone His life-giving light on them, and gave me great comfort. He provided friends—a couple who were living through what I was experiencing, one who needed my encouragement to walk the path I'd just traveled, and some who didn't fully understand but wanted to love me where I was.

Today I live with the knowledge that with all his health issues, my husband may not make it through the day. And while I don't like that, I'm okay with it. Because I wrestled with God. I got honest with Him. And in the end, He still wrapped His arms around me and assured me that He is trustworthy.

LESSON 3: PREPARATION

Finally, I've learned to build resilience. General Dees explains this process very well in his book *Resilient Warriors*. With his permission, I will quickly summarize it for you here, but I encourage you to pick up his book as he explains these in more depth and includes Scripture for study.

First, you must know your calling. One of the reasons Kathy and I started this book with the basics of what a wife is called to do is because it is critical to your foundation. The most successful people have specific written goals that they look to regularly.

When I see God, I want to hear, *"Well done"* (Matthew 25:14–30). To meet that goal, I must know what my calling is and what it looks like within the parameters of my life. That requires prayer, focus, and determination. Hard work? Yes. Exhausting? At times. Worth it? Absolutely.

Second, you must know your enemy. The success of any mission depends upon knowing who you are up against, and our enemy is not very imaginative. Satan still uses the same techniques he applied throughout the Old Testament. He's good at tripping you up through your own weaknesses, so consider that and implement guards to help. Staying out of certain places, avoiding certain people, and being honest with an accountability partner are all steps you may need to take.

But sometimes our enemy blindsides us, whether through the betrayal of a friend, a natural disaster, or a sudden medical issue. We cannot adequately prepare for some events. This is when it is critical to know your God and your calling. If you hang onto the truth that God is good and trustworthy, you'll make it through these storms.

Third, you must know your friends. In our culture of social media, we tend to have a lot of friends, but it would be wise to take General Dees's advice: "One must be careful not to confuse quantity with quality in the area of friendships" (page 94). It's important to work on deep relationships with two or three others, women with whom you can share your dreams and fears as well as recipes, lunches out, and children's play dates.

Let me offer a caution here: women should be best friends with their husband and with other women. I know some of you bristle at this, and believe me when I say that I understand many of the reasons some women choose guy friends over other girls. But trust me. If the ladies in your life are causing you grief, either you need to take to heart what they are telling you, or they are the wrong friends.

This doesn't mean that you cannot have a guy as a friend. I have two men in my life whom I consider brothers. I pray for their safety when they deploy and look forward to seeing them whenever possible. If you listened to our conversations, you would think we were siblings the way we tease each other. And I know without any doubt that if I really needed them, they would both do whatever was necessary to help.

But my primary friendships are with the wives of these men. I place most of my focus on their wives and children, and it is with their wives that these men place their loyalty. All of our inside jokes are fully known by their wives, and the ladies are included on occasional emails between us. When something is on my heart or when I have great news to share, it is the women I call.

I value these men in my life. And because of the value I place on them, I place a higher value on their families. I work to protect their family, guard my family, and keep boundaries clear. I encourage you to evaluate where you share your heart.

Fourth, you must know your equipment. Just as our men have a massive amount of both offensive and defensive equipment they take with them to battle, Christians have spiritual battle gear. The best summary of this armor is in Ephesians 6:10–18:

> Finally, be strong in the Lord and in his mighty power. Put on the full armor of God, so that you can take your stand against the devil's schemes. For our struggle is not

against flesh and blood, but against the rulers, against the authorities, against the powers of this dark world and against the spiritual forces of evil in the heavenly realms. Therefore put on the full armor of God, so that when the day of evil comes, you may be able to stand your ground, and after you have done everything, to stand. Stand firm then, with the belt of truth buckled around your waist, with the breastplate of righteousness in place, and with your feet fitted with the readiness that comes from the gospel of peace. In addition to all this, take up the shield of faith, with which you can extinguish all the flaming arrows of the evil one. Take the helmet of salvation and the sword of the Spirit, which is the word of God.

And pray in the Spirit on all occasions with all kinds of prayers and requests. With this in mind, be alert and always keep on praying for all the Lord's people.

Each piece of armor is important and requires practice to get better at using. Just as an athlete must practice with all his equipment, a Christian should consciously practice with his own gear. Including the sword of the Spirit.

This passage in Ephesians clearly defines the sword as being the Word of God. The only offensive weapon Paul tells us to pick up is God's Word, and when we go into battle, the Word must already be hidden in our hearts, memorized in our minds. In the middle of a fight, you do not always have time to stop and learn a new verse. It works best if a verse is already there, ready for the Holy Spirit to bring it to mind. I encourage you to work on this, whether it's through some formal program like the Navigator's *Topical Memory System* or informally, by challenging a friend or your children to learn a verse a week.

Fifth, you must deploy with the right mindset. I promise you, it's far easier to go into battle with a great mindset than trying to fix it while in the midst of battle. Romans 12:2 says we are to renew our minds so we can be transformed. This instruction becomes even more powerful in combination with Philippians 4:4–8:

> Rejoice in the Lord always. I will say it again: Rejoice! Let your gentleness be evident to all. The Lord is near. Do not be anxious about anything, but in every situation, by prayer and petition, with thanksgiving, present your requests to God. And the peace of God, which transcends all understanding, will guard your hearts and your minds in Christ Jesus.

> Finally, brothers and sisters, whatever is true, whatever is noble, whatever is right, whatever is pure, whatever is lovely, whatever is admirable—if anything is excellent or praiseworthy—think about such things.

Yes, I understand how difficult it is to follow these directives from Paul while your home is a war zone. So please imagine this is coming with every ounce of love within me: Tough! The pity party that's so easy to throw is not helping. But following God's Word and cooperating with your Heavenly Father brings forth all the blessings of His promises—including an abundant life!

No, your circumstances may not change, particularly in the first several days or weeks you are working through this. But change will come. Your outlook will improve. And you will know God's trustworthiness and provision like you can only dream of at this moment. So take my hand, look up, and find something true, something noble, something lovely, and hang onto it. And next time you feel despair, or pain, or anger—do it again.

Finally, you must develop and rehearse *Actions on Contact*. Many combat wives are familiar with all the paperwork that must be done prior to deployment to a hazardous area. Similar actions are taken throughout life. Guardians are discussed when a couple begins to have children, or living wills and other advance directives may be considered prior to major surgery.

If you're not currently living within a crisis, sitting down and purposely working through each aspect of this process will save you stress when trouble comes. If you are in the middle of suffering, then just work through each part the best you can. Remind yourself what your calling is and who your enemy is. Pray, asking God to show you one or two women around you who could become your support beams. And get into the Bible, seeking out God's truthful encouragement.

Your life right now may not be pretty, and if you are living with a wounded warrior then it probably is not easy. Don't give up! God is your secret to success. He sees you, loves you, and wants to walk through this time with you.

You are not alone.

CHAPTER 13

FINAL THOUGHTS

Now to Him who is able to do immeasurably more than all
we ask or imagine, according to His power that is at work within
us, to Him be glory in the church and in Christ Jesus throughout
all generations, for ever and ever! Amen.

—Ephesians 3:20–21

FROM CARRIE

Years ago, a friend sent me an email, one of those stories that get passed around to everyone in your email address book. I have no idea who the original author is, but I would like to share it here for you.

> As I faced my Maker at the last Judgment, I knelt before the Lord along with the other souls. Before each of us laid our lives, like the squares of a quilt, in many piles. An Angel sat before each of us sewing our quilt squares together into a tapestry that is our life.

But, as my Angel took each piece of cloth off the pile, I noticed how ragged and empty each of my squares was. They were filled with giant holes. Each square was labeled with a part of my life, the challenges and temptations I faced. I saw hardships that I had endured, which were the largest holes of all. I glanced around me. Nobody else had such squares. Other than a tiny hole here and there, the other tapestries were filled with rich color. I gazed upon my own life and was disheartened.

Finally the time came when each life was to be displayed, held up to the light, the scrutiny of truth. The others rose, each in turn, holding up their tapestries. So filled their lives had been.

My Angel looked upon me and nodded for me to rise. My gaze dropped to the ground in shame. I hadn't had all the earthly fortunes. I had love in my life, and laughter. But there had also been illness, death, and false accusations that took from me my world as I knew it. I often struggled with the temptation to quit, only to somehow muster the strength to pick up and begin again. I had spent many nights on my knees in prayer, asking for help and guidance in my life. I had often been held up to ridicule which I endured painfully, each time offering it up to the Father in hopes that I would not melt beneath the judgmental gaze of those who unfairly judged me. And now, I had to face the truth. My life was what it was, and I had to accept it for what it had been.

I rose and slowly lifted the combined squares of my life to the light. An awe-filled gasp filled the air. I gazed around at the others who stared at me with eyes wide. Then, I looked upon the tapestry before me.

Light flooded the many holes, creating an image. The face of Christ. Then our Lord stood before me, with warmth and love in His eyes. He said, "Every time you gave over your life to Me, it became My life, My hardships, and My struggles. Each point of light in your life is when you stepped aside and let Me shine through, until there was more of Me than there was of you.

Your life may not look pretty. You've seen in the pages of this book moments where Kathy and I truly failed. But God sees you and Christ loves you. They want to take the ashes of your life and make them beautiful (Isaiah 61:3).

We've covered a lot of ground, and in many of these chapters, we know that we've just scratched the surface. What I know of the complexities of life tells me that you may have as many questions now as when you started, but hopefully we've encouraged you.

No matter your situation, if you and I could sit down together, I would tell you three things. First of all, breathe. Just take a moment and breathe deeply. I don't have the knowledge to tell you all the medical and psychological science behind it, but I know this: the act of taking a moment to get quiet and breathe deeply will still your soul. It will calm your nerves. It will steady you for the moment like little else can. Breathe, my friend.

Second, pray. I'm hoping that by now you were expecting that word of advice from me. Over the years, as I faced deployments, quick moves, uncertain schedules, and my own fears, prayer did more to change me and my perspective than any other thing I can name. No, it didn't always change my circumstances, but so often, simply allowing God to give me His perspective helped me to deal with the problems before me.

Last, find a Christian friend. Or two. Someone who will not just go to lunch or relax and watch a movie with you, but a lady who will remind you to seek God first and who wants you to remind her of the same truth. A woman you can call at 2 a.m. when fears overtake you, or on whose doorstep you can unexpectedly appear when a call comes down the line about an injury on your husband's team; a friend who may become like a sister to you, whom you will call long after one or both of you PCS.

By taking the time to breathe, seeking God's opinion, and having a person you can lean on at your side, there's nothing the military can throw at you that you can't hand over to your Heavenly Father and watch Him cover you in blessings. I want that for you. I want you to thrive within this governmental system that burns out so many families.

And I believe that you really can do this, and do it well.

FROM KATHY

By their fruit you will recognize them. Do people pick grapes
from thornbushes, or figs from thistles? Likewise every good tree
bears good fruit, but a bad tree bears bad fruit.
—Matthew 7:16–17

This spring, when we were working in the garden, several little sprouts were growing and I had no idea what they were. I told my daughter we would simply have to wait and see what fruit was produced in order to determine what plants they were. But honestly, we should be able to tell what type of plant is growing while it is still fairly small, so we can anticipate a particular fruit. If we have tomato plants growing where we wanted watermelons, then we will have to remove the plants by the roots and either discard them, or transplant them. If you want to change the fruit, you must change the root.

Everyone knows, when they plant a seed, that the plant and fruit that come from the seed will be as its parent plant was. If you plant an apple seed, you will get an apple tree, and the fruit you gain will be apples. You wouldn't expect to get an orange from an apple seed.

And yet in our lives we often plant seeds but expect to see a different plant spring up. We hope for peace, joy, and patience in our lives, yet we plant strife, anger, and complaints. Why do we think that we will get good fruit if we aren't planting good seeds?

The foundation of truth in our lives must spring forth from the living Word of God. If we hope to have good fruit, such as those listed in Galatians 5:22–23, we must learn to plant the right seeds and water them liberally with the Word daily, all while standing in the light of the Son. Without the planting of salvation in our lives, which is possible only through faith in Jesus and the payment He made for our sins, the life we seek will evade us.

Once we begin with the planting of salvation, we can begin to grow truth. But we must take care that the weeds of deception do not stay intertwined with our new budding roots of truth. Lies can choke out truth and destroy the planting of the Lord, so we must make an active effort to begin plucking them from the soil of our hearts.

The devil is a thief who comes only to steal, kill, and destroy (John 10:10). Jesus says of Satan in John 8:44, "He was a murderer from the beginning, not holding to the truth for there is no truth in him. When he lies, he speaks his native language, for he is a liar and the father of lies." To engage in deception on any level, whether consciously or not, is to follow Satan. In order to move forward in our fruit inspection, we must look at the seeds we planted, or those that were planted within us as children by our parents or grandparents. Remember, fruit comes from seeds.

Looking at our lives can be painful. But when we begin to look through the eyes of truth, we can see clearly and can begin to take steps to cultivate our hearts and allow God to prune and shape us as He wants to. Staying close to the Lord through the reading of His Word is essential. If we don't renew our minds with the watering of the Word, we will not recognize the difference between the early sprouts of lies and truth.

Remember the tomatoes and watermelons? They look very similar when small. But, given time, you can see the difference. We must be keen gardeners of righteousness. We must keep diligent eyes upon our hearts and allow the Lord to weed and prune as necessary in our lives to ensure a healthy life and abundant, good fruit.

Recently, a young military bride I had gotten to know quite well moved to Florida with her husband's PCS there. She had been an eager servant of the Lord within our church and was always full of life and joy. She was a godly wife and mother of two small girls.

As soon as they arrived at their new home, she tried to plug into activities with her little girls and meet moms. Their family began church hunting right away. They tried a few and settled on one that didn't feel like home, but the preaching was solid and they wanted to try to plug in somewhere quickly.

But try as they might they couldn't seem to connect. Her girls couldn't make friends and were actually treated meanly by many children at school and at church. My friend's husband deployed almost immediately, so my friend pressed in harder to find friends, but could find none.

My experience with this woman was that she was a friendly, hard-working, joyful lady who was not afraid to put herself out there for people. When she began experiencing her woes, she prayed harder and then tried harder. But then DCF (Department of Children and Families) showed up at her door because someone turned her in for being abusive to her girls. She had no idea if it was a random citizen, a neighbor, someone from her kid's karate class, or a church member who had accused her.

She was completely blindsided by this assault. She truly had no idea what to do or think. The social worker inspected her home and interviewed her kids and determined everything to be false and dropped all charges. But now this woman who readily put herself out there for others was terrified to reprimand her kids in public, so she opted more often than not to stay home. She didn't engage with people anymore. She didn't trust anyone. What a waste and what a defeat, for her and for all the folks who were missing out on what God could have brought them through her.

Remember the father of all lies? Satan is truly out to steal, to kill, and to destroy whatever he can within you, to render you ineffective for kingdom work. He doesn't have to make the lie he whispers initially be believed, as he did with my friend. She is a great mom. She would never abuse her children, nor would she condone such behavior from anyone else.

But what about the lies she now believes? That she can't trust anyone. That no one in that town will ever understand her or care about her and her family. That she mustn't discipline her children according to the Word of God for fear someone will take her kids from her and accuse her of being cruel to them.

The enemy would love to keep this vibrant woman alienated. She knows how to walk out the Word of truth in her life, marriage, and parenting, and the enemy fears that. So he struck at the very heart of her. Her family. Her children. All too often he strikes at our marriages. Anything he can do to plant seeds of doubt, fear, alienation, hurt, and defeat, he will do.

You must know his tactics. You must know that he doesn't take a break when you are especially vulnerable or down. He doesn't play fair. He strikes harder when he thinks he can win a victory. He loves to kick us when we are down. You must not listen to him.

It is not your neighbor, the rude lady at church, the hateful commander at your husband's work, or even your husband himself causing you problems in your life. It is the enemy of your soul planting seeds within you, and you allow them to grow. You cultivate them by harboring fear and unforgiveness, and watering them with bitterness. Your thoughts become the fertile soil where these lies not only sprout but begin to spread out and take over other areas of your life.

Your thoughts then stretch and envelope insecurity and doubt, consuming them until all you have is a living weed of untruth in your mind that is so large you can no longer see truth. Your emotions and expectations are all devoured by the lies. This process can happen so subtly and effectively that you won't see anything but what the enemy meant for you to see. And sometimes you choose to walk in the deceptive comfort of your flesh and selfishness, believing your enemy's lies that you are better off there.

I'm glad to say that my friend did not give into all of those weeds of untruth. She decided to get mad at the devil. She decided to overcome him and his lies by diving into the truth of God's Word, and, holding steadfastly, she allowed God to cultivate within her a spirit of forgiveness and mercy. She has been and still is reaching out for new friendships and trusting God for her life right now.

In which areas of your life have you allowed Satan to plant seeds of deceit? In your parenting? In your relationship with your husband? Have you believed lies about yourself, about your worth and beauty? Perhaps you never had loving parents or you were in some way left uncovered and unprotected in childhood. Perhaps, like me, you have placed your value and worth in your own strengths and accomplishments rather than in God. Perhaps you have believed the lies that you have never and will never be loved or understood.

Your God wants to deliver you from all untruth and bring you into the light of life. In all that Carrie and I have laid before you in this book, we encourage you beyond all things to remember His amazing love for you. It is God's greatest desire to pursue you and show you all truth through Jesus Christ.

There are many things we are called to do in our lifetimes. But God's purposes in our stations in life are always the same. No matter what the different seasons of life bring, we are all here for one purpose: to bring glory to God. When we are bringing glory to Him, we are direct beneficiaries of that glory, because He has united with us in an extension of His infinite love and mercy.

The grace He lavishes on us is amazing. That His Spirit resides within us and He partners with us to do His will never ceases to astonish me. My feeble brain can barely wrap around the knowledge that He gave up everything to pursue a wretched sinner such as me. Or even though He is so profound in His strength and might, that He would use me despite my weaknesses and frailty. Only His glory could shine so brightly that the dullness of my heart could even remotely reflect the grace that shines through Him.

And yet He never stops pursuing us. He never stops loving us. He never stops using the mess we make of our lives and somehow, miraculously, turning it around to cause blessing and growth and beauty. Truly, beauty for ashes! (Isaiah 61:3).

Proverbs 31:30–31 says, "Charm is deceptive, and beauty is fleeting; but a woman who fears the Lord is to be praised. Honor her for all that her hands have done, and let her works bring her praise at the city gate." When we begin to see the beauty that Christ sees in us and begin to seek what He sees of worth, we are rewarded with a life filled with the good fruit we have longed for in our lives and we become a witness for others to see and partake.

When we can truly lay every area of our life down before this Heavenly Father and when we can trust in His Word, then we can and will begin to live in truth. Darkness will lose its power in our lives. 2 Corinthians 3:16–18 says, "But whenever anyone turns to the Lord, the veil is taken away. Now the Lord is the Spirit, and where the Spirit of the Lord is, there is freedom. And we all, who with unveiled faces contemplate the Lord's glory, are being transformed into His image with ever-increasing glory, which comes from the Lord, who is the Spirit."

The truth is that you are loved with an unfailing love. The truth is that you are called to an extremely high calling as a warrior's bride. The reality is, your God believes in you so much He will entrust this calling to you. He didn't just ask you to endure this place, He is asking you to embrace it. He has all the strength you need to not only find peace, but extreme joy in your life, if you will but lay down your life and receive His gift.

From the depths of my heart, I want you to receive this great gift from your Heavenly Father. I have been in hard places in this life and have learned that our God is faithful. He is working all things together for my good, because I love Him. Are you willing to trust today that He loves you, your husband, and your life within the military so much that He went to all extremes to tell you?

Carrie and I are praying with you today for your great journey of hope and purpose. Precious sister, we encourage you to embrace the cross. Embrace the Word. Embrace your warrior, and in that place embrace the liberty of your beautiful high calling.

RECOMMENDED RESOURCES

Several military resources are available to you and your husband for counseling that we suggest you prayerfully consider using. We strongly encourage the use of godly pastors and counselors, as well as strong Christian sisters, to help you through your times of trials, as we believe true change occurs only when founded on truth: God's Word.

Chaplains are a resource available to you within your husband's unit and at the main Chapel. They have numerous options to assist you and are usually eager to do so. Sometimes your spouse may frown on approaching a chaplain for assistance, but other counseling and therapy groups are available on military installations. They vary by base, but the chaplain should be able to help you plug into the options available to you. He may even have a recommendation of a private counselor or church where you can seek help.

Another resource that is available to all branches of the military is the MFLC Program (Military and Family Life Counseling Program). These free services are provided for non-medical, short-term, situational problem-solving issues within your home. They seek to do marital, individual, family, and children's counseling specifically geared towards the unique challenges military lifestyles face. The licensed clinical counselors are very flexible and can meet anywhere on or off post as long as it isn't in a home. They do not keep records, which may appeal to soldiers who would like to keep their personal lives away from their command's knowledge. Legally, MFLC counselors are required to report all cases that could deal with suicide or homicide, but all other situations are kept confidential.

PWOC (Protestant Women of the Chapel) is another resource available at many installations worldwide. A chapel-based ministry, it is a great place to connect with other women who are striving to place a priority on Bible study, prayer, and spiritual growth. If you are Catholic, don't let the name scare you away—PWOC groups accept all women who want to know more about Christ.

These resources are listed in alphabetical order by book title or web address. This list is not all inclusive, but includes items we found helpful:

MILITARY-SPECIFIC BOOKS AND WEBSITES FOR TRAUMA, PAIN, AND HEALING

When War Comes Home: Christ-centered Healing for Wives of Combat Veterans by Christopher Adsit, Rahnella Adsit, and Marshele Carter Waddell

www.whenwarcomeshomeretreats.com – Marshele Carter Waddell's website. Includes a blog, resources, and information for retreats designed for families dealing with PTSD issues.

www.MHNGS.com – Military & Family Life Counseling Program supporting service members and their families.

MILITARY-SPECIFIC BOOKS AND WEBSITES FOR ENCOURAGEMENT AND GROWTH

Faith Deployed: Daily Encouragement for Military Wives and *Faith Deployed . . . Again: More Daily Encouragement for Military Wives* by Jocelyn Green. Also, www.faithdeployed.com – Jocelyn Green's website. Includes a blog, a list of resources, and links to the Faith Deployed network.

The 5 Love Languages Military Edition: The Secret to Love That Lasts by Gary Chapman and Jocelyn Green

God Strong: The Military Wife's Spiritual Survival Guide by Sara Horn. Also, www.wivesoffaith.org – Sara Horn's website. Includes a blog, a way to find a group local to you, and information for their support groups called Survival Sisters.

Home Builders Bible Studies by Family Life Ministries:

- *Defending the Military Marriage* by Lt. Col. Jim Fishback

- *Making Your Marriage Deployment Ready* by Mike and Linda Montgomery and Keith and Sharon Morgan

- *Defending the Military Family* by Lt. Col. Jim Fishback

Hope for the Home Front: Winning the Emotional and Spiritual Battles of a Military Wife by Marshele Carter Waddell

Resilient Warriors by Robert F. Dees, Major General, U.S. Army, Retired

MARRIAGE AND FAMILY BOOKS AND WEBSITES FOR TRAUMA, PAIN, AND HEALING

Breaking Free (Updated Edition): The Journey, The Stories by Beth Moore

Real Marriage: The Truth About Sex, Friendship, and Life Together by Mark and Grace Driscoll. Also the Real Marriage sermon series found at http://marshill.com/media/sermons.

MARRIAGE AND FAMILY BOOKS AND WEBSITES FOR ENCOURAGEMENT AND GROWTH

Becoming the Parent God Wants You To Be by Kevin Leman (NOTE: Other resources by Leman include *Have a New Husband by Friday, Have a New Kid by Friday* and *Making Children Mind Without Losing Yours*)

Boundaries: When to Say Yes, How to Say No to Take Control of Your Life by Henry Cloud and John Townsend (NOTE: Other resources by Cloud and Townsend include *Boundaries in Marriage, Boundaries with Kids, Boundaries with Teens,* and *Boundaries for Leaders*)

www.familylife.com – Dennis and Barbara Rainey's website dealing with marriage, parenting, and faith issues.

Financial Peace, The Total Money Makeover or any other resources by Dave Ramsey. Another great option for biblical financial advice and resources is Crown Financial Ministries at www.crown.org.

For Men Only: A Straightforward Guide to the Inner Lives of Women by Shaunti and Jeff Feldhahn. Also, *For Parents Only: Getting Inside the Head of Your Kid* by Shaunti and Jeff Feldhahn, and Lisa Rice. And *For Women Only: What You Need to Know About the Inner Lives of Men*, and *The Surprising Secrets of Highly Happy Marriages: The Little Things That Make a Big Difference* by Shaunti Feldhahn

Intimate Issues: Conversations Woman to Woman by Linda Dillow and Lorraine Pintus

Laugh Your Way to a Better Marriage by Mark Gungor. While this also comes as a book, we highly recommend the DVD series.

Margin: Restoring Emotional, Physical, Financial, and Time Reserves to Overloaded Lives by Richard Swenson

Marriage Undercover: Thriving in a Culture of Quiet Desperation by Bob Meisner, Audrey Meisner, and Stephen W. Nance

www.mynewday.tv – Bob and Audrey Meisner's website, with lots of great information and resources for marriage.

The Power of a Praying Wife by Stormie Omartian

Praying God's Will for My Daughter and *Praying God's Will for My Son* by Lee Roberts

BIBLICAL/APOLOGETIC BOOKS AND WEBSITES

Any books by E.M. Bounds on prayer, to include *The Complete Works of E.M. Bounds: Power Through Prayer; Prayer and Praying Men; The Essentials of Prayer; The Necessity of Prayer; The Possibilities of Prayer; Purpose in Prayer; The Weapon of Prayer*

The Case for a Creator: A Journalist Investigates Scientific Evidence That Points Toward God, The Case for Christ: A Journalist's Personal Investigation of the Evidence for Jesus, and *The Case for Faith: A Journalist Investigates the Toughest Objections to Christianity* by Lee Strobel. Also, www.leestrobel.com – Lee Strobel's website. Includes a newsletter, videos, and a schedule of where he's speaking.

Essential Truths of the Christian Faith by R.C. Sproul. Also, www.ligonier.org – R.C. Sproul's website. Includes broadcasts, devotions, books and links to free eBook downloads.

Finding Peace in Life's Storms by Charles Spurgeon

Mere Christianity by C.S. Lewis

My Utmost for His Highest by Oswald Chambers. Also, www.utmost.org – Includes more information on Oswald Chambers, devotions, blogs, and other great resources.

precept.org – Kay Arthur's website. Includes online lessons and Bible study programs.

The Problem of Pain by C.S. Lewis

Why I Believe by D. James Kennedy

Kathy Barnett

Married at age eighteen, Kathy began her journey with Sam right out of high school. Having always had a love of reading and writing, she pursued a degree in English Language and Literature while beginning their family. After teaching for one year, the Lord called Kathy home to minister to her own children through homeschooling and to serve Sam while he was busy serving in the US Army.

God had a beautiful plan of faithfulness and joy lined up for Kathy in exchange for her previous personal marriage, family, and career goals. Twenty-four years, nine children, and more than a dozen deployments resulting in over ten years of separation in their marriage, finds Kathy still seeking obedience to her Father's plan.

Recently retired, Kathy and her husband reside near Ft. Bragg, NC, where they continue to raise their family and minister to the needs of the military within their church and community. She loves running on long roads, reading long books, and having long conversations about what Jesus has done in her life. Her heart is to see people find freedom in Christ—her greatest joy is seeing that liberty become reality.

For more information about
KATHY BARNETT
please visit:
www.facebook.com/TheWarriorsBride
WarriorBride90@gmail.com

Carrie Daws

Over the years, God rewrote Carrie's dreams to include being a stay-at-home mom and a writer. She started by simply writing weekly devotionals online, before a mentor at the Christian Writer's Guild encouraged her to try writing fiction. However, even in her fiction books, Carrie's stories are based on the struggles of real people and convey the hope that God never abandons His people.

After almost ten years in the US Air Force, Carrie's husband medically retired; they now live in Virginia with their three children. Besides writing, she stays busy homeschooling and volunteering within military ministries.

More than anything, Carrie strives to write clean fiction and encouraging non-fiction that demonstrate practical Christianity. She says, "I didn't want to be embarrassed for my daughter to pick up any of my books. But I also wanted to do some exploration. Imagine what your life would look like if you stood up to your greatest fear. Or someone close to you deeply believed you were made for more! I want my readers to find the courage for those things, and that's what compels me to write."

For more information about
CARRIE DAWS
please visit:
www.CarrieDaws.com
@CarrieDaws
www.facebook.com/Carrie-Daws
Contact@CarrieDaws.com

For more information about
AMBASSADOR INTERNATIONAL
please visit:

www.ambassador-international.com
@AmbassadorIntl
www.facebook.com/AmbassadorIntl